BEHAVIOR PROBLEMS
OF PRESCHOOL
CHILDREN

BEHAVIOR PROBLEMS OF PRESCHOOL CHILDREN

DIAGNOSIS AND TREATMENT

By

ELINOR VERVILLE, Ph.D.

Consulting Psychologist
Former Director
Central Wyoming Counseling Center
Casper, Wyoming
Tulsa County Child Guidance Clinic
Tulsa, Oklahoma
Mayes County Guidance Center
Pryor, Oklahoma

CHARLES C THOMAS • PUBLISHER
Springfield • Illinois • U.S.A.

Published and Distributed Throughout the World by

CHARLES C THOMAS • PUBLISHER

2600 South First Street

Springfield, Illinois 62717

© *1985 by* CHARLES C THOMAS • PUBLISHER

ISBN 0-398-05052-X

Library of Congress Catalog Card Number: 84-8740

With THOMAS BOOKS *careful attention is given to all details of manufacturing and
design. It is the Publisher's desire to present books that are satisfactory as to their physical
qualities and artistic possibilities and appropriate for their particular use.* THOMAS
BOOKS *will be true to those laws of quality that assure a good name and good will.*

Printed in the United States of America
Q-R-3

Library of Congress Cataloging in Publication Data

Verville, Elinor.
   Behavior problems of preschool children.

   Includes bibliographies and index.
    1. Child psychopathology. 2. Family psychotherapy.
I. Title. [DNLM: 1. Child Behavior Disorders.
2. Child, Preschool. WS 350.6 V57lb]
RJ499.V47 1985   618.92'89   84-8740
ISBN 0-398-05052-X

To
Very Important Preschoolers
Tim, Karen, and Sarah

PREFACE

AN alien creature, the preschooler: mysterious, fierce, startling, appealing. What does one do with him?

Most psychologists avoid him. Many child guidance clinics turn away preschool clients. Others enroll them in a diagnostic nursery and after weeks of observation, staff members hazard a guess about what is wrong.

The staff at one guidance center groaned when the director announced that their next project would be the rehabilitation of small misfits from the neighborhood's Head Start nursery school. Finally, two non-professional aides, two social workers, and one psychologist undertook the task, the reluctant psychologist only because she was put in charge. No other psychologist at the center would have anything to do with the program.

Strong-arming the preschooler who has behavior problems is a tradition which spotlights not only the psychologist's preference for the familiarity of conversation with adult clients, but also his ignorance of young children. Dozens of books about the antics and motivations of adolescents regularly appear. Child guidance centers welcome six- to twelve-year-olds by the hundreds. No one seems interested in the troubled preschooler.

True, there has been a recent flurry of research about him. Scholars are finding that infants are much more alert, intelligent, and self-sufficient than previously was thought. They report that older preschool children are generous and sympathetic (not new information to their mothers and nursery school teachers). But instruction in how to manage behavior problems is woefully scarce.

This is too bad; more than at any other time in his life, the child is both flexible in performance and dedicated to pleasing adults. It is easy to replace ruinous actions with new, sound habits.

This book, written to entice students and practicing clinical psychologists to venture into the preschooler's world, has four parts.

The first describes the normal child with a year by year account of his achievements, the worries of his parents, and the ordinary problems they face together. The section begins with a review of external forces, other than age, which bend the boy or girl in predictable directions and account for some of his attitudes and actions.

The second part reports on long-standing behavior problems, why they developed and what can be done about them. This section also includes a discussion of the unique difficulties of handicapped boys and girls, whom the psychologist often is charged with helping.

The third part details the diagnostic techniques which ensure a thorough study of the child and reveal the factors responsible for his deviant behavior.

The fourth part deals with treatment and tells how to teach parents in private consultations, remedial classes, and preventive classes. The section starts with a compassionate and realistic look at the mother and father the psychologist must aid.

Names and identifying characteristics of families whose children are described have been changed.

Special thanks go to Mrs. Randy Thrower, whose account of events in her family's life vividly pictures the bittersweet education small children give their parents.

The preschool child — eager, thoughtful, persistent, and funny — is a joy and a challenge. He and his struggling parents deserve the conscientious, knowledgeable help of behavioral scientists.

Elinor Verville
Littlelon, Colorado

CONTENTS

PART III. DIAGNOSIS

PART IV. TREATMENT

BEHAVIOR PROBLEMS
OF PRESCHOOL
CHILDREN

Part I.
The Normal Child

Chapter 1

EXTERNAL AGENTS OF BEHAVIOR

G ENES and jobs, neighbors and fate touch the child. His sex, birth order, and race cannot be changed; yet they drive him in set directions. Knowing how external agents direct behavior, adults can understand and counterbalance forces which cause trouble for the preschooler.

His characteristics, his family, and his community tell on his life.

THE CHILD

Physique

Some small children have obvious physical imperfections: they are too fat, too tall, or too tiny. They have freckles or big ears. They limp or suffer from strabismus. Comments, either sympathetic or mocking, distress and shame them.[27]

A preschooler with a chronic illness seldom feels peppy. Irritable and hard to manage, he is hard to like. If he is hospitalized often, he backslides to helplessness. Emotional trauma from hospitalization is most severe for the youngster between seven months and three years of age.[39]

Some accident-prone children break bones, cut themselves, knock out teeth, and hurt most of the time. Their parents scold, pay the doctor, and worry.

A premature baby, who may appear early because of lax prenatal care,[38] starts life a lap behind the full term infant. Clear or subtle differences in physical and intellectual growth last for months, even years. Some parents, overprotective, rebuff the premature's tries for independence.[3,20]

The attractive, coordinated, healthy boy or girl develops on schedule. He handles himself well in games; he fearlessly climbs trees and jumps into swimming pools. He and his parents gloat over his physical prowess.

Intelligence

The child of low intelligence does not walk, speak, control elimination, feed, or dress himself at the age other youngsters do. Embarrassed and frustrated, his parents hound him to do better. Or they may label him "Dummy" and pretend he's not there.

The preschooler of high intelligence eagerly practices self-management, talks glibly, masters puzzles, and recalls details of adult-forgotten events. His delighted mother and father brag about him to neighbors; he knows he is the star in their lives.

The boy or girl with average intelligence fares best in families unconcerned with academic excellence. If his parents are well-educated, they may dream of a future doctor in the family and the youngster's abilities seem meager.

Dull, bright, or average, the child's achievements routinely are compared with those of brothers and sisters when they were his age. Soon he thinks of himself as grandly special or strangely defective.

Some parents, hedging against future trouble, enroll the child in an educational nursery school where he studies shapes and sizes but never plays. Or they drill him daily in counting, printing the alphabet, and coloring neatly. Burned out at five years, the youngster ignores his kindergarten teacher's directions.

Sex

Boys

Preschool boys throw, run, and jump better than preschool girls.[24] Their high metabolic rate and their smooth movement of large muscles guarantee that they'll feel fine when they run and climb, not so fine when they must sit still. Constantly on the go, they run off from their mothers,[18] get hurt, [35] and often are in hot water with adults.[5]

Boys focus on one object at a time, exploring and experimenting.[4] They take apart alarm clocks and tables; they pound a hundred nails into the garage door; they pour sand into the car's gas tank. Concentrating, they miss much: the red stoplight as they walk to kindergarten, their mother's call to come to lunch. Unseeing and unhearing, they often are punished for destructiveness and disobedience.

They believe this treatment unfair and reject it by developing toughness to criticism and indifference to others' wishes. Unable to win adult praise, they gain self-respect by testing themselves against peers. Over and over, they challenge and scorn other boys and girls. Soon they have slipped into the lifelong competitiveness of their sex.

At school, they wriggle in their seats, consider rules unimportant, and cannot read or write because the small muscles in their hands and eyes are uncoordinated. Parent disapproval is compounded by teacher disapproval, ample cause for the high rate of personality and behavior problems in young boys.[12,34]

Girls

Preschool girls meet adult standards more quickly than boys can. With a rapidly-maturing central nervous system, they easily achieve dryness. They talk early and fluently, so they can say what they want, get their own way, and understand parental requests. Because they use their hands well, they eat neatly, manage buttons carefully, and play for long periods with puzzles, board games, crayons, and dolls. Parents like and admire their quiet efficiency.

Girls notice everything, including adult frowns and silences which signal displeasure. Equating approval with right and wrong, they blame themselves when parents are unhappy; their lifelong search for others' esteem begins.

They want and seek adult praise, so they obey rules and stay out of trouble. They correctly judge their own behavior as desirable and that of boys as undesirable.[14]

At school, their success with words, crayons, and orders highlights their competence and wins smiles from teachers.

Because of her sex, a preschool girl can identify with both her mother and her woman teacher or caretaker, the key, indispensable people in every young child's life. Imitating them, bossing paper doll families, criticizing her wild younger brother, she feels as important as they are. Not until the later elementary years do girls begin to question their worth.

Ordinal Position

Oldest Child

First-born children must struggle. They have been described as lacking confidence, aggressiveness, and leadership[16] and also as being seclusive, gullible, anxious, and quickly defeated. Some are hostile and easily angered.[17] Phillips[26] states that 73 percent of the boys and 85 percent of the girls referred to clinics for behavior problems are oldest children.

The first child suffers from amateur parenting. Burdened with his care, facing startling new problems, expecting too much of him and themselves, his mother and father treat him erratically. They venture into emotion-based, unproductive, and inconsistent ways of getting him to do what they wish.

The oldest child models himself on both parents and, trying to act as they do, fails often. His behavior always is more mature than that of younger siblings,[23] but stretching for high standards wearies and irritates him.

Middle Child

The middle child has three models, each unique. Less dependent on his parents than is either his older brother or younger sister, he may or may not try to please them.

Often he finds his own niche in life. He becomes socially expert, scholastically superior, or athletically skilled. When he is older, he gains confidence and independence by devoting hours to astronomy, story-writing, carpentry, baking, or stamp-collecting.

Youngest Child

The youngest child is kept infantile. His mother has time to dress and feed him forever; she dreads losing her snuggling, adoring, final baby. She protects him from the orders and attacks of older siblings, so he cheerfully pesters them, setting habits of dealing with others which make him unpopular. The older children speedily wash dishes, dust, and rake leaves, so the youngest never is asked to lend his inexpert hands to chores. He lags in ability, adaptation, and self-sufficiency.

Hazy barriers block growth and strength. With too many models, his personality fractures like a smashed mirror. He is the one who witnesses for years the troubles of each family member. What happens to those who are older and more able than he frightens him and he retreats. Even if he tries hard to improve his skills, he cannot match older brothers and sisters. He lives with clear evidence that he amounts to little.

Special Status

The Only Child

The only child is bedeviled with overwhelming attention, either supportive or destructive. His parents, with no other youngsters for comparison, can be far off the mark in their goals for him. And, not totally committed to family life, they may resent the interruption of preferred adult activities by the need to donate time and effort to the child's rearing. But they feel guilty about selfishness and, soothing conscience, take the youngster along whenever they go out. No one has a good time.

Even when his parents are reasonable in their treatment, the only child believes they are unjust because he never hears a sibling criticized. Every day, he must try to manage and please two adults, each of whom has a different idea of how he is to act. He is the odd one of the trio, so he feels lonely and sometimes panicky.[37]

Twins

Same-sex twins are most alike during their first year.[7] They tend to develop and to react similarly because they experience many of the same events.[2]

As toddlers, twins form a private club, complete with a secret language, and delight in each other's ability to make awesome messes and outwit their parents. Content with each other, they fail to adjust to and find friends among other children. School gives them a second chance to make their way independently.

They hear themselves compared by every adult who knows, or even meets, them: "Nicole is so much more friendly than Nancy"; "Roger's the athlete of the two, isn't he?"

One twin will be better-looking, more obedient, or healthier than the other and parents prefer the youngster who best fits their dreams.

One leads; the other follows. The leader may feel confidence in himself but concern for his twin. The follower may feel smothered and inadequate. If the twins are a boy and girl, the girl takes charge. Because she matures more quickly, she dominates her brother and both may grow up atypical of their sexes.

The Adopted Child

Adults adopt for many reasons, some of which have little to do with fondness for children. Many adoptive mothers and fathers, shaky about their feelings toward and knowledge of children, let their youngster do whatever he likes. Others, burdened with a sense of deep responsibility, snap at his every move.

The spectre of heredity hovers, and some parents blame the child's background for misbehavior or personality quirks.

Sometimes an adoptive parent resents the youngster: he comes first in a spouse's affections; he causes new, unwelcome problems in daily living; or his presence underlines the couple's own inability to produce children.

Such conflicting, upsetting adult emotions create insecurity in the adopted child. But even when he is reared well by loving and sensible parents, he feels alone and unwanted at times.[37]

The Illegitimate Child

Over 500,000 babies are born annually to American teenagers, half are illegitimate.

Most are being kept by their mothers, not released for adoption as they once were. But few adolescents are ready to sacrifice time and freedom to infant care. Soon a young mother thinks of her off-spring as a nuisance. Her boy- and girl-friends, equally uninterested and unskilled, act as occasional baby-sitters, sometimes neglecting or abusing the child.

Or a grandmother may be saddled with his care. Tired and resentful, she ignores or over-punishes the youngster and he grows up anxious, undisciplined, and impulsive.

The Child of Divorce; the Stepchild

Bewildered victims of divorce, small children are sure their own failure to eat their carrots or pick up their toys caused the breakup.[33] They believe they will never see their fathers again. Newly divorced mothers and fathers, guilty, angry, and afraid, offer little discipline or training to their confused children.

Three-year-olds whose parents were recently divorced could neither play naturally nor get along with other people. A year later, they still were disobedient and immature. Two years later, girls had regained their confidence, but boys were disliked by both peers and teachers even after their behavior improved.[15]

If his mother or father marries again, the child must win the approval of stepparents. This may not be easy. The new husband or wife, jealous of the former mate, degrades the youngster, an all-too-obvious and perpetual reminder of the previous marriage. Often, the natural parent protests the new spouse's correction and criticism of the child and the preschooler discovers that he is free to defy the stepparent. The new marriage founders and the child is credited with sinking it.

THE FAMILY

Size

If the preschooler is one of four or more children, he rarely can count on personal attention from his parents. Needing it, he sometimes seeks and gets adult notice by starting fights and breaking rules. With this technique, he ensures frequent punishment for him-

Behavior Problems of Preschool Children

self and status as the bad boy in the family. Worse, he settles into lasting habits of aggressiveness.

With each addition to the large family, problems mutliply and money must stretch. Beleaguered and weary, parents give only haphazard training to their brood.

In big families, an older youngster usually is assigned responsibility for a younger one. His unwise counsel, ridicule, commands, or over-concern can stifle and depress the preschooler.

Socioeconomic Status

Lower Class

Poor adults, discouraged and angry, may neglect or abuse their preschoolers. Although poverty does not harm the child, the attitude of his parents toward themselves and society bounces off him. He feels guilty and bad without knowing why.[32]

Lower class mothers tend to speak and play less with their children than do middle class mothers.[6,40] The boys and girls watch more television,[1] do less well on intelligence tests,[25,31] are more often rated socially immature,[25] and are less willing to accept peers' leadership than are middle class youngsters.[9] Boys have only bottom-level career aspirations.[22]

Middle Class

Preschoolers from middle class families do better both in development and behavior.[31] Their mothers consider them easy to get along with[32] and they direct them less than lower class mothers do their children. Middle class fathers help out by looking after the children some of the time and thus get to know them better.

At present, half of all women with children hold jobs, with the increased numbers primarily from the middle class. Four million working mothers have children under the age of three; eight million preschool children are cared for by others.[8] If the sitter or nursery teacher is stable, sensible, and affectionate, the youngster benefits. His over-busy parents may be more indifferent to his needs than his paid caretaker. But some sitters neglect, frighten, or abuse the young child.

Upper Class

Wealthy parents nearly always turn over the care of a preschooler to a nurse. Occupied with travel, job and community duties, and a barrage of dinners and parties, they see their offspring at set times and make decisions about his education and recreation without knowing what he's really like.

The child becomes close to his nurse if she's available for comforting and proud announcements. He may resent his parents' deserting him for more attractive pursuits.

Times change. Both middle and lower class mothers hold jobs; both attend child-rearing classes. Now there are fewer differences between their management of children and their response to certain behaviors than formerly.[6,13] Upper class mothers, more sensitive to the needs of their children than they once were, enjoy looking after sons and daughters and seek help promptly if there is trouble.

Race and Nationality

Despite major gains in assimilation and equality of opportunity, minority children still must battle for self-respect.

Mahan[21] states that attitudes about their own race tend to stabilize when youngsters are four years old. Rohrer[28] found that black preschool children look down on themselves. Since 1970, the divorce rate for black couples has doubled; 70 percent of poor black families are headed by women.[30]

Mexican-American children hesitate to leave their own group.[28] Chinese, Japanese, Korean, Cambodian, and Vietnamese boys and girls also remain within their own ethnic circles. Their immediate families include uncles, aunts, and grandparents, each of whom adds his bit to the youngster's rearing.

Steady exposure to American ways and language are needed so the child can learn when he enters school.[36] Head Start classes improve confidence and skills for minority children.

Values

Religion

The church school class or nursery can be unpleasant, especially for the toddler. Each time he goes, there are strange teachers and new classmates. Most Sundays, he would rather stay home.

When he is older, he begins to realize that church is honorable and purposeful and he feels good about being part of it.

Because of his parents' religion, the child differs from his playmates. If they are fundamentalists, he hears diatribes against dancing, card-playing, and movies. If they are Christian Scientists, he is ashamed when he is ill. If they are Catholic, he is awed by ceremony, ritual, and rules. If they are Jewish, he celebrates Hanukkah, not Christmas, and wonders why. If they are Mormon, he learns that tea and coffee are tabu.

Hobbies and Diversions

In some families everyone jogs, swims, and exercises. The imitating preschooler beams at what he can do and tries to do better.

For other mothers and fathers, learning is paramount. The child goes to story hour at the library and brings home a dozen books at each visit. His parents coach him in the alphabet and read him stories from the classics. Older, he spends hours every day with books.

Some adults entertain constantly. They produce their preschooler at each event to greet guests and recite nursery rhymes. Intrigued by parties and people, he learns early to seek applause with performance at social gatherings.

Parents may spend spare time hunting fossils, skin-diving, building furniture, playing the guitar, camping, flying, cooking, sculpting, or studying genealogy. The child tags along, joining in when allowed, and develops similar hobbies.

Ethical Standards

One preschooler's mother and father obey every law. They never cheat on their income tax or exceed the speed limit. Another child's parents smirk as they pocket an apple in the grocery store, scoot through the red light, and return a dropped radio to the store for refund, claiming defective workmanship.

Some adults listen to neighbors' worries, take cookies to an elderly widow, wrap gifts for poor children at Christmas, and invite foreign students to dinner. Others spend money on cars and clothes they can't afford, indulge themselves with liquor, drugs, and expensive entertainment, seek friends' and relatives' attention and help, and brush off requests from others for their assistance.

The small child, observing, copies his parents' ethical ways.

THE COMMUNITY

The Neighborhood and Neighbors

Although neighborhoods are composed of people whose socioeconomic status is roughly similar, the particular families living there make a difference in the preschooler's experiences.

The block may swarm with children of all ages. If so, the young boy or girl stays exhausted from running with and after hordes of playing youngsters. Or, families in the neighborhood may consist only of retired couples or those with a teenager or two. If so, for his first five years, the preschooler plays alone.

The neighbors make a difference in his parents' lives and thus, in his. If a neighbor drops in uninvited for daily coffee and conversation, his busy mother turns angry and tense. The youngster gets splashed with her spill-over irritation.

One neighbor may shout at him for walking on his newly-sown grass; another may complain about his climbing on the fence; still another may object to his addressing her as, "Mary," not "Mrs. Olson."

Or, the neighbors are friendly. One offers a cooky every time he knocks at the door. Others help when his father is moving furniture or come over when his mother needs an emergency sitter.

The attitudes and actions of neighbors influence the small child's feelings toward people outside his family.

School

Teacher

If the preschooler attends nursery or day school, he gets used to the differing methods and standards of several teachers.

But if he meets his first and only teacher in kindergarten, he

bases his prediction for educational pleasure or horror on her manner. If she is brusque and critical, he fears public humiliation. If she
hurries and pushes, he is strung tight and sleeps restlessly. If she
turns on the TV to "Sesame Street" and abandons her pupils to do as
they like with toys and crayons, he believes that school is for amuse-
ment. If she feebly protests when a child disobeys or turns her back
on the youngster who hides and resists, he thinks of school as a
chaotic, unsafe place.

But if his teacher plans the day carefully, alternates games and
songs with stories and table work, teaches by repetition, arranges for
everyone to succeed at something, and calmly handles behavior and
emotional problems, he loves her and likes school.

Classmates

At first, most five-year-olds are wary of classmates. They are
dangerous strangers.

Much of the kindergartener's year is spent learning to ignore
classmates so that he can hear and follow the teacher's directions.
The young scholar who entertains, challenges, or comforts other
boys and girls is distracted from learning and exits kindergarten
knowing little more than he did on his first day there.

If he can keep up with classmates in most activities, he likes being
with them. If he falls behind, is ridiculed, or is left out, he hates
them and makes excuses to stay home from school.

Tasks

Academic requirements vary at different schools. A few even
schedule a full day of kindergarten.

In some classes, youngsters are drilled in the alphabet and word
recognition. They seldom relax with songs and marching games.
They are assigned homework every night. If the five-year-old cannot digest what the teacher stuffs into him nor sit still while she tries,
he is worried and unhappy.

In other schools, little instruction is attempted. Free play takes
most of the time, no help is given youngsters unfamiliar with scissors
and crayons, and children are not taught the alphabet nor asked
questions about stories read to them. Knowing little, they find the

demands of first grade overwhelming. Many fail.

The young child's impressions of school and of his place there linger for years and affect his ability to learn.

REFERENCES

1. Braithwaite, V., and Holman, J.: Parent observed behaviours of preschool television watchers. *Australian Journal of Psychology, 33:* 375, 1981.
2. Burlingham, D.: *Twins: A Study of Three Pairs of Identical Twins.* New York, Intl Univs Pr, 1952.
3. Caplan, H., Bibace, R., and Rabinovitch, M. S.: Paranatal stress, cognitive organization and ego function: A controlled follow-up study of children born prematurely. *Journal of Child Psychiatry, 2:* 434, 1963.
4. Daldry, A. D., and Russell, P. A.: Sex differences in the behavior of pre-school children with novel and familiar toys. *Journal of Genetic Psychology, 141:* 3, 1982.
5. Eaton, W. O., and Keats, J. G.: Peer presence, stress, and sex differences in the motor activity level of preschoolers. *Developmental Psychology, 18:* 534, 1982.
6. Farran, D. C., and Haskins, R.: Reciprocal influence in the social interactions of mothers and three-year-old children from different socio-economic backgrounds. *Child Development, 51:* 780, 1980.
7. Freedman, D. G., and Keller, B.: Inheritance of behavior in infants. *Science, 140:* 196, 1963.
8. Friedrich, O.: What do babies know? *Time, 122* (7): 52, 1983.
9. Fu, V. R.: Preschool leadership-followership behaviors. *Child Study Journal, 9:* 133, 1979.
10. Griffore, R. J.: *Child Development.* Springfield, Thomas, 1981.
11. Gullo, D. F.: Social class differences in preschool children's comprehension of *wh* questions. *Child Development, 52:* 736, 1981.
12. Haring, N. G., and Phillips, E. L.: *Educating Emotionally Disturbed Children.* New York, McGraw, 1962.
13. Harmon, D., and Kogan, K. L.: Social class and mother-child interaction. *Psychological Reports, 46:* 1075, 1980.
14. Hartley, D.: Infant-school children's perception of the behaviour of same- and opposite-sexed classmates. *British Journal of Social Psychology, 20:* 141, 1981.
15. Hetherington, E. M., Cox, M., and Cox, R.: Play and social interaction in children following divorce. *Journal of Social Issues, 35:* 26, 1979.
16. Hurlock, E.: *Child Growth and Development,* 4th ed. New York, McGraw, 1970.
17. Lahey, B. B., Hammer, D., Crumrine, P. L., and Forehand, R. L.: Birth order x sex interactions in child behavior problems. *Developmental Psychology, 16:* 608, 1980.

18. Ley, R. B., and Koepke, J. E.: Attachment behavior outdoors: Naturalistic observations of sex and age differences in the separation behavior of young children. *Infant Behavior and Development, 5:* 195, 1982.
19. Liss, M. B.: Patterns of toy play: An analysis of sex differences. *Sex Roles, 7:* 1143, 1981.
20. Lubchenco, L. O., Horner, F. A., Reed, L. H., Hix, I. E., Jr., Metcalf, D., Cohig, R., Elliott, H. C., and Bourg, M.: Sequelae of premature birth. *American Journal of Diseases of Children, 106:* 101, 1963.
21. Mahan, J.: Black and White children's racial identification and preference. *Journal of Black Psychology, 3:* 47, 1976.
22. Malone, C., and Shope, G.: Career expectations of primary grade children related to socioeconomic status. *Gifted Child Quarterly, 22:* 322, 1978.
23. McDavid, J. W.: Imitative behavior in preschool children. *Psychological Monographs, 73:* (486), 1959.
24. Morris, A. M., Williams, J. M., Atwater, A. E., and Wilmore, J. H.: Age and sex differences in motor performance of 3 through 6 year old children. *Research Quarterly for Exercise and Sport, 53:* 214, 1982.
25. Nettelbladt, P., Uddenberg, N., and Englesson, I.: Sex-role patterns, paternal rearing attitudes, and child development in different social classes. *Acta Psychiatrica Scandinavica, 64:* 12, 1981.
26. Phillips, E. L.: Cultural vs. intrapsychic factors in childhood behavior problem referrals. *Journal of Clinical Psychology, 12:* 400, 1956.
27. Podolsky, E.: How the child reacts to his physical defects. *Mental Hygiene, (N. Y.), 37:* 581, 1953.
28. Rohrer, G. K.: Racial and ethnic identification and preference in young children. *Young Children, 32:* 24, 1977.
29. Sandler, I. N.: Social support resources, stress, and maladjustment of poor children. *American Journal of Community Psychology, 8:* 41, 1980.
30. Schreiner, T.: Blacks gain in schooling, lag in income. *USA TODAY, 1:* August 22, 1983.
31. Silva, P. A., McGee, R., Thomas, J., and Williams, S.: A descriptive study of socio-economic status and child development in Dunedin five year olds. *New Zealand Journal of Educational Studies, 17:* 21, 1982.
32. Simonds, M. P., and Simonds, J. F.: Relationship of maternal parenting behaviors to preschool children's temperament. *Child Psychiatry and Human Development, 12:* 19, 1981.
33. Tomlinson-Keasey, C.: *Child's Eye View.* New York, St Martin, 1980.
34. Touliatos, J., and Lindholm, B. W.: Congruence of parents' and teachers' ratings of children's behavior problems. *Journal of Abnormal Child Psychology, 9:* 347, 1981.
35. Tush, B. R.: Bruising in healthy 3-year-old children. *Maternal-Child Nursing Journal, 11:*165, 1982.
36. Valencia, R. R., Henderson, R. W., and Rankin, R. J.: Relationship of family constellation and schooling to intellectual performance of Mexican-American children. *Journal of Educational Psychology, 73:* 524, 1981.

37. Verville, E.: *Behavior Problems of Children.* Philadelphia, Saunders, 1967.
38. Wortis, H., Heimer, C. B., Braine, M., Redlo, M., and Rue, R.: Growing up in Brooklyn: The early history of the premature child. *American Journal of Orthopsychiatry, 33:* 535, 1963.
39. Yarrow, L. J.: Separation from parents during early childhood. In Hoffman, M. L., and Hoffman, L. W., eds.: *Review of Child Development Research,* Vol. 1. New York, Russell Sage, 1964.
40. Zegiob, L. E., and Forehand, R.: Maternal interactive behavior as a function of race, socioeconomic status, and sex of the child. *Child Development, 46: 564, 1975.*

Chapter 2

BIRTH TO ONE YEAR

WRINKLED, red, and wet, his eyes and hands scrunched tight, the newborn promises little. But in a brief twelve months, this useless, helpless waif magically turns into an upright human who explores, tests, laughs, gives, and obeys. He can entertain and control both himself and others.

ACHIEVEMENTS

Off to a good start during his first three months, the infant holds up his head and looks around, sights on moving objects, and recognizes colors and shapes.[7] He rocks, kicks, and rolls from side to back. He smiles and gurgles. His grasp on bottles and rattles grows firm.[19]

Between three and six months, he reaches for and inspects toys, shifting them from hand to hand. He deliberately turns over, pushes himself into his crib corner, sits propped with a pillow, laughs, plays with his toes, grins when his mother picks him up, and gabbles new sounds.

Between six and nine months, he sits alone and tries creeping and crawling. Interesting sounds or tiny objects captivate him and he pats his twin in the mirror. He loves the playfulness of his parents but puckers up when a stranger tries the same antics. He understands some words and joins society by copying his big brother's head-shaking, spoon-banging, and waving.[15]

In the final three months of his busy year, he gets on his own two feet. He pulls up, stands alone, and walks when led. He "talks" by repeating the same syllable over and over, but also uses a genuine word or two.[10] He plays patty-cake, amuses himself when alone, manages both spoon and cup, and makes friends by handing over a toy.

Sociable and competent, he has come a long way.

PARENT CONCERNS

As their baby changes, so do his parents. Scared, exhausted, ignorant, and worried, they continually must adapt themselves to the needs and demands of this strange little person who lives with them.

Swinging between emotional high and lows of adoring their tiny, sweet, cute, soft, cuddly infant and despairing over smelly diapers, mountains of laundry, inexplicable crying, and overwhelming responsibility, the mother and father lose quantities of confidence.[18] They question their ability to make common-sense decisions.[1] Chess *et al.*[5] describe the perplexed parents of a crying, misbehaving six-month-old. Guilty and fearful, sure their baby suffered from anxiety they had created, they cut all ties with friends and stayed home to suffer with him.

Parents who don't know what to expect[3] are sure that the infant isn't developing properly. He doesn't eat right and won't burp; his stools are like nothing they've ever seen. There are splotchy birthmarks on his face and rashes on his body; he has bow legs and scaly hands.[9] Is he retarded? Can he hear and see?

Their fears for him and themselves are heightened by the corrections and warnings of their own parents. At the doctor's office, in the neighborhood, or at family get-togethers, the mother and father anxiously compare their baby with others.

Luckily, time and experience erase their dismay.

TYPICAL PROBLEMS

Emotion

Crying

Crying signals that something is wrong. A weary, tense mother joins her infant with tears of her own during the first draining weeks.

Hunger, indigestion, fatigue, illness, discomfort, or hypersensitivity to stimulation can cause sporadic fretting or hours of steady crying.[16]

A loud noise or sudden movement provokes tears. When something is taken from him, the infant cries in protest.

Dunn[8] reports that babies delivered under general anesthesia were more irritable than those who were not. Also, girls were calmer than boys; perhaps anesthesia for circumcisions causes the difference.

Usually the baby can be soothed by rocking, petting, cuddling, swaddling, or sucking. After six weeks, his digestive system works more smoothly and evening crying from colic ceases.

A mother's instant rescue during the first months can be replaced with gradually lengthened delay, which teaches both parent and child to tolerate discomfort for short periods.[18]

Anger

The infant shows his mettle by six months of age. No longer can he be maneuvered to suit his parent's whims. Angrily, he bats away the cup of orange juice; he yells and twists to escape diapering; he furiously pulls off the cap placed on his head. At any time, for no good reason, he screams and kicks and flails his arms.

Nearing a year, sometimes the angry child holds his breath until he turns blue. His frightened mother backs off and gives in; the youngster discovers that violence wins him his way.[18] Breath-holding is even more common during the second year.[13]

The storming baby can be diverted. Handing him a new or favorite toy prevents resistance to dressing. Offering orange juice when he is bored, not fascinated with play, heads off temper stirred by interruption. Tossing or swinging him about when he kicks, yells, or holds his breath makes it impossible for him to continue.

Affection

Parents are distressed when their baby appears disinterested in them. Normally an infant is charmed by his smiling, talking mother and father, especially after he reaches six months of age.[8] But breaks in contact between parent and child cool affection.

In one study, infants cared for solely by their mothers were compared with those whose care was shared by a second woman. At six months, the babies looked after only by their mothers were less irritable and easier to handle than the others, and at one year they were more active and more socially and emotionally responsive. Also, the mothers were more tolerant and self-confident than mothers who shared child care with a sitter or relative.[12]

A father who plays with and looks after his infant becomes close to him. The baby knows and trusts his father just as he does his mother.

Fear

Brazelton[4] states that the baby fears strangers when he is four to five months old, again at eight months, and also at one year. At four months, he can differentiate between faces; at eight months, he is startled by peculiar or unexpected overtures; and at one year, he worries that the unknown person will replace his parents or seize his toys.

Often he shows fear when he is in a place strange to him: *e.g.*, at the beach[6] or in a jammed shopping center. Sometimes he cries frantically when taken outside. The new sensations of prickly grass as he crawls or the eerie feel of the breeze which touches his cheek frighten him.

If his parents walk off into another room, leaving him in his playpen, he instantly lets out a bellow, his fear-and-rage message that someone must stay with him.

Fear can be damped. A stranger should keep his distance and busy himself with the adults. He should wait for the infant to stare at or approach him. When the baby is frightened by new surroundings, cuddling and soft talk help. Letting him put his foot into the shifting sand while safe in his father's arms wards off panic at the beach.

Several times each day he must fall asleep in his own crib, away from his parents, but when he is up, one adult can stay in sight. When his mother is working in the kitchen, his playpen can be moved near the door.

Feeding

Feeding troubles start at birth. The nursing mother doesn't know if her baby is getting enough milk and she worries. The annoyed mother of the bottle-fed infant, who falls asleep after guzzling only one ounce, knows that won't do. He'll be awake and crying for more in fifteen minutes.

Older, now strapped in a high chair, the baby grimaces as his mother inserts cereal into his mouth. He promptly pushes it out with his tongue and the gooey stuff dribbles over his chin and bib. When she tries green beans and plums, he acts the same way.

There's more trauma ahead: the mother must take away bottles and also allow her inept baby to feed himself with fingers and an upside down spoon.

Problems aren't inevitable. The nursing mother can weigh her baby before and after feeding till she's sure he's doing fine. The mother of the bottle-fed infant can jiggle him to keep him awake and sucking so he gets two or three ounces every three hours when he first comes home. He'll work up to four or five ounces by six weeks and six or eight by three months. Then feedings can be cut to four or five a day. Stuffing a bottle in his mouth every time he cries leads to a fat baby and hours of extra handling.

Spit-out solid foods aren't necessarily disliked. They're merely strange for the baby to manage: he knows only about liquids and sucking. The chief reason for giving solid food during the early months is not to keep him healthy, it's to accustom him to the spoon and to new textures and tastes.

Normally a baby handles and gums on crackers when he is six months old. By ten months, he grabs the spoon from his mother and, mimicking her, tries to feed himself.[16] If he's allowed to practice, he does a neat job of it within two or three months.

Graduating from bottle to cup is easy if the baby is given sips of water, fruit juice, and small amounts of milk in a cup by nine months. Gradually, milk in the cup is increased and that in the bottle decreased. By the time he is a year old, his bottles can be put away.

Sleeping

At first the infant's sleeping time is a see-saw affair: it ranges from fifteen minutes to five hours. But soon, usually by six weeks, he gives up his 2 A.M. feeding and his weary parents get their first full night's sleep. By three months, when he's put to bed at six or seven, he sleeps until morning.[2]

The baby takes three naps during the day until he is six months old, then naps once in the morning and again in the afternoon. The one-year-old vacillates between one and two naps, but is cranky if his one nap is short or comes too late in the day.

During his first weeks, the baby wakes often if he has not been fed enough. When he is older, he resists sleep if he is picked up each time he fusses, kept up late, or not held to a regular schedule.[11]

He will sleep well if he is put in his crib at the same time each day and left alone. His fretting soon stops; most undisturbed babies fall asleep within twenty minutes.

If he sleeps too long during naps, he can be wakened so that he is ready to sleep at night.[18]

Independence

The normal, healthy infant is active and exploring from the moment of birth.[14] He has an inborn need both to survive and to master obstacles.[4]

He asserts his independence by investigating, climbing, resisting dressing, and staggering off in the opposite direction when his parents call. He is not being bad: he is proving that he is a learner and a doer.

Planning prevents his experiments in independence from harming him or distressing his mother and father.

Clothes which can be slipped on speedily divert parent-infant

battles. Beads, pins, and other swallowables can be spotted and removed; ash trays can be kept clean; leftover pet food can be discarded promptly. Because high chairs tip over and chests of drawers
fall on an eager climber, the child needs watching and the furniture
stabilizing.

When he toddles off in the wrong direction, his mother can catch
and turn him around so he's headed the way he should go.

Emotional storms, feeding and sleeping irritants, tries for independence: all can be managed.

REFERENCES

1. Austin, G., Oliver, J. S., and Richards, J. C.: *The Parents' Guide to Child Raising.* Englewood Cliffs, P-H, 1978.
2. Beardslee, C.: The sleep of infants and young children: A review of the literature. *Maternal-Child Nursing Journal, 5:* 5, 1976.
3. Bigner, J. J.: *Parent-Child Relations.* New York, Macmillan, 1979.
4. Brazelton, T. B.: *Infants and Mothers.* New York, Delacorte, 1969.
5. Chess, S., Thomas, A., and Birch, H. G.: *Your Child Is a Person.* New York,
Viking Pr, 1965.
6. Church, J.: *Understanding Your Child from Birth to Three.* New York, PB, 1976.
7. Cohen, L. B.: Our developing knowledge of infant perception and cognition.
American Psychologist, 34: 894, 1979.
8. Dunn, J.: *Distress and Comfort.* Cambridge, Harvard U Pr, 1977.
9. Gersh, M. J.: *How to Raise Children at Home in Your Spare Time.* New York, Stein
& Day, 1966.
10. Gesell, A.: *The First Five Years of Life.* New York, Harper, 1940.
11. Hurlock, E. B.: *Child Growth and Development,* 4th ed. New York, McGraw,
1970.
12. Hurlock, E. B.: *Personality Development.* New York, McGraw, 1974.
13. Kanner, L.: *Child Psychiatry,* 4th ed. Springfield, Thomas, 1972.
14. Sherrod, K., Vietze, P., and Friedman, S.: *Infancy.* Monterey, Brooks-Cole,
1978.
15. Smart, M. S., and Smart, R. C.: *Children.* New York, Macmillan, 1967.
16. Spock, B.: *Baby and Child Care.* New York, Dutton, 1976.
17. Stewart, B. J.: Mother-infant care unit. In Walters, C.E., ed.: *Mother-Infant
Interaction.* New York, Human Sci Pr, 1976.
18. Verville, E.: *Behavior Problems of Children.* Philadelphia, Saunders, 1967.
19. White, B. L.: *The First Three Years of Life.* Englewood Cliffs, P-H, 1975.

Chapter 3

ONE TO TWO YEARS

A ONE-YEAR-OLD is a little person programmed for trouble-making. He deliberately disobeys, slyly smiling and sneaking glances at his daddy as he twists knobs on the costly stereo. He makes spectacular messes, dumping wastebaskets, ripping labels from cans, and dragging out every shoe in his parents' closet. Nearly every day he injures himself: he crashes into the corner of the coffee table, pulls the iron on top of himself, falls off the back porch, and cuts himself on opened tin cans.

Because his mother and father now start teaching him to fit into polite society, the toddler's days are studded with prohibitions, warnings, and punishment. The adorable baby has disappeared. In his place stands a Challenge.

ACHIEVEMENTS

The one-year-old walks alone, both forward and backward. Often he disdains the proffered but restraining hand, and thus falls off curbs and wanders into traffic. Before the year is over, he climbs stairs and kitchen cabinets, kneels, jumps, trots, and kicks a ball.[9]

He can, when asked, point to his nose, eyes, and hair or to a pictured dog, spoon, baby, or chair. When his second birthday arrives, he has a vocabulary of 300 words and can produce two- and three-word sentences. His union of noun and verb describes, explains, and commands. He talks to himself, his toys, and his grandfather in a mystifying jargon of sounds, complete with inflections and fraught with meaning.

He welcomes home his father with jumps and squeals, cries loudly and bitterly when his parents leave him with a sitter, shows off for his mother, and gives the visiting neighbor a kiss. Helpfully, he puts his toys in the toy box, gets his coat when his daddy starts for the door, fetches dishes off the table and throws them in the sink, and digs into the grocery sack to hand his mother cans to put away.

He is an important member of his family and his world.

PARENT CONCERNS

Parents want their child to be like them in activity level and interests; usually, there's a fair match. But sometimes eager, athletic adults beget a youngster who calmly sits playing with one toy or studying magazine pictures. Quiet, scholarly parents watch with growing unhappiness the perpetual motion of their experimenting, running, shrieking small child. Such characteristic traits show themselves more during the second year of life than the first.

Parents of the one-year-old nurse their ongoing concern that the child is not developing properly. They worry about his garbled sounds and meager vocabulary. They frown when his staggering walk ends in a crashing thud. They fear he never will master the intricacies of using a potty-chair[5] or stacking plastic rings on a post.

Because he is both mobile and curious, they must rearrange their home to protect him and their belongings. Prized mementoes, once proudly displayed, must be hidden away. Medicines and cleaning fluids must be stored on high shelves. Gates must be installed across stairs and kitchen entries; hooks must be hammered on doors.

A dozen times a day the adults stare at their bare living room, drag out the step-stool, and unlock gates to get from one room to another. Because of the child, life is fettered.[11]

COMMON PROBLEMS

Independence

The one-year-old's attempts at independence are like pendulum swings. One moment he gleefully bounces up and down on the bed, ignoring stern orders to stop at once. The next, he is sucking his thumb and snuggling with his mother.[2] His quick switches from outlaw to infant demonstrate again that most growth comes in fits and starts.

As he tries to be his own man, his despairing parents cope with unending trouble. At night and at naptime, he escapes his crib to appear, all smiles, in the living room, bent on playing with his mother and father.[3] Bored with the steady appearance of meals, his appetite fading, he pounds his spoon into his mushy apricots, cheerily spits spinach into his mother's face, reaches for his father's beer, and relentlessly drops overboard the mashed potatoes and chopped chicken his mother has fixed for him.[10]

Again and again he turns on lights, runs from his mother, and grabs the paper his father is reading, his persistence labelled stubbornness by his tired parents.

Nuisance though they are, his independent ways mean that he is alert, self-confident, and determined, not bad traits in such a small, ineffectual person.

He must be taught and protected while he experiments.

A twenty-month-old girl died in a night fire at her home because weeks earlier her parents had given up trying to keep her in her bed. They allowed her to plop down and sleep wherever she chose. That night, they could not find her.

The child who leaves his bed always must be returned to it.

When he shows by playing with his food that he is not interested in it, he should be let down from his high chair and sent out of the kitchen. He quickly learns that if he wants something to eat, this is the time and place for it.

If he persists in forbidden acts, he can be distracted with a toy, removed to another room, or deposited temporarily in his playpen. When parents always back up "no" with action, eventually the child stops trying to provoke them.

Toilet Training

Long months of excitement, disappointment, punishment, and frustration await parent and child as toilet training begins. The constant attention to toileting, with its exaggerated joy or distress, can affect the relationship between tutor and pupil all day, every day, and for years after training finally is achieved.

Toilet sessions should be brief, non-emotional, and regular, beginning when the child is able to succeed some of the time. Given the need for maturation of the nervous system and close attention by the toddler, instant dryness is impossible.

Success should be greeted with, "Look at that!" not, "You wonderful, marvelous child!" and lapses with, "Oh-oh!" not, "How could you!"

Speech

Some one-year-olds talk all the time, but no one can figure out what they're saying. Their jargon sounds like speech. Obviously the child is communicating, seriously and intelligently.[11]

Parents who do not understand the youngster's sounds fret that he makes no sense and worry that his recognizable vocabulary is so limited.

They need only be patient and have faith. If they talk to him, read to him, listen to him, and repeat what they believe is his meaning, speech develops easily.

The boy or girl who rarely speaks usually has been over-questioned or pushed to talk.[8] Parental quarreling or constant correction of his poor enunciation also silences him.

Emotion

The infant's screams baffled and disturbed his parents, but the one-year-old's emotion makes sense to them. Knowing that he is afraid of the jumping kitten or is angry at being interrupted at play, they consider his reactions reasonable and may back away from their job as teachers. If they do, serious and lasting problems develop.

If the child always cries when left in a nursery or with a sitter, his sympathizing parents go nowhere without him. If sometimes they must, they sneak out when he's not looking and the youngster, unable to trust them and ever more anxious, never lets them out of his sight.

If he kicks and yells at bedtime, his understanding parents let him stay up until they go to bed. Soon his temper rules the household and, exhausted from emotion and lack of sleep, he falls behind age-mates in achievement and self-control.

If he shrieks at a shadow, lightning, a large dog, or a pounding train, his alarmed parents berate the fearsome object and cluck in pity. Before long, he hides behind his mother or a chair a dozen times daily.

Rather than using the young child's emotion to guide their actions, a mother and father can explain events briefly with words and demonstrations. Then they must do what is best for the child — leaving him with the sitter, putting him to bed early — proving to him that he can endure difficulties and that he can count on them to take charge.

Exploration

Exploring his world, the one-year-old creates disorder and disaster for his harried parents.

He prefers dragging out his mother's pots and pans to playing with his carefully selected "educational" toys. With his father's keys, he scratches a permanent design on the gleaming wood of the front door. He grabs the pen his mother left on the kitchen table when she answered the phone and scribbles all over the wallpaper. Proudly announcing, "Light!", he pulls on the dresser scarf and the lamp topples to the floor. He tenses every muscle in his body and grandly heaves his rubber ball straight at his father's face and glasses.

One mother wrote about a typical scene with Kathy, eighteen months, and Lisa, five months.

> The last time Mama saw them, the girls were in their room, the baby just up from a nap and lying on the single bed waiting for her bottle. Kathy is happily pretending to brush her teeth with a red toothbrush confiscated from the bathroom. While the bottle cools, Mama and Daddy have a short conversation in the living room.

Suddenly from the girls' room came sharp screams of pain and anger. The baby! In alarm, Mama and Daddy rush in. Kathy sits by the baby on the bed, holding her sister's hand and sobbing hysterically. The toothbrush is nowhere to be seen.

Mama picks up the baby, red-faced, teary, still screaming, and Daddy gets Kathy.

"What happened? Kathy, what's the matter?"

Kathy tries to explain but is crying so hard that all the adults hear is, "Sorry, Sissy."

It's assumed that Kathy tried to brush Lisa's non-existent teeth.

Both girls fuss on and off for a few more minutes, but soon Lisa is taking her bottle in calm forgetfulness. Mama and Daddy are proud of the way Kathy stayed with the baby, even though she was upset and scared.

Conclusion: more than likely it was all Mama's fault anyway.

Close watching and a sense of humor reduce wear and tear on parents. But nothing can prevent minor crises and major destruction as the one-year-old explores and experiments his way through his lively second year.

REFERENCES

1. Adler, S., King, D., and Hodges, A. L.: *A Communicative Skills Program for Day Care, Preschool, and Early Elementary Teachers.* Springfield, Thomas, 1982.
2. Austin, G., Oliver, J. S., and Richards, J. C.: *The Parents' Guide to Child Raising.* Englewood Cliffs, P-H, 1978.
3. Beardslee, C.: The sleep of infants and young children: A review of the literature. *Maternal-Child Nursing Journal, 5:* 5, 1976.
4. Gesell, A.: *The First Five Years of Life.* New York, Harper, 1940.
5. Hurlock, E.: *Child Growth and Development,* 4th ed. New York, McGraw, 1970.
6. Kanner, L.: *Child Psychiatry,* 4th ed. Springfield, Thomas, 1972.
7. Lombardo, V. S.: *Paraprofessionals Working with Young Children.* Springfield, Thomas, 1981.
8. Sherrod, K., Vietze, P., and Friedman, S.: *Infancy.* Monterey, Brooks-Cole, 1978.
9. Smart, M. S., and Smart, R. C.: *Children.* New York, Macmillan, 1967.

10. Verville, E.: *Behavior Problems of Children*. Philadelphia, Saunders, 1967.
11. White, B. L.: *The First Three Years of Life*. Englewood Cliffs, P-H, 1975.

Chapter 4

TWO TO THREE YEARS

THE two-year-old's life tempo approaches frenzy as he storms, mimics, runs, and tries himself for hours every day. His "No!" is clear and automatic. Both creating and copying, he garners dozens of new skills. Contacts with other boys and girls initiate him into the startling manners and morals of his own generation. Always, he is exhausted, both from the pace he sets and the kaleidoscope of events with which he copes.

ACHIEVEMENTS

He handles himself well, so the two-year-old attempts daring athletic feats. Before the year is out, he has taught himself to jump off the porch steps, zip down a short slide, and climb to the top of the jungle gym.

His small muscles give better service. He can spear cut-up meat with a fork; he rarely spills his milk by accident.

Sanitation sets in. He pushes a brush up and down on his four front teeth, manages a brief contact with soap and water when told to wash his hands, and some time during the year achieves dryness, although he has sporadic accidents for another year or two.

He wants to do it himself, so he pulls off his socks and shirt and wiggles into his pajamas when they are laid out on the floor.

Now he turns on lights because he wants to see better, not merely to practice switch-flipping. He plays alone, in his room or out-of-doors, checking on his mother every few minutes to make sure she still is nearby. He shares some playtime, not always pleasantly, with other children.

Jargon doesn't work, so he converts to true speech. With longer sentences and many new words, he gets across to everyone what he knows and wants. He loves games and singing. He can sort objects by shape, color, and size.[10]

By the end of the year, he has acquired a hundred new physical, intellectual, social, and self-help skills, each a block in the steady building of his self-esteem and confidence.

PARENT CONCERNS

His mother and father are sure he is getting out of hand. He does not come when called, follow orders to fetch and carry, eat his dinner, stay in his yard, or keep his thumb out of his mouth. He marches to a different drummer and they see their control slipping away.

His social habits worry them. Left in a nursery for a half-day so his imprisoned mother finally can go somewhere without him, he screams in fear and fury. Introduced to strange children, he bites them, hides his head in his mother's lap, or both. The adults abhor these distressing signs that he's a born bully or sissy. They puzzle over how they'll make him charming and popular.

His efforts to grow up try their patience and get him into trouble. Again and again he painfully pushes at the button on his coat; it won't go through its hole, but he loudly refuses parental help. He reaches above his head for the mower handle and does his best to shove the heavy machine through the grass; the handle bounces and hits him on the head. Hauling himself to the lowest branch of the tree is not enough and he crawls up to the next, and the next; then he can't get down. Helping his mother, he drags his twelve-pound baby sister from her crib and lugs her to the kitchen. She is too much for him and he drops her with a thud on the floor.

As he works hard at extending himself, his mother and father vacillate uneasily between encouraging his originality and protecting him from harm.

COMMON PROBLEMS

Negativism

Mothers and fathers brace themselves for the "Terrible Twos" and the predicted string of refusals and temper.[14]

A two-year-old's negativism takes many shapes. Besides the plainly-spoken "No," the small child may stiffen his body to prevent being placed on the potty, collapse into limpness when it's time to leave the grocery store, or put on a dramatic show of screams and kicks which frightens his mother into giving up her plans for him to come eat lunch.[2]

Because he spends increasingly shorter amounts of time touching his parents and cuddling,[3] he convinces them that both they and what they want are of less and less concern to him.

A two-year-old who is completely docile and always obedient isn't developing normally. At this age, the child defies his parents to prove that he's entitled to make decisions about his life and that he's too important to boss around.[7] Also, if he is to get along with other boys and girls, he must practice asserting himself. His parents, permanently stuck with him, are ideal for his purposes.

More often than not, the two-year-old rebels just to see what will happen. Rarely does he have firm convictions about his wants. The mother and father who never hear his objections and, without please, explanation, or arguments, lead or carry him to where he must go, manage negativism with minimum trouble.[14]

Learning

The young child's drive to perfect skills and gain knowledge is strong. He learns most by imitating his parents: he dabs his mother's powder on his face and shirt; clumps through the house in his father's boots; pours sugar and Kool-Aid® and cereal and pepper into a bowl and stirs up his own chef's special; and cuts his face while scraping it with his father's razor.

Parents are copied not only in what they do but in mood and speech. Heather spanks her dolly and orders, "Stop that!" Eddie can't get the back door open, socks it with his fist, and shouts, "God-damnit!"

The two-year-old mimics his same-sexed parent most.[1] Lamb[8] notes that fathers give more attention to sons than to daughters after their first year. The difference in adult interest aids the child's identi-fication with the same-sex parent.

Lapses in behavior modeling are frowned on. The small boy who cries easily, retreats often, clings to his mother, and avoids his roughhousing father is urged to mend his ways. The small girl who swears, kicks, and throws toys is considered out of step by everyone.[7]

To achieve a firm and lasting sexual identity, the child needs to acquire the characteristics of his own sex during this year and the next.[11]

Two-year-olds not only mimic, they also are creative, choosing activities from all they see and hear. They haul rocks in wagons, hold tea parties with dolls, stage dogfights with hand-held airplanes, and build fences, towers, and houses with blocks.[15]

Some of the new ideas lead to destructiveness. To find out what happens when he does this to that, the young child pulls eyes out of dolls' heads, yanks wheels off trucks, rips up books, dunks his teddy bear in the toilet, cuts notches in drapes, sticks pins in balloons, and hammers dents in the coffee table.

Ridiculing or punishing the two-year-old's attempts to learn squelches his enthusiasm and turns him away from his parents as trusted models. Instead, he can be given his own equipment — a toy shovel, carpet sweeper, lawn mower, baking utensils — so he can identify with his mother and father and practice new skills.

Destructiveness lessens when razors, scissors, cosmetics, and hammers are kept out of reach. Toys should be few and inexpensive. If damage he does is repairable, the youngster should help: he can tape torn pages and hang up a soaked teddy bear to dry.

Playing means learning for the two-year-old, so parents should provide plenty of time for it and a place where he can play alone. For short periods every day, the adult should both play with him and let him join them at work.

Playmates

The small child's first regular contacts with other boys and girls begin, contacts which can determine his reactions to other people for a lifetime.[4] If other children frighten or bully him, he believes everyone will treat him this way. So he avoids playmates and grows up lonely and immature.[5]

Usually, with age-mates, he plays near but not with them. His first getting-to-know-you feelers include grabbing the other youngster's toy and giving him a shove. Later, with seasoning and adult counseling, he becomes more affectionate and less pushy.

Older playmates will treat him as a doll, laugh at him, and run off with his toys,[14] so it's essential that his chief companions match him in social development.

By the end of the year, the small child who is flexible in response, stands up for his rights, and holds his playmates' interest enjoys social contacts.[12] But if initial reactions of aggression or retreat have solidified, other youngsters dislike him.[13] The two-year-old's behavior with other boys and girls does not change for eight years.[6]

As their child climbs into the social ring, his parents turn into referees and coaches. Time and again they cringe when their youngster either attacks or runs from playmates. They swell with indignation when another boy or girl calls their names, knocks him down, or escapes with his favorite ball.

They can help. Although they should not force the two-year-old to play with youngsters who boss and degrade him, neither do they need to defend or remove him from the normal give-and-take of age-mates. If they don't interfere, soon their child will work out his own solution to attacks. They need to train themselves to stay calm, rather than get angry, when there is trouble between playmates.

If their child always is the aggressor, they can have him practice, with them, other ways of treating playmates. They also should monitor their own actions to make sure they do not teach hostility by over-punishing or rejecting him.

Whether or not a mother and father are happy with their child's social behavior, they should see that he regularly has the chance to be with boys and girls his own age. He'll never do better if he's confined to home and their company.

Fatigue

Much of the two-year-old's negativism and fussing is spawned by fatigue. A whirlwind, he tears from place to place and is battered with overstimulation. Some is self-induced, but the rest is caused by his constant exposure to talkative adults, noisy television, and shopping trips with parents which short-change him on sleep.[2]

Fear and tension tire him. Older children delight in scaring the young child with tales of ghosts in the basement and bears in the bushes. His father's growls and playful wrestling after supper overexcite him.[14] Television cartoons keep him taut and anxious. Many two-year-olds sleep poorly, unable to shed the strain of their busy days.[7]

Because the child will not seek the rest he needs, parents regularly should interrupt his exhausting activities with quiet breaks during which he can listen to stories and records.[9] The television should be kept off, jaunts away from home should be limited, and older children prevented from frightening him.

Every day, without exception, he should have a two-hour nap after lunch and twelve hours' sleep nightly. The hour before bedtime should be peaceful, not exciting.

The parents' reward is a calmer, easier-to-manage child who enjoys what he does and gains steadily in knowledge and adaptability.

REFERENCES

1. Austin, G., Oliver, J. S., and Richards, J. C.: *The Parents' Guide to Child Raising.* Englewood Cliffs, P-H, 1978.
2. Church, J.: *Understanding Your Child from Birth to Three.* New York, PB, 1976.
3. Dunn, J.: *Distress and Comfort.* Cambridge, Harvard U Pr, 1977.
4. Hurlock, E.: *Developmental Psychology,* 5th ed. New York, McGraw, 1980.
5. Hurlock, E.: *Personality Development.* New York, McGraw, 1974.
6. Kagan, J., and Moss, H. A.: *Birth to Maturity.* New York, Wiley, 1962.
7. Kanner, L.: *Child Psychiatry,* 4th ed. Springfield, Thomas, 1972.
8. Lamb, M. R.: Paternal influences and the father's role. *American Psychologist, 34:* 938, 1979.
9. Langford, L. M., and Rand, H. Y.: *Guidance of the Young Child,* 2nd ed. New York, Wiley, 1975.
10. Lombardo, V. S.: *Paraprofessionals Working with Young Children.* Springfield,

Thomas, 1981.
11. Mischel, W.: Sex-typing and socialization. In Mussen, Paul, ed.: Carmichael's *Manual of Child Psychology*, 3rd ed. New York, Wiley, 1970.
12. Müller, A.: Über die Entwicklung des Leistungs-Anspruchsniveaus (On the development of a level of aspiration). *Zeitschrift für Psychologie, 162:*238, 1958.
13. Murphy, L. B.: Coping devices and defense mechanisms in relation to autonomous ego functions. *Bulletin of the Menninger Clinic, 24:* 144, 1960.
14. Verville, E.: *Behavior Problems of Children*. Philadelphia, Saunders, 1967.
15. White. B. L.: *The First Three Years of Life*. Englewood Cliffs, P-H, 1975.

Chapter 5

THREE TO FOUR YEARS

TALKING like a Gatling gun, friendly and competent, his baby fat run off, the three-year-old fools his parents into thinking he is grown up.

He's not; he proves it by his rambling, ceaseless speech, his emotional explosions, his carelessness with toys and clothes, and his regression to infantile behavior.

ACHIEVEMENTS

The three-year-old's coordination improves. He can manage the alternate pedaling of trike-riding and by year's end, pump himself on his swing. He throws and catches his beach ball more accurately and, trying to bat, swipes a stick at it and whacks it around the back yard.

He plays alone for twenty minutes or longer, imaginatively creating busy worlds crowded with miniature farm animals, cowboys and Indians, dolls, cars, boats, and planes. He learns to use scissors, paste, crayons, and paint. He likes to play in sand and water.[4] Now he wants to use a real rake on the leaves, not a toy one, and do real baking, not pretend. He likes stories, especially those he hears often, and he corrects the wily parent who skips a sentence.

He is handy to have around. He dresses himself, painfully, his shirt on backwards and his buttons askew; he gets cleaner because he plays longer with soap and water; he manages toileting alone. He follows directions, runs errands, and regularly helps by dusting and setting the table.

Socially and emotionally, the three-year-old matures.[9] He empathizes with a crying, hurt child.[13] He loosens ties to his mother and strengthens them to his father and siblings.[3] He appropriates anyone and everyone as audience and tells lengthy stories about what he has seen or done.[1] He knows the physical and behavioral differences between boys and girls and acts in accord with his own sex.[11] Girls avoid conflict, try to please, and busy themselves cutting and coloring; boys ignore rules, brag, and play with blocks and toy vehicles.[10]

An interesting, alert companion, the three-year-old likes what he is and what he can do, but he is puzzled and worried by others' treatment of him and by situations new to him.

PARENT CONCERNS

A mother and father expect, from their three-year-old, the miracle of adult behavior.[6] They are disappointed. Their small "grownup" continues to fail in independence and self-control: he hides when visitors come; he stages fierce tantrums; he refuses to play with a neighbor child.

Also, old as he is, he should mind. *He knows better,* his parents tell themselves when he slams the front door and drops his dirty socks in the wastebasket.

But the child cannot manage perfection. One study found that older preschoolers (3 to 6 years) obeyed only 51 percent of the orders mothers gave.[4]

Misjudging the three-year-old's abilities, some parents try to force him to behave more maturely. Other mothers and fathers protect themselves from witnessing the child's mistakes and failures by waiting on and isolating him. Fixating on these rearing methods and continuing them for years, both adults and child are miserable.

COMMON PROBLEMS

Talkativeness

The three-year-old is a non-stop talker, delighted with his new ability to snare attention with speech. His vocabulary stretches to 1,600 words by the time he reaches four years. During his waking day he is silent for only nineteen minutes and his longest quiet period is four minutes.[1]

Curious, he asks hundreds of questions. His constant "Why?" annoys his busy mother, who suspects that he is less interested in answers than in being noticed. Some meaningless questions screen real concerns: parent fights, death, sex differences, witches, and deformity.[12]

Parents can temper the child's conversational storm by sitting down, several times daily, just to talk. Letting the youngster help with work provides a natural setting for verbal interchange. When he chats on and on and his mother is too preoccupied to listen and answer, she should tell him so, adding that he is free to talk if he expects no reply.

Emotion

Anger, fear, and jealousy now are conspicuous and purposeful. Older, the child spots more possibilities for harm and he worries.

The unthinking rebellion of the two-year-old is replaced with sturdy anger. The three-year-old knows what he wants and, practiced at standing up for himself with playmates, he vigorously opposes parental wishes.[7]

Fear was rare and temporary before; now it is frequent, acute, and lasting.[5] The child spies a ladybug or swinging crane and grabs his mother's leg in panic; he refuses to try the unsteady swing or the towering slide; he cries and breaks away when his father leads him toward the lake. Disgusted, his parents tell him he's too big to act like a baby.[12]

By now he may have acquired a baby brother or sister and his jealousy is constant and dangerous. He may pinch or smother the infant, instruct his mother to take him back to the hospital, or revert to sucking on a bottle, wetting, and crying. His tired mother, counting on him to look after himself and cause no trouble, resents the turmoil he brews.[12]

Emotional upsets can be managed. When the child throws a tantrum he should be isolated and his wishes ignored. But when he is calm, parents can and should let him make decisions which don't affect his health, safety, or others' rights.

Fear is natural in the observant three-year-old. Explanations help; shaming and forcing don't. Letting him set his own pace for investigating what he fears strengthens courage.

Jealousy emerges because the youngster believes his parents value the baby's traits more than they do his. He mimics the infant to regain approval. If that fails, he tries to get rid of his rival. Parents need to be firm about not letting him harm the baby, but give him private time daily, keep his routine the same, let him help care for his tiny brother or sister, and praise him often for what he can do that the infant cannot.

Carelessness

As his parents often remind him, the three-year-old does not appreciate how hard his father works to buy him clothes and toys, nor how hard his mother works to keep things nice. He is both careless and messy, regularly losing one shoe or one mitten, leaving dolls and books out in the rain, and strewing toys all over the house.[12] His father swears as he trips over a truck; his annoyed mother kicks aside doll dishes and blocks as she cooks dinner.[2,8]

He is told to pick up his toys and put his clothes in the hamper, but thirty minutes later he still is working placidly with his Lego® blocks, his room a madhouse of littered belongings. Neatness and care of possessions are concepts he does not grasp.

Matters can improve. So there's less to look after, parents can put away all his toys but six, changing them weekly for a different set. Toys should be off-limits in certain rooms: *e.g.,* the kitchen, bathroom, and parents' bedroom. Regularly before naptime, dinner, and bedtime, toys can be picked up. While he learns, his mother can share the task. Then she should watch and admire while he does it himself. He needs reminding that toys are outside and must be rescued from the weather.

Tossing his soiled clothes in the hamper can be part of supervised bedtime routine. If he loses clothes, he should search for them. He can put away his clean clothes after they're laundered and learn that each has its place. The fewer clothes he has, the less the disorder.

Unfortunately, parents who demand neatness in their three-year-old must set the example. There can be no more scattered magazines and newspapers, dropped jackets, and kicked-off shoes. No longer can dishes be piled unwashed in the sink or tools left out on the work counter. When standards for adult and three-year-old are the same, the child's indifference to order seems more natural.

Regression

Not only does the three-year-old backslide emotionally (his parents believe), he also forgets everything he has ever learned. At meals, he uses his spoon or his fingers, not his fork. Instead of walking, he crawls. Smelly puddles appear on the floor and smelly stains on his underwear.[12] His mother and father wonder what's going on. What has happened to their reliable child?

Underneath all his peculiar antics, he's still there. But reliability bores him: now that he knows what to do, he doesn't think he needs to prove he can do it. Besides, he's too busy mastering what's new — talking up a storm and building friendships — to waste time and energy on old stuff.

Parents who scold and shame him for babyish actions bring out the mule in him. He'll persist with crawling and finger-eating; he'll blandly announce that the lady visitor made the puddle. It's best if a mother and father don't over-excite themselves about temporary regressions. Casual corrections and praise for mature behavior usually will head the three-year-old back to normal.

REFERENCES

1. Bereiter, C.: Fluency abilities in preschool children. *Journal of Genetic Psychology, 98:* 47, 1961.
2. Bigner, J. J.: *Parent-Child Relations.* New York, Macmillan, 1979.
3. Breckenridge, M. E., and Murphy, M. N.: *Growth and Development of the Young*

Child, 8th ed. Philadelphia, Saunders, 1969.

4. Forehand, R., Gardner, H., and Roberts, M.: Maternal response to child compliance and noncompliance: Some normative data. *Journal of Clinical Child Psychology, 7:* 121, 1978.
5. Gesell, A., and Ilg, F. L.: *Infant and Child in the Culture of Today.* New York, Harper, 1943.
6. Hurlock, E. B.: *Child Growth and Development,* 4th ed. New York, McGraw, 1970.
7. Kanner, L.: *Child Psychiatry,* 4th ed. Springfield, Thomas, 1972.
8. Neisser, E. G.: *Primer for Parents of Preschoolers.* New York, Parents, 1972.
9. Newman, B. M., and Newman, P. R.: *Infancy and Childhood.* New York, Wiley, 1978.
10. Rubin, K. H.: The social and cognitive value of ps toys and activities. *Canadian Journal of Behavioural Science, 9:* 382, 1977.
11. Thompson, S. K.: Gender labels and early sex role development. *Child Development, 46:* 339, 1975.
12. Verville, E.: *Behavior Problems of Children.* Philadelphia, Saunders, 1967.
13. Zahn-Waxler, C., Radke-Yarrow, M., and King, R. M.: Childrearing and children's prosocial initiations toward victims of distress. *Child Development, 50:* 319, 1979.

Chapter 6

FOUR TO FIVE YEARS

H E'S a stranger, this sassy, rejecting, fly-apart four-year-old. His baffled, hurt mother and father wonder what's got into him. Something has: he's moving from the safe familiarity of home into a wide and wooly world.[7,10] It's an ordeal for him and his family.

ACHIEVEMENTS

The four-year-old's erratic emotion can blind his parents to solid achievement.

His muscles work well. He can manage both a standing and running broad jump. He throws a ball overhand, strongly. He keeps his scissors feeding straight on line.[3,4]

He can count to four and recite both nursery rhymes and TV ads. He understands opposites: *slow* and *fast, up* and *down*. He knows that a cow gives milk, a window is made of glass, and ears are for hearing. He draws unrecognizable pictures and interprets them for anyone who asks.

He likes games, both with children and adults. He compromises with friends on what to do and how to do it. For long periods, he plays happily alone, sometimes with lively drama.

He dresses himself efficiently; he combs his hair. But left to handle his daily bath, he prefers playing with soap and water to washing with them.

He's curious,[2] and he sticks to what he starts.[3] Running errands
and doing chores, he tries to do things right. He can remember and
follow as many as three directions given at the same time if he's
alerted first.

Versatile, determined, and energetic,[6] the four-year-old
strides upwards toward the misty peaks of personal and public competence.

PARENT CONCERNS

Friendliness between parents and child evaporates. Small playmates replace the adults as favored companions and models. Sarcas-
tically, the youngster parrots his mother's correction, "Settle down!"
— words and tone. He argues loudly when told he cannot play outdoors after supper and, finally defeated, yells, "You're an old
meany!" The racket he makes and the rejection he slams at them
anger his mother and father.[12]

They are dismayed and puzzled by the contrast between his defiance of them and his shaken confidence. Fear keynotes his actions.[1] Guilt shadows his life: he blames himself for spilling the peas
and for his parents' divorce.[2] Wounded, he's awash in tears when
playmates run off and leave him. In vain, he tries to smother his uncertainty by bullying younger children, opposing adults, and bragging.

"I did that very fast," he announces and, "My dad has a zillion
dollars."

Also, during this year, it's obvious that the child is developing
normally as a member of his own sex or he is not. Mischel[11] reports
that the masculine preschool boy has a warm relationship with his
father and values his approval; the feminine girl sees her mother as
warm, gratifying, and important. The child himself is aware of a
spectrum of differences between the sexes and his choice of behavior
reflects his experiences with each sex. Boys who play with dolls and
girls who won't distress their mothers and fathers.

COMMON PROBLEMS

Hyperactivity

Giggling and screaming, twirling till dizziness flings him to the ground, hilariously tossing books and toys, jumping on beds and off couches, growling and squeaking, twisting his mouth and crossing his eyes, the four-year-old appears to have lost all good sense. Momentarily, he has. He's bent on impressing playmates with what a jolly fellow he is and on convincing himself that he's having a splendid time.[15]

His frenzied activity not only tires him, but also, distracted, he hurts himself and damages furnishings.[13] Adults can halt the out-of-control youngster's perpetual motion by sitting down with him for a story or starting him on a quieter project. Thompson[14] found that four-year-olds whose nursery school teachers gave suggestions, information, and help when needed were more sociable and less hostile and destructive than four-year-olds left to their own devices.

Indecency

Testing society's limits, the four-year-old tries out an assortment of scatological terms. He shouts at a vexing playmate, "You dirty do-do!" and he sometimes hollers "Shit!" and "Asshole!" — words he hears adults and teenagers use.

Boys and girls play "doctor," examining each other's genitals to see if what they've heard is true. Often they grasp their own. Boys urinate outdoors, usually with friends watching.[15]

None of this behavior signals sudden depravity. Swearing is imitative, a union of words and emotion the child often witnesses. Parents can suggest substitutions: "You old cow!" and "Criminentlies!" as well as set an example of cleaner speech.

Curiosity causes youngsters to study the anatomy of the opposite sex. Parents happening on the self-conducted lessons should not show shock or anger; such negative, strong reactions linger to trouble boys' and girls' sexual interest for years. Instead, they can tell the youngsters that people don't show these parts of their bodies in public. Then or later, the adults need to find out what questions the children have about body differences. These should be answered and the clear statement made that each sex is important; neither is superior to the other.

Grabbing his genitals is a reflex action of the ill-at-ease or frightened young child. It should be treated as bad manners, not bad morals. Instead of slapping the child's hand and scolding him, a parent should say only, "That's not polite." Telling the youngster what to expect and what to do before thrusting him into situations which may make him uneasy also helps.

The preschooler is sure that, when he dashes off to the bathroom, his playmates will vanish. Taking care of his needs on the spot prevents that risk. Punishment won't help for long. Instead, the youngster can be told that, although urinating behind a bush in the countryside is all right, doing the same thing in his back yard offends neighbors and harms lawns. His mother should promise that she'll stay with his friends and make sure they don't leave when he must go to the bathroom.

Playmates

Boys and girls spend time with playmates of both sexes, but usually prefer those of their own sex.

If there is only one other youngster in the neighborhood, the two children may be together every waking hour. Each copies the other[1] and parents fume when their unsullied child sports his best friend's swagger, stutter, icy stare, shoulder shrug,[15] or contrary opinions.[8]

Belligerency — put-downs, commands, name-calling, and shoves — becomes a way of life. Each youngster tries his best to stake his claim to kingship over peers struggling to do the same.[9] Fair play is a lost notion; many four-year-olds meet all comers with bullying and cruelty.[10]

Parents can muffle both imitation and aggression.

Imitative behavior is experimental: the child sees a friend blinking his eyes or kicking furniture and does the same thing to learn how it feels. A mother and father need only say that they'd rather he didn't do that; it's not like him.

Belligerence wanes when youngsters don't spend hours daily together. Constant stimulation and competition breed fatigue and edginess. Four-year-olds can be limited to 90-minute play sessions thrice weekly. With time to play alone, doing as they choose, they grow more confident and then feel less need to fight others.

Regular private time with parents also helps boys and girls to get along better with peers. Children secure within their families explore the outside world with little anxiety or distress.[5]

Attacks on Parents

Parents are outraged when their four-year-old turns on them, calling names, refusing orders, accusing them of favoritism, and grimly shouting, "I hate you!"

Such attacks are bluff and bluster; they in no way evidence the child's true feelings. Even though his behavior is guaranteed to estrange his mother and father, the youngster desperately wants them to understand, respect, and love him. Only four and unskilled in tact, he acts as he does because this is how he shores up his integrity with playmates. Also, after a session of ego damage from peers, he explodes at home because he can't tolerate one more command or rebuff.

Parents needn't and shouldn't permit the child to develop a habit of insolence. They can answer his "I hate you!" with "Too bad, I like you," and leave the room. Soon the small battler will show up wanting to be friends again.

When he refuses to clear the table, he should be told that his help is needed and he must do the work. If he runs outside into the snow without boots, he should be brought back to put them on.

Working and playing with him daily, praising him for good qualities and good deeds, and planning family fun — games, picnics, songfests, and trips to the zoo or airport — parents weave a sturdy tie to themselves, a lifeline which steadies their four-year-old in his encounters with peers.

REFERENCES

1. Austin, G., Oliver, J. S., and Richards, J. C.: *The Parents' Guide to Child Raising.* Englewood Cliffs, P-H, 1978.
2. Bigner, J. J.: *Parent-Child Relations.* New York, Macmillan, 1979.

3. Gesell, A.: *The First Five Years of Life.* New York, Harper, 1940.
4. Gesell, A., and Ilg, F. L.: *Infant and Child in the Culture of Today.* New York, Harper, 1943.
5. Hartup, W. W.: The social world of childhood. *American Psychologist, 34:* 944, 1979.
6. Heimgartner, N. L.: *Behavioral Traits of Deaf Children.* Springfield, Thomas, 1982.
7. Hurlock, E.: *Developmental Psychology,* 5th ed. New York, McGraw, 1980.
8. Hurlock, E.: *Personality Development.* New York, McGraw, 1974.
9. Jersild, A. T.: *Child Psychology,* 7th ed. Englewood Cliffs, P-H, 1975.
10. Kanner, L.: *Child Psychiatry,* 4th ed. Springfield, Thomas, 1972.
11. Mischel, W.: Sex-typing and socialization. In Mussen, P., ed: Carmichael's *Manual of Child Psychology,* 3rd ed. New York, Wiley, 1970.
12. Neisser, E. G.: *Primer for Parents of Preschoolers.* New York, Parents, 1972.
13. Stewart, B. R.: Development differences in the stability of object preferences and conflict behavior. *Child Development, 29:* 9, 1958.
14. Thompson, G. G.: The social and emotional development of preschool children under two types of educational program. *Psychological Monographs, 56:* (5), 1944.
15. Verville, E.: *Behavior Problems of Children.* Philadelphia, Saunders, 1967.

Chapter 7

FIVE TO SIX YEARS

TALL and capable, with thousands of plus and minus events to guide him, the five-year-old embarks on his adventure with life. He's unique, unlike any one of his peers, with distinctive ways of coping with frustration, managing people, and looking after himself.

These brief summaries of psychological examinations of four children about to enter kindergarten highlight differences among them.

Marc B. Average intelligence. Siblings, ages 14, 12, 2. He is uncertain, inattentive, and refuses to try tests. Motor coordination is good; speech is unclear. His mother interferes and controls. She appears angry, with no knowledge of or interest in Marc's needs.

Julia K. Average intelligence. Siblings, ages 13, 11, 9, 7. Busy and talkative, she sings at times, and never hesitates to attempt what is asked. She brags about how well she does and dramatizes everything from block-stacking to ball-kicking. Her mother is relaxed and accepting.

Frank W. Average intelligence. No siblings. He refuses to follow instructions, grabs test materials, and makes demands. His mother is ineffectual and admits she gives him his way, placates him with gifts, dresses and sometimes feeds him.

Anita H. Dull intelligence. Siblings, ages 3, 1. She rarely stirs from her chair and her movements are awkward. She continues working at tasks she cannot do. There is no spontaneous talk. Her mother pretends interest but clearly is embarrassed by Anita's failures.

Ready or not, the five-year-old now must take a giant step toward independence.

ACHIEVEMENTS

In many ways, he is ready. Since birth, he has doubled his height and quadrupled his weight. His nervous system has developed to 90 percent of its adult size. Eye-hand and body coordination are good; sensory perceptions are accurate.[3] The five-year-old can balance on one foot, hop, and by the end of the year, skip. Marching or dancing, he keeps reasonably good time to music.[5] This is the year he learns to skate and handle a sled.

He knows his address and phone number and he can answer questions about stories read to him. He is a problem-solver and likes to figure out things. He can copy a square and a triangle[5] and draw a person, complete with shoulders and neck. Some time during the year he will add dots, lines, and squiggles for the missing eyes, nose, and mouth.

He talks well, recalling minute details of his experiences. He is beginning to understand concepts and organize what he sees into appropriate groups. He likes board games and he can print his name.

He manages all his dressing, including the jacket which zips, but will not be able to tie his shoes until he is nearly six. He pays the clerk for his candy bar and walks to school alone. Helping out, he makes his bed, washes dishes, and puts together sandwiches and pudding. He entertains and keeps an eye on younger siblings.

Because he's a bit serious, he's dependable, obedient, concerned for others, and welcomes direction and routine.[7] He likes clothes, which must be the same kind worn by classmates. He likes his classmates, too, and looks forward to being with them at school.

Trusting himself and others, eager to achieve and make friends, conscientious and reliable, the five-year-old is a credit to himself and his family.

PARENT CONCERNS

Mingled worry, pride, and hurt hound a mother and father when their child enters public school. How will he do? Is he as smart as he seems? What will the teacher think of him? What if he fails? His school performance frames his future and his parents wait tensely for his first report card.

They are concerned about how other boys and girls will treat him. He's their little one, vulnerable and naive, and they know it's rough out there. They dread dealing with his tears and their own anger when peers isolate or manhandle him.

And, school-time ushers in growing-apart time.[13] Suddenly their pride and joy is on his own, pleased to march with his own generation and to adopt his teacher as surrogate mother. Parental opinions and facts take second place to those relayed from school. The mother and father suffer as their child deserts them for new interests and new attachments.

COMMON PROBLEMS

School

It's not only parents who have mixed feelings about school: so does the child. Every day is different. Some are winners: he's chosen first for the relay; he can tell his teacher it's Columbus Day; he catches on fast to the new song. Other days are miserable: a small girl growls, "I don't like you!"; his teacher announces in public that he's putting his LEFT foot forward instead of his right; and classmates hog the crayons he needs for his picture of a lion. Often he feels strange and alone. Sometimes he fears his teacher and her demands.[12] Ulcers are common in kindergarteners[1] and tics appear during this year.[11]

Some apprehensive parents spend years getting their child ready for school. They study books which describe how to teach infants to read. They turn on TV programs which instruct toddlers in the meaning of *under* and *over*. They buy educational toys by the dozens.[15] A mother or father may sentence their preschooler to endless daily sessions of reciting letters and counting.[11]

Some parents currently are advocating starting youngsters in public school at the age of four, an idea frowned on by educators. Elkind,[4] preaching against pushing children, reports that four- and five-year-old black youngsters drilled hours daily learned to read. But, demonstrating their skill, their voices were subdued and their faces sad.

The child should be prepared for school not with drills but with experiences.[8] His mother can read to him;[2] his father can take him hiking, to a farm, to the museum, to the circus, and to the hardware store. He can learn to handle kindergarten's tools: paste, crayons, and scissors.[12] He should be taught to manage his clothing, including boots and buttons. He can practice walking to school. If he does chores, he knows he is capable; if he obeys family rules, he knows he is likeable.

And he needs regular contacts with boys and girls his age, so he knows what to expect from peers and can cope with challenge. If he doesn't go to a day care center or nursery school, he can be taken to church school and vacation Bible school. There, he'll get used to classmates, schedules, and teachers' directions.

Safety

The five-year-old experiments with danger. He takes up with strangers, strikes out alone for the shopping center, slices into a package with a butcher knife, turns on his father's power saw to speed up his airplane-building, and sets fires. Because parents cannot and should not monitor every move he makes, the preschooler must be taught to look out for his own safety.

Films and instruction programs teach the young child how to repulse the adult who entices him to get into a car or who approaches him sexually. Parents and youngster should review together what he should say and do.

If he habitually wanders off, he must be stopped. To teach him never to leave home without permission, he should be escorted everywhere for two weeks, even next door to his friend's house. If he slips away, then he must stay inside for a day.

Rules about what he may and may not do should be clear, issued one at a time, and enforced rigidly: *e.g.*, power tools are off limits.

Hand tools, knives, and matches always are handy, so the youngster must be taught how to use them carefully. With supervision and practice, he will do so.

Outside Opinions

The socially sensitive five-year-old is embarrassed when he fails to measure up to his own or others' expectations.[6] His parents, even more sensitive, are angered and shamed by outsiders' negative opinions of their child.

The teacher calls to say that the youngster doesn't know his address, can't carry a tune, hides under her desk, won't help put away toys, and cries a lot. Relatives comment that he's spoiled; neighbors complain that he tramples their flowers; playmates announce that he hits them.[14]

Parents, resenting the unpleasant messages, have three choices. They can defend their son or daughter, which often makes matters worse; they can scold and punish the youngster, which may not be justified; or they can solve the problem each indictment presents.

When a teacher reports that all is not well at school, parents need to keep in close touch with her and follow any reasonable suggestions she has for new ways of managing the child. If nothing changes, then they'll need the direction of a knowledgeable psychologist. Critical relatives may be pacified with, "Perhaps you're right." Neighbors' complaints should be heeded and the child kept out of their yards. Playmate squabbles are best resolved by telling the youngsters either to work out their differences or stop playing with each other for the rest of the day.

Unsolved Problems

Unsolved problems are an irritant and an embarrassment.

A kindergartener, his parents believe, should long ago have gotten over such babyish habits as bedwetting, dawdling, erratic eating, and thumbsucking. When their son or daughter asks for help at tasks other five-year-olds manage alone, throws tantrums, whines, clings to them, and avoids other children, they are disgusted.

If, for years, they have shown patience and understanding, they now are weary and annoyed because his behavior has not improved. If they have tried criticism and punishment, they now try even harder. Unsolved problems convince child and parents that they are failures. Discouraged, they bog down in deep ruts of faulty, harmful attitudes and actions.[10,14]

But this is no time to settle in; this is the time to take a new heading. Parents who dislike their child's behavior should sort it out and choose one problem at a time to work on. Deciding how to manage this one in a new way, they can do so until it disappears. Every time a mother and father teach the youngster to overcome an unwanted action, everyone in the family is proud.

From crying, wriggling infancy, the five-year-old has traveled far. But he has miles yet to go. Behavior problems may block his path.

REFERENCES

1. Austin, G., Oliver, J. S., and Richards, J. C.: *The Parent's Guide to Child Raising.* Englewood Cliffs, P-H, 1978.
2. Bakwin, H., and Bakwin, R. M.: *Clinical Management of Behavior Disorders in Children.* Philadelphia, Saunders, 1966.
3. Breckenridge, M. E., and Murphy, M. N.: *Growth and Development of the Young Child,* 8th ed. Philadelphia, Saunders, 1969.
4. Elkind, D.: *The Hurried Child.* Reading, A-W, 1981.
5. Gesell, A.: *The First Five Years of Life.* New York, Harper, 1940.
6. Gesell, A., and Ilg, F. L.: *Infant and Child in the Culture of Today.* New York, Harper, 1943.
7. Heimgartner, N. L.: *Behavioral Traits of Deaf Children.* Springfield, Thomas, 1982.
8. Hurlock, E. B.: *Child Growth and Development,* 4th ed. New York, McGraw, 1970.
9. Jersild, A. T.: *Child Psychology,* 7th ed. Englewood Cliffs, P-H, 1975.
10. Kagan, J., and Moss, H. A.: *Birth to Maturity.* New York, Wiley, 1962.
11. Kanner, L.: *Child Psychiatry,* 4th ed. Springfield, Thomas, 1972.
12. Neisser, E. G.: *Primer for Parents of Preschoolers.* New York, Parents, 1972.
13. Stith, M., and Connor, R.: Dependency and helpfulness in young children.

Child Development, 33: 15, 1962.
14. Verville, E.: *Behavior Problems of Children.* Philadelphia, Saunders, 1967.
15. Weinberg, R. A.: Early childhood education and intervention: Establishing an American tradition. *American Psychologist, 34:* 912, 1979.

Part II.
Problems

Chapter 8

EATING

THERE are 3,000 feeding contacts during the child's first two years. Some, or many, are disappointing or disastrous.[10]

Concerned parents, wanting the child to eat what is good for him and as much as they do, fret when he doesn't. But if they prod and push, threaten and coax, matters rapidly deteriorate.

Eating problems include weaning failures, food refusal, overeating, pica, dawdling, and vomiting.

WEANING FAILURES

Within eighteen months after birth, the child must dispense with bottles and drink from a cup. He must add solid food to his totally liquid diet. He must graduate from mushy fruits and vegetables to chewy, stringy ones. No longer will an adult ladle food into his mouth; he must do it himself. One baby protests each change in diet or procedure; another accepts life's mysteries with calm curiosity.

Weaning from the bottle should start when the baby is nine months old and extend over a four- or five-month period. An ounce or two at a time, milk is transferred from bottle to cup for one feeding. The process is repeated for all other feedings in turn. If the child habitually takes a bottle to bed, a favorite toy is a welcome replacement.

Once the baby is used to the cup, it's better not to allow an occasional bottle as a treat. He won't understand why sometimes that's okay and other time she gets a stern turn-down. Trying to find out, he'll scream and storm.

The small child who spits out his first strained peaches or later refuses junior and table food is merely observing that something strange is happening. He's not suggesting he hates what's offered. Trying the new food again in a day or two usually works. If he's been gumming crackers he holds himself, changing to solid foods at meals is easier.

Persistence may be needed. One weak, tired boy, seven years old, still ate only strained foods. His mother, alarmed by a bout with diarrhea he suffered when he was eleven months old, never taught him to eat food suited to his age.

Bernal[5] describes a four-year-old girl who ate only strained foods because, at nine months, she had choked on string beans. Now every mealtime was a wild scene of pleas, lectures, and tantrums as her parents tried to get her to eat table food. The little girl was started on a program which rewarded her for trying a new food. Eight months later she had gained three pounds and regularly ate fifty different foods.

Before he's a year old, the baby grabs the spoon his mother holds and tries to jam it into his mouth. If he's allowed to practice and helped only at the end of meals,[17] he'll be feeding himself smoothly and neatly by fifteen months.

FOOD REFUSAL

The regular refusal of food often starts when the child is between one and two years.

It's then that his appetite normally dwindles. During his first year, he triples his weight. During his second, he gains only three to five pounds and no longer needs huge amounts of food.

Gersh[8] writes that a healthy child, left alone, will regulate his own diet. A pint of milk and two ounces of orange juice daily, plus meat, fruit, and vegetables eaten several times weekly, will do him nicely.

Because the toddler needs less food, he is likely to eat well only once a day, usually at noon. Parents, not realizing why he nibbles at breakfast and supper, think something is wrong and press him to eat more. Fascinated by their concerned attention, he loudly refuses.

Also, now older, he takes meals with the family and the distractions delight him. He doesn't get what the adults have, so he reaches for his mother's coffee and his father's barbequed ribs.[12,18] His mother tells him to stop wiggling; his father orders him to quit pouring milk on his tray.

An older brother announces that he hates broccoli and shoves his plate away. The preschooler promptly sweeps his dish to the floor with a vigorous, "No!" Copying his elders' food rejection, he launches a new and enduring mealtime habit of turning down food.[4]

He's not hungry and won't eat if he's sick, irritable, tired, or cooped up in the house all day. Often he's bored with the routine of thrice-daily meals.

The adults' reaction to food refusal can break the chain or weld stronger links. If a hesitant mother anxiously pleads with her child to eat, he's thrilled with his power to control her mood and actions and, glowering, he refuses. But more often, it's parent power which takes over.

A mother and father are upset when the toddler declines costly food which took time and effort to prepare. They're determined to make him eat. His father takes off his belt and lays it across the table.[18] His mother warns that he'll get sick and die. Before he tackles breakfast, he must down the shriveled peas and cold potato he left at last night's dinner. He may not leave the table until he cleans his plate, even if it takes two hours.

There's no way he can eat now: fear and anger lock every digestive muscle and gland.

A new regime can change a child's fixed habit of food refusal.

He should eat alone, away from adults who scold, watch, threaten, or beg. When he says or shows by playing that he is through, he should be excused and any remaining food discarded.[19]

Amounts should be tiny — one-quarter of a hamburger, three ounces of milk, a teaspoon of mashed potatoes. If he's not given much, he'll eat it all and ask for more.[9]

At first he should have only food he likes, except for pie, corn chips, and tea, which fill his stomach but do nothing for bones and muscles. After a week, less favored foods gradually can be served.

Straight-sided dishes, small glasses, and child-sized, straight-handled spoons and forks make eating easy to manage.

Some parents don't permit snacks, reasoning that the youngster surely will be hungry for meals if he's not eaten for five hours. But it doesn't work; he still won't touch dinner. Because he eats less than ever, both his stomach and appetite shrink.

With contrasting logic, other parents convince themselves that the child who won't eat meals will starve, so they let him fill up all day long on cokes and cake. And he does starve, because he gets too few foods which nourish him.

It's best if the youngster who refuses food at meals is given fruit juice and graham crackers mid-morning and mid-afternoon. Apple slices and carrot and celery sticks, to which he can help himself any time, can be kept in the refrigerator.

A worried mother can record, privately, everything her child eats during the day. As time goes on, the list will lengthen. Also, she can substitute fruits for vegetables he dislikes and bread for the cereal he won't touch, knowing he's not missing out on vitamins and minerals he needs.

If a mother and father don't care what their preschooler eats or leaves at meals, keep table time pleasant, and enjoy their own food, the young child will eat what his body requires.

OVEREATING

A child grows fat both because he overeats and because he is inactive. Current theory posits the growth of fat cells when an infant is fed too much, but Bruch[6] states that obesity rarely occurs in the absence of environmental influences. She cites the case of a one-year-old boy, twice as heavy as he should have been, who later dropped to normal weight. As he grew older, he was encouraged to be active, and the running, jumping, climbing, and throwing he did burned off excess pounds.

Extreme inactivity teams with immaturity and social isolation. The fat youngsters studied by Bruch were sulky and over-sensitive. They bullied younger children. Usually their mothers were dominant, emotional, and protective. Their fathers were docile. They were either only children or had but one sibling.[2,18]

Some parents heap food on youngsters' plates because they themselves had little to eat when they were growing up. Others pressure a son or daughter to eat as a gesture of concern. Sometimes the child was unwanted; bestowing extra food atones for guilt.

Endocrine abnormality rarely is responsible for excess weight, nor is there inherent neurological damage or delayed locomotor function in obese children.[6] Heredity may play a part: if one parent is overweight, 50 percent of the children are; if both parents are overweight, 80 percent of the children are. But a loaded table and an enticing example may have the same effect.

The overeater needs to bestir himself. The television should be off and the child required to play outdoors daily.

He needs interests other than food. Nursery school, trips to the zoo and the airport, playmates, and a variety of toys will help.

Eating habits must change. Skim milk and normal servings should replace huge portions. Because preschoolers trust their parents to do what is right, they won't fuss forever when quantities are restricted.

All youngsters trying to cut down on eating do better when parents do not nag or warn. A mother and father should limit food consumption, praise the child for his good qualities, and promote independence, activity, and friendships. To untangle their own deep involvement in the child's life, they should seek new interests and closer ties to each other.

PICA

Pica is perverted appetite for non-foods. All small children taste twigs and leaves and gnaw on crib railings to ease tingling gums, but some consume everything within reach.

Ames[1] describes a sixteen-month-old girl who ate only sand. Even when she was offered both eggs and heavily-peppered sand, she ate the sand.

Kanner[11] reports that the two-and three-year-olds he studied consumed polish, buttons, rugs, clothes, plaster, dirt, coal, ashes, paint, feces, bugs, newspaper, thread, wallpaper, soap, beads, blankets, egg shells, string, match heads, and splinters. Some of these children ate regular meals; others refused all food. Many were retarded. Most were neglected.

The consequences can be severe. Wads of thread and hair obstruct the intestines, and anemia and constipation develop.

Lead poisoning can occur. Modern paints are lead-free, but peeling paint and crumbling plaster in old houses are dangerous. Other sources of lead are dust, newsprint, gift wrap, cosmetics, and health food supplements.

Indications of poisoning include visual-motor deficit, short attention span, restlessness, impulsiveness, and easy distractability.[2,11,14,16] Untreated survivors of heavy intoxication may suffer convulsions, retardation, paralysis, blindness, behavior and speech abnormalities.

Although the death rate has dropped from 66 percent to under 5 percent since treatment by chelating agents (which bind lead and remove it from the body) was started in the 1960s, lead poisoning is a current, unrecognized health problem.[14] Of two million children screened by the Center for Disease Control between 1973 and 1977, 7 percent had too much lead in their systems. Eighteen thousand youngsters were treated.

To counter pica, the child needs to be so closely supervised that he puts nothing harmful into his mouth. He needs good food, regularly offered, and improved general care. The preschooler needs to play and work with his parents daily. Hugging helps. Some children in Kanner's study promptly dropped their pica habit when mothers quit work and stayed home with them.

DAWDLING

The dawdler daydreams through meals, holding food in his mouth and not bothering to chew or swallow.

Sometimes he dawdles through breakfast because he's neither fully awake nor yet hungry. At day's end, he's exhausted, with no energy left for eating.

Slow eating is adopted as habit if the preschooler was not allowed to feed himself when he was ready to do so. Before he was a year old, he concluded that getting food inside him was a grown-up's job, not his.[7,19]

If his mother and father prod and scold at meals, his appetite vanishes and his eating halts.

Or, if the youngster knows that he must nap or sit on the toilet when the meal ends, he pokes at his food to delay unwanted bed and bathroom sessions.[4]

Many exasperated parents give up waiting for the child to eat and feed him themselves, a solution which guarantees that he will continue to dawdle.

Her can learn to eat more efficiently. So he won't be distracted or need to listen to adults urging him on, he should eat alone.

He should be given only small amounts; the sight of an enormous pile of food discourages him. Breakfast can be delayed for an hour after he wakes. By then he'll be both active and hungry. To calm and rest him for dinner, he can be called in from play thirty minutes before the meal is ready.

Food uneaten after thirty minutes should be removed without comment. The youngster quickly learns that if he wants his meal, it's up to him to eat it while it's there.[18]

VOMITING

Frequent vomiting troubles parents. They rightly suspect illness, overfeeding, allergies, or infections and these possibilities must be checked. But there may be other causes.

A child forced to eat gags and then vomits.

If he is over-excited, angry, crying hard, or worried by visits, parties, or going to sleep in a strange bed, his muscles play tricks on him and food comes up.

When vomiting distresses his parents and leads to soothing, gifts, and victory in disputes, the preschooler learns to bring up the contents of his stomach whenever he chooses.[11]

Parents of the habitual vomiter need a doctor's assurance that the child is not ill. They must train themselves to become indifferent to how much or how quickly the youngster eats at mealtime. If it then seems obvious that he vomits to control them, they should show little sympathy, never change decisions which have set off the vomiting, and teach the young schemer to clean up the mess he makes.

REFERENCES

1. Ames, L. B.: *Child Care and Development.* Philadelphia, Lippincott, 1970.
2. Bakwin, H., and Bakwin, R. M.: *Clinical Management of Behavior Disorders in Children,* 3rd ed. Philadelphia, Saunders, 1966.
3. Bernal, M. E.: Behavioral treatment of a child's eating problem. *Journal of Behavior Therapy and Experimental Psychiatry, 3:* 43, 1972.
4. Breckenridge, M., and Murphy, M.: *Growth and Development of the Young Child,* 8th ed. Philadelphia, Saunders, 1969.
5. Brody, S.: Preventive intervention in current problems of early childhood. In Caplan, G., ed. *Prevention of Mental Disorders in Children.* New York, Basic, 1961.
6. Bruch, H.: *Eating Disorders.* New York, Basic, 1973.
7. Edge, P.: *Child Care and Management.* London, Faber & Faber, 1962.
8. Gersh, M. J.: *How To Raise Children at Home in Your Spare Time.* New ork, Stein & Day, 1966.
9. Ilg, F. L., Ames, L. B., and Baker, S. M.: *Child Behavior.* New York, Har-Row, 1981.
10. Jersild, A. T.: *Child Psychology,* 7th ed. Englewood Cliffs, P-H, 1975.
11. Kanner, L.: *Child Psychiatry,* 4th ed. Springfield, Thomas, 1972.
12. Langford, L. M., and Rand, H. Y.: *Guidance of the Young Child,* 2nd ed. New York, Wiley, 1975.
13. Leach, P.: *Your Baby and Child.* New York, Knopf, 1982.
14. Lin-Fu, J. S.: Lead poisoning in children — what price shall we pay? *Children Today, 8:* 9, 1979.
15. Schaefer, C. E., and Millman, H. L.: *Therapies for Children.* San Francisco, Jossey-Bass, 1977.
16. Smith, H. D., Baehner, R. L., Carney, T., and Majors, W. J.: The sequelae of pica with and without lead poisoning. *American Journal of Disease of Children, 105:* 609, 1963.
17. Spock, B.: *Baby and Child Care.* New York, Dutton, 1976.
18. Verville, E.: *Behavior Problems of Children.* Philadelphia, Saunders, 1967.
19. Verville, E.: What to do when your child refuses to eat. *Parents' Magazine, 27:* 42, 1952.

Chapter 9

SLEEP

THE preschooler who gets too little sleep is irritable. If he wins daily contests about bedtime and rest, he also is anxious and unsure of his parents' ability to look after him. A mother and father who fail to teach their child to go to bed and to sleep feel guilty, worried, and angry.[5]

Resistance, restlessness and bad dreams, and night wandering are problems with which parents must deal.

RESISTANCE

Resistance To Sleep

By the time he is three months old, the newborn infant has fallen into regular sleep habits. His inner mechanisms now operate smoothly, so that air bubbles and lumpy milk no longer distress him. He takes two short naps and one longer nap during the day and he sleeps ten to twelve hours straight at night. This dependable series of time-outs cheers adults.

But it never happens if jittery parents, hearing the baby's settling-down whimpers, hurry to pick him up, feed, and entertain him. At three months, he no longer needs such soothing.[7] Soon the mother and father are sure he cannot fall asleep in his crib; he must

71

be rocked to sleep. And they are right. Constantly held and fussed over, the infant is too keyed up to relax. Getting him to sleep at night becomes a wearying, tedious chore.

Even the small child who always falls asleep on time, in bed, changes when he reaches his second birthday. Suddenly he's on the run for hours and, excited by his thrill-a-minute pace, he cannot wind down at day's end.[11] As long as possible, he keeps himself awake calling for a drink, crying pathetically, or summoning his mother for no reason at all. Parents who appear on demand, let the child up, play with him, and then try to put him down again have it all to do over again five minutes later.

Some preschoolers stay awake because they're afraid. A lively imagination crowds the child's room with fierce bears, ghosts, giants, and bad men, remnants of grand stories told by an older sister and of television's pictured threats and attacks.

A before-bed, friendly wrestle with his father, who growls ferociously, keeps the young child tense and half-afraid.[12]

The loud, angry sounds of parental quarrels frighten him so that he cannot sleep.

Sometimes the young child is deserted while he sleeps. He wakes to find a stranger in the living room and his mother and father gone. For weeks, he fights sleep so his parents can't again slip away without his knowing.[11]

Too often, a preschooler refuses to stay in bed unless his mother lies down with him. One tiny mother curled up in her youngster's crib every night.[12]

Some small children always are taken into the mother's bed when the father is out of town. This comforts her but makes sleep more difficult for the youngster, who is banished to loneliness when his father returns.

Many preschoolers routinely are permitted to sleep with parents if they wake in the middle of the night and announce that they are frightened. They learn in this way to get out of bed, not stay in it.

Sometimes the young child hears his parents talk about their own meager sleep and he quickly adopts their life-style as his own.[3]

Resistance To Bedtime

Some young children not only resist sleep, they object strongly to going to bed. Directing the nightly drama, they insist that daddy give the bath, mommy produce the chocolate milk and two cookies, and big brother rad the story. Every step is prolonged and embellished until the young lord finally condescends to get into his bed.[7]

The preschooler dislikes leaving his family and the exciting things they're doing (reading the paper and washing the dishes) to be alone in the dark by himself. If he is rushed off to bed,[9] sent there as punishment, or at times rewarded by being allowed to stay up, his natural aversion to being separated from the family is strengthened.[12]

There's trouble if bedtime rests on parental convenience. After a late nap or an evening shopping trip, one night he gets to bed at ten o'clock. The next, he's bundled off right after supper. Knowing that he stands a chance of postponing bed-going because the timing really doesn't matter to his mother and father, he objects loudly every night.

Common sense and consistency solve the problems.

The preschooler should go to bed at the same time every night, neither being taken out in the evening nor kept up when company comes. His afternoon nap also should come at the same time daily and end early enough so there is no interference with night sleep.[3,9]

A full hour should be allowed for relaxing before lights out. A bath with time to play, putting away toys and clothes, toileting, a drink of water, one story, and conversation should be routine, slow-paced, and pleasant.[11]

Once the child is in bed, parents must forget he exists. They must not answer his pitiful pleas or urgent demands.[6] Ever. When he knows for certain that he cannot entice his mother or father into his room, he stops trying. Most children fall asleep within twenty minutes after being put to bed.[3]

Lying down with the child or permitting him in the adults' bed only convinces him that he is too young and helpless to sleep alone. He's not. A stuffed animal is good company; a parent can sit by the youngster's bed if he's frightened by a nighttime storm. The preschooler also may have a night light and permission to turn on his room light briefly for a look around if he's afraid. His courage grows as he gets through night after night by himself. In time, he welcomes the security of his own bed.

It's sensible for different people to put him to bed occasionally so he'll sleep even if the routine varies. His father can take over a time or two each week. Then the child will get to bed on schedule when his mother is gone for the evening.

When both parents go out and a sitter is hired, the preschooler should talk and play with her before going to bed. Sometimes the sitter can put him to bed while his parents still are there. Even if he's too young to understand what they are saying, his mother and father must always tell him where they are going and when they will return.

He should not be sent to bed as punishment, allowed to watch TV after supper, or permitted to win arguments for staying up later.

Going to bed and to sleep can and should be an ordinary, expected part of daily life.

RESTLESSNESS AND BAD DREAMS

Restlessness

Overactive youngsters stay that way at night. Some toss about, wave their arms, jerk, and grind their teeth while sleeping. Talking is not unusual. Sometimes names of parents and playmates are repeated, but often the child's words cannot be understood. Occasionally, the small boy or girl cries out.[2,7]

Bad Dreams

Nightmares

A preschooler has much to fear. He is so small that the world seems peopled with giants. In his nightmares they are huge, powerful, and menacing. He hears tales of evil witches and ghosts; they too appear in his dreams.

A nightmare lasts only a few minutes. If the child wakens, or his parents wake him, he knows who they are, where he is, and he can recall the dream.

Night Terrors

Vivid and frightening, the night terror may last for twenty minutes. The child is disoriented. He may seem to be awake and fending off an attacking dog or threatening burglar. He sweats profusely, cannot be calmed, and does not recognize his parents. When finally wakened, he remembers nothing of the experience.[7]

Night terrors are common in tense, anxious children.[2] Herzog[4] reported both night terrors and nightmares in three preschool childrenwho lost their fathers through divorce or separation.

To ensure more restful sleep, parents need to determine if the child's daily life is over-exciting or too busy. The youngster should alternate active play with quiet time for stories and listening to records. Play with other children can be cut to an hour three days a week and older playmates banned. The television should be turned off completely.

Parental arguing in the preschooler's presence should cease. Angry scolding and punishing should be limited to serious rule infractions. Talking with the child about what scares or worries him may reveal misconceptions and fears which yield to explanation.

Kellerman[8] describes a frightened five-year-old boy who kept himself awake for hours each night. Taught how to conquer his fears and rewarded for sleeping well, he quickly overcame his problem.

NIGHT WANDERING

Night wandering can be fun for the child, but it also can harm him: he may play with matches or knives while he is up at night alone. And he needs his sleep.

Wandering can start when the toddler first learns to climb out of his crib. If he joins his parents each evening in the living room and they, entranced with his cleverness, are pleased to see him, he rightly concludes that night life is delightful.

Once accustomed to leaving his bed, he does so at will.

Three-year-old Mary often got up at night and, while her parents slept, looked at magazines, emptied ashtrays, and tidied up the living room. Other children are not content to entertain themselves. They rouse their parents to come play with them.[12]

An early morning wanderer may get into trouble. Up before his parents, he often goes outside and prowls the neighborhood. Four-year-old Jason climbed into a neighbor's car, released the brake, and rolled backwards down the driveway into a tree across the street. His sleeping parents knew nothing of his solitary adventuring.[12]

When a child habitually gets out of bed instead of remaining in it, changes are needed. Each time he leaves his bed he should be returned to it immediately and told that this is a time for sleeping.

While the child is learning, a chain or hook on the outside of his door can be attached. The fastening should permit the door to open a few inches, but not wide enough for the preschooler to leave his room. It can be removed as soon as he regularly remains in bed.

Also, the wanderer should have large doses of attention and a good time with parents and friends during the day. If he does, he won't need to create his own fun at night.

REFERENCES

1. Anders, T. F.: Neurophysiological studies of sleep in infants and children. *Journal of Child Psychology and Psychiatry and Allied Disciplines, 23:* 75, 1982.
2. Bakwin, H., and Bakwin, R. M.: *Clinical Management of Behavior Disorders in Children.* Philadelphia, Saunders, 1966.
3. Faègre, M. L., and Anderson, J. E.: *Child Care and Training,* 8th ed. Minneapolis, U of Minn Pr, 1958.
4. Herzog, J. M: Sleep disturbance and father hunger in 18-28-month-old boys: The Erlkönig syndrome. *Psychoanalytic Study of the Child, 35:* 219, 1980.
5. Hirschberg, J. C.: Parental anxieties accompanying sleep disturbance in young children. *Bulletin of the Menninger Clinic, 21:* 129, 1957.
6. Ilg, F. L, Ames, L. B., and Baker, S. M.: *Child Behavior.* New York, Har-Row, 1981.
7. Kanner, L.: *Child Psychiatry,* 4th ed. Springfield, Thomas, 1972.
8. Kellerman, J.: Rapid treatment of nocturnal anxiety in children. *Journal of Behavior Therapy & Experimental Psychiatry, 11:* 9, 1980.
9. Langford, L. M., and Rand, H. Y.: *Guidance of the Young Child,* 2nd ed. New York, Wiley, 1975.
10. Leach, P.: *Your Baby andChild.* New York, Knopf, 1982.
11. Spock, B.: *Baby and Child Care.* New York, Dutton, 1976.
12. Verville, E.: *Behavior Problems of Children.* Philadelphia, Saunders, 1967.

Chapter 10

ELIMINATION

PROBLEMS with elimination breed hostility between child and parent. Months of toilet training discourage both the weary instructor and the erring youngster. Regression, enuresis, constipation, or encopresis humiliates the preschooler and angers his mother and father.[25]

TRAINING

Bowel Training

Bowel training may start when the infant sits alone, at about nine months. When his straining and red face announce that a movement is *en route,* he is placed on the potty chair. There he associates the feel of the seat with defecation. Often he urinates at the same time.[12,23]

If he's left alone with the soft, smeary product of his efforts, he fingerpaints the wall with it. To prevent this, only snug diapering and speedy removal of feces from the pot are needed.

Bladder Training

Most children are ready for bladder training between 15 and 20 months.[24] By then they stay dry for at least two hours, a sign that the nervous system is developing control over involuntary urination.

For successful training, the youngster must (1) recognize the sensation of a full bladder, (2) hold urine until he reaches the toilet, and (3) release his contracted muscles when he gets there. Boys, with more slowly maturing nervous systems, require longer practice than girls and have more continuing elimination problems.[5]

There's no need to train for night dryness. A child dry during naps soon stays dry at night;[9] he achieves this between two and three years of age.[23] Less urine is produced when the child is quiet, so the bladder does not fill up during sleep.

Training requires a regular routine. The toddler is placed on the toilet before and after meals and naps, and every two hours in between. A small potty chair is less frightening than the adult toilet and allows the youngster to manage by himself. He should wear clothing, including training pants, which he can remove easily.[15]

Watching siblings or playmates use the toilet helps him learn. So do compliments on his success.[24] Praise need not be lavish, nor should it include the comment that he could do as well all the time if he would try. Failures should receive little fanfare.

Misunderstandings

A preschooler in training points to the puddle he's just made on the kitchen floor, grins, and proudly announces, "Tinkle!" His startled mother is sure he's trying to make a fool of her. He's not. Finally connecting urination with this new word and knowing his mother is showing unusual interest in the whole business, he's letting her know he shares her enthusiasm.

Or, after a dash to the bathroom and a patient, useless wait, the child lets go with a splashy stream the instant he's off the chair. Again, he's not trying to disappoint or out-maneuver his mother. It's only that he has not yet mastered the final step in training: release. Sitting there, tense with hope that success and smiles are near, his muscles stay tight. Off the potty, the Big Moment over, he relaxes and urine pours out.[3,25]

REGRESSION

A trained child who reverts to erratic wetting baffel his parents, who are sure he can do better. Often he cannot, but reasons for back-sliding can be unearthed.

Regression after the birth of a sibling is common. Sometimes the jealous boy or girl imitates his rival to win parental approval. More often the older youngster is distracted by schedule changes and household upheaval. Sometimes, in anticipation of the new arrival, his training came too early to take hold.

The ill, tired, or over-excited child relapses to wetting and soiling.[10] If he is kept up late, watches frightening TV programs, and lives in a noisy, busy, crowded household, control is easily lost.[25]

Also, if his parents quarrel or playmates shove him around every day, he stays anxious and tense, oblivious to body signals. He may worry that a strange sitter is replacing his parents and not notice that he needs to go to the toilet. Or he may dread the bathroom because of unpleasant sessions there or fear of the flushing toilet.

After both child and mother consider training accomplished, inattention sets in. The youngster now concentrates on his speech or getting along with playmates. His mother, busy with visiting relatives, a child's illness, or a move, neglects his regular bathroom trips. Soon he again is wetting unpredictably.[25]

Regression can be halted. A mother and father need only keep the child on normal eating and sleeping routines and watch for signs that he needs to go to the toilet. They should give him regular, daily attention and protect him from over-exciting or frightening situations. Taking or sending him to the bathroom at two-hour intervals alerts him again to toileting needs.

ENURESIS

Enuresis is involuntary urination in a child over three years of age, although night wetting in boys under four is not unusual. Nineteen percent of five- and six-year-olds are enuretic, two-thirds of them boys.[7,21]

Enuresis disrupts families. Parents revile and punish. The child lives with chronic anxiety, impaired peer relationships, and lowered self-esteem.[7] Bedwetters have been described as rigid, aggressive, dependent, insecure, isolated, and rejected.[11] But Berg[4] found a majority of the enuretic children he studied were well-adjusted.

Many enuretic boys are overly dependent on their mothers. They cannot compete with other boys and do not enjoy being with them. Enuretic girls tend to take on more than they can handle. They try to out-do boys and are uncomfortable with girls.

There are many reasons for enuresis.

A number of children, lonely and dissatisfied with themselves, become enuretic when they start school and must endure daily doses of competition and aggression from classmates.[25]

A few unhappy, isolated youngsters admit that they wet the bed because they are unwilling to leave their warm covers for a trip to the bathroom.

Kaffman and Elizur[11] found that delayed training promotes enuresis. Of six- to eight-year-olds whose training had begun between 15 and 19 months of age, 95 percent had dry beds; of those whose training started between 20 and 26 months, only 80 percent did.

Sometimes a preschooler, jealous of an infant sibling, continues wetting to win parental attention. Even scoldings are better than abandonment.[12]

Some small children ignore wetting because their parents do. The adults also were bedwetters and claim that "weak kidneys" run in the family. They fail to train the child thoroughly, they expect him to wet, and they make no effort to keep him clean. One little boy slept in the hall every night on blankets reeking with urine.[25]

Other young children can't overcome enuresis because parents get too upset when they wet. The anxious child, dreading furious punishment, loses all control.[6] Many youngsters lie awake for hours, fearful of wetting once their eyes close. Enuretics often are described as heavy sleepers. Some are, but many are the victims of too little sleep.

A few youngsters actually are difficult to rouse, no matter how much sleep they get. Others have undetected bladder abnormalities and infections which cause persistent wetting. Every enuretic child should be examined by a physician to rule out physical problems.

Enuresis need not continue forever.

Many children, as they mature and are encouraged, cease wetting by themselves. Schaefer and Millman[21] report a spontaneous cure rate of 14 percent in five- to nine-year-olds. But if treatment can erase the problem before then, everyone benefits.

Treatments have ranged from reasonable to desperate. Surgery has been tried. Mechanical devices, hypnosis, diet changes, enforced bed rest, drugs, shaming, and severe punishment all have been considered solutions.[12]

Some parents forbid evening drinks. Others take the child to the toilet once or several times during the night. But fluid restriction only makes the preschooler thirsty; getting him up assures him that the problem is his parents' to solve.[25]

Most children overcome enuresis when they are made responsible for keeping dry and also know that other boys and girls have done so.[12]

Using a calendar chart works for many. The child puts a star on the chart for each night he keeps his bed dry; five stars win him an ice cream cone, a trip to the zoo, or a toy. Proud of his stars and delighted with his presents, he gradually ceases wetting.

Children can be taught to hold urine. Kimmel and Kimmel[13] describe two four-year-old girls who were encouraged to drink liquids freely at any time. If they could hold urine for five minutes (they watched the clock hands) after stating that they needed to go to the toilet, they won a prize — pop, candy, or cookies. The holding time required to get a treat was increased in increments of three to five minutes and in only a few days, the girls could retain urine for thirty minutes. Within a week, they had stopped their bedwetting.

Mowrer and Mowrer[19] cured three- to thirteen-year-old children of enuresis within four to eight weeks. The youngsters slept on a mat wired to ring a bell when drops of urine wet it. When they were wakened by the bell, they got up, turned off the bell, and went to the bathroom. Conditioned to the bell's warning, they anticipated its signal when wetting was imminent and made it to the bathroom in time.

Some pediatricians give antidepressant drugs, such as imipramine, to enuretic youngsters. Meadow[17] reports that 40 percent of children given this drug became dry, but that relapses were frequent.

He also says that the drug is expensive, addictive, and may have dangerous side effects.

Day wetting ends in half of the children who learn to stay dry at night.[21] If an over-excited or resistive boy or girl still wets in the daytime, re-training is needed. The child should be sent or taken to the toilet every two hours, but kept on the seat no longer than five minutes.

When he shows by jumping about and holding his genitals that he needs to go to the bathroom, his parents should insist that he do so. If he fears the flushing, an adult can do this for him once he is finished and gone.[25]

Enuretic children need to grow more independent and learn to fit in with same-sex peers. A boy should work and play with his father, spend less time with his mother, do chores daily, and play away from home with other boys. A girl should mix up cakes and have good times with her mother, playing, singing, and talking. She should regularly play with other girls her age, both at her own home and theirs. If she is trying too hard to best all comers, the whole family should lower its standards for achievement.

CONSTIPATION

Their child's constipation worries parents. Some do not know that a healthy youngster may not have a daily bowel movement. Breast-fed babies often defecate only every other day and may continue the habit as they grow older.

Some alarmed mothers take control of their preschooler's evacuation.[12,14] They give daily enemas and laxatives; they force the youngster to remain on the toilet for long periods of time. One mother, every day, spent an exhausting two hours in the bathroom with her three-year-old daughter, reading stories to her and pleading with her to move her bowels. Nothing happened.[25]

Such extreme efforts often make the problem worse. The daily use of suppositories, enemas, and laxatives reduces muscle tone and thus lessens the child's ability to empty his bowel when he needs to. Forcing and pleading disturb the preschooler, who becomes tense and worried by his inability to please his parent.

Often a busily playing preschooler, afraid that friends will vanish while he goes to the bathroom, ignores signs that he needs to defecate. When no response is made to bowel contractions, they cease. Fecal material accumulates and the child postpones evacuating because he knows it will be time-consuming and painful.

Gersh[8] points out that some children do not move their bowels regularly because they must do so on an adult toilet. The same muscles retain and expel feces; therefore the child needs to have his feet on the floor so he can push harder.

Gersh also notes that constipation tends to be hereditary, and that constipated and non-constipated children show different patterns of muscular motility.

The constipated child can be helped.

Parents should be told that children differ in the frequency of movements and that daily evacuation is unnecessary. But if the child, when younger, had a preferred time of day for moving his bowels, he can be sent to the bathroom regularly at that time. With a set schedule, time to attend to defecation is guaranteed.

If there is no preferred time, the youngster can be sent after breakfast and after dinner to try for ten minutes to move his bowels. He should have no entertainment or company, nor should there be family activities going on which he hates to miss.

Laxatives and enemas should not be used without a doctor's approval, and they should be phased out as soon as possible. Prunes and molasses, plus plenty of water, help soften the movement so the child does not dread passing it.[25]

ENCOPRESIS

Encopresis is persistent soiling by a child over two years of age. Most adults find encopresis incomprehensible, but there are a number of reasons which account for it.

Some youngsters never have been adequately trained.[1] Others are retarded or brain-damaged and learn slowly.[16] With sustained instruction, nearly all of these acquire control.

Pick[20] identifies constipation as the single most significant cause of encopresis. Feces are retained until the bowel is distended and no contractions occur. The bowel loses its capacity to absorb water and finally, driblets or masses of fecal material are expelled.[8,12]

Psychological factors are cited. Parents of encopretic children have been described as compulsive, over-intellectualizing, isolated individuals.[22] They both distance themselves from the child and infantilize him. Communication is faulty and repressed anger is strong.[2] Sheinbein[22] recommends therapy for parents of encopretics.

Soiling may follow coercive bowel training.[1] It also has been considered a devious form of resistance by usually compliant children.

Many preschoolers, sure they can hold the movement and reluctant to leave play, wait too long. Others fear the bathroom.[26] These children relieve themselves wherever they happen to be, often hiding feces behind the couch or in the closet to avoid punishment.[12]

In some busy households, no time or privacy is allowed for defecation, so constipation, then soiling, results.

Upset parents ridicule the child, describe his sin to teachers and visitors, dose him with medicines and vitamins, make him wash soiled clothing, and punish him fiercely.

It's better to re-train him. He needs once again to attend to the feel of a signalling bowel and go promptly to the bathroom.

To re-learn the sequence, he should sit on the toilet twice a day for ten minutes, attempting to evacuate. Flexing bowel muscles improves tone and reminds the youngster how they feel and what they are for.

If soiling does not decrease within two weeks, the preschooler can be required to try three or four times daily. Disliking interruption of his play time, he will learn. Optimism by parents and rewards for success both help.

Wright[27] has taught parents to re-train their encopretic children. Rewards (time alone with the parent, toys, money, trips) are given for cleanliness; penalties (extra chores, loss of play time) are imposed for soiling. Evacuation is triggered by suppositories and enemas. Regular emptying of the bowel not only prevents soiling but also permits the colon to regain its shape and tone. After two weeks of cleanliness, the child gradually is weaned from suppositories and enemas. The process takes 15 to 20 weeks.

Threats, punishment, and forcing the child to stay on the toilet for hours are counterproductive. Rebelling at this unfair treatment, the youngster soils in revenge, a motive which originally played no part in his encopresis.[25]

REFERENCES

1. Anthony, E. J.: An experimental approach to the psychopathology of childhood: Encopresis. *British Journal of Medical Psychology, 30*: 146, 1957.
2. Baird, M.: Characteristic interaction patterns in families of encopretic children. *Bulletin of the Menninger Clinic, 38*: 144, 1974.
3. Bakwin, H., and Bakwin, R. M.: *Clinical Management of Behavior Disorders in Children,* 3rd ed. Philadelphia, Saunders, 1966.
4. Berg, I.: Child psychiatry and enuresis. *British Journal of Psychiatry, 139*: 247, 1981.
5. Breckenridge, M., and Murphy, M.: *Growth and Development of the Young Child,* 8th ed. Philadelphia, Saunders, 1969.
6. Faegre, M. L., and Anderson, J. E.: *Child Care and Training,* 8th ed. Minneapolis, U of Minn Pr, 1958.
7. Fritz, G. K., and Andrews, T. F.: Enuresis: the clinical application of an etiologically based classification system. *Child Psychiatry and Human Development, 10*: 103, 1979.
8. Gersh, M. J.: *How To Raise Children at Home in Your Spare Time.* New York, Stein & Day, 1966.
9. Ilg, F. L., Ames, L. B., and Baker, S. M.: *Child Behavior.* New York, Har-Row, 1981.
10. Jersild, A. T.: *Child Psychology,* 7th ed. Englewood Cliffs, P-H, 1975.
11. Kaffman, M., and Elizur, E.: Infants who become enuretics: A longitudinal study of 161 kibbutz children. *Monographs of the Society for Research in Child Development, 42*: 1977.
12. Kanner, L.: *Child Psychiatry,* 4th ed. Springfield, Thomas, 1972.
13. Kimmel, H. D., and Kimmel, E.: An instrumental conditioning method for the treatment of enuresis. *Journal of Behavior Therapy and Experimental Psychiatry, 1*: 121, 1970.
14. Langford, L. J., and Rand, H. Y.: *Guidance of the Young Child,* 2nd ed. New York, Wiley, 1975.
15. Leach, P.: *Your Baby and Child.* New York, Knopf, 1982.
16. Lempp, R.: Zur Ätiologie des kindlichen Einstuhlens (The etiologyof fecal soiling in children.) *Zeitschrift für Psychotherapie and Medizinische Psychologie, 6*: 206, 1956.
17. Meadow, R.: Drugs for bed-wetting. *Archives of Disease in Childhood, 49*: 257, 1974.
18. Meyerhardt, O.: Al hamekhanizm shel hartavat layla (On the mechanism of enuresis nocturna.) *Harefuah, 52*: 258, 1957.
19. Mowrer, O. H., and Mowrer, W. M.: Enuresis — a method for its study and

treatment. *American Journal of Orthopsychiatry, 8*: 436, 1938.

20. Pick, W.: Fecal soiling due to paradoxic constipation. *American Journal of Diseases of Children, 105*: 229, 1963.
21. Schaefer, C. E., and Millman, H. L.: *Therapies for Children.* San Francisco, Jossey-Bass, 1977.
22. Sheinbein, M.: A triadic-behavioral approach to encopresis. *Journal of Family Counseling, 3*: 58, 1975.
23. Spock, B.: *Baby and Child Care.* New York, Dutton, 1976.
24. Tomlinson-Keasey, C.: *Child's Eye view.* New York, St Martin, 1980.
25. Verville, E.: *Behavior Problems of Children.* Philadelphia, Saunders, 1967.
26. Walker, C. E., and Werstlein, R.: Use of relaxation procedures in the treatment of toilet phobia in a 4-year-old child. *Behavior Therapist, 3: 17, 1980.*
27. Wright, L.: *Handling the encopretic child. Professional Psychology, 4*: 137, 1973.

Chapter 11

SPEECH

THE preschool child who speaks well grows in knowledge, self-control, power, social approval, attentiveness, and pride.

Reciting facts and reporting events, he remembers them. Coaching himself on what is forbidden, self-discipline strengthens. Announcing his wishes, he commands parental attention and service. Both playmates[12] and adults admire him as he studs his conversation with what he believes, does, plans, and owns. As he watches, listens, recalls, and then talks, he can snare interest, promote ideas, entertain, and dispense news. He is rightfully pleased with himself.

DEVELOPMENT

Skill with speech, like motor development, progresses in ordered stages. By six months, the infant's eating and breathing mechanisms work smoothly and he is free to turn his attention to making sounds.[13] As he babbles, German gutterals, Scottish burrs, and French trills can be heard. *L* and *r* are difficult sounds; some youngsters cannot manage these until they are seven years old.[9]

Most children use one to three words at 12 months and twenty-two at 18 months.[6] By then the toddler talks often to himself in a jargon of his own, complete with inflections and sounding exactly like true language. He repeats others' words and phrases, whether or not he understands them, and he catches meanings sooner than he can express them. By two years he has a vocabulary of 300 words and speaks in two- and three-word sentences. At three years, he knows 900 words and has mastered most sounds.[22] By the time he is five, he has a vocabulary of 2,000 words, he uses correct syntax, and his speech is clearly understandable.[15]

Preschoolers speak more when parents translate their one-word "sentences", name objects, describe surroundings, and correct the child's mispronunciations.[21]

Single children and those with better-educated parents develop the most extensive vocabularies.[6]

Norman-Jackson[16] found that 24- to 42-month-old siblings of good second-grade readers spoke in longer sentences than preschool siblings of poor readers. Five years later, the more verbal youngsters also were good readers, suggesting a familial influence on the acquisition and use of language.

DISORDERS

Speech disorders hamper the child's ability to progress intellectually, socially, and emotionally. They may cause serious damage to self-respect and lead to behavior problems. They include delayed speech, articulation defects, voice disturbances, stuttering, and mutism.

Delayed Speech

Some preschoolers rarely speak; others use words in a babyish or unintelligible way.

Deafness delays speech. If the youngster cannot hear, he cannot imitate sounds.

Neurological damage may cause aphasia, difficulty in understanding or expressing language. If the injury is congenital, sometimes the child suddenly develops acceptable speech when he is four or five years old. If the brain is harmed by accident or infection, speech may be lost temporarily. Recovery time ranges from a few weeks to two years.[3]

The mentally retarded preschooler will not talk early or well. The parents of attractive, obedient four-year-old Michael could not understand why he said nothing but, "Muh-uh-duh." Testing revealed that the child had an I.Q. of 45.[23]

Twins often lag in speech development. Using sounds which mean something to each other, they care little about communicating with others. Once they start school, they quickly learn to speak as everyone else does.[5]

A bilingual home confuses and slows the child. Smith[18] reports that monolingual preschoolers use a greater variety of words than children in families speaking two languages.

A youngster reared in an institution or hospitalized for long periods is slow to talk. His needs are taken care of automatically, with no request from him. There is scant possibility of personal attention from caretakers. Because he has no reason to speak, he does not.

If his home is bare and there is little to intrigue him, or if his parents rarely talk, the preschooler remains passive and silent.[22]

Debilitating emotion is a prime cause for retarded speech. Overprotected and smothered in parental anxiety, an infantile youngster almost never expresses his own thoughts.[2,13] Nor does the preschooler whose parents are critical and perfectionistic: they constantly question him, urge him to talk, and then deride both his pronunciation and his ideas.[17] Still other mothers and fathers quarrel, shout orders, or signal indifference by ignoring the child's questions and stories.[19] To him, talking means trouble, so he avoids it.

Young children who don't entertain themselves with jargon or who depend on gestures to get service block their own speech development.[22]

Much can be done for the preschooler who falls behind in word communication.

If he's three years old and rarely talks or if he uses single words more than sentences, he should be examined for deafness, neurological deficit, and intelligence.

The child who cannot hear or who has neurological problems should attend a nursery school for the deaf. There, he'll learn to read lips, make sounds, and acquire vocabulary. Early instruction prevents a serious and enduring speech problem in the future.

The mentally retarded child will learn to speak, but he takes longer to master and remember words than a normal boy or girl. Parents and siblings must speak to him often, rather than ignore his presence because they are sure he will not understand.

The preschooler with delayed speech can be trained to learn a few words at a time, starting with names of objects he sees daily.

He learns that speaking pays when his parents give him what he wants when he asks for it. If gestures replace words, the habit can be phased out gradually. His mother can "misunderstand" one or two gestures daily, then three or four, until the youngster concludes that grownups aren't bright enough to know what he wants unless he tells them.[22]

Parents need to avoid questions, rapid speech, and complex sentences when they talk to the child. If they are critical, overprotective, or excessively quiet, they can learn to moderate their ways.[14]

Playing regularly with a normally-speaking, friendly child also helps the youngster. Soon he imitates his playmate's conversation and tries to hold his interest. His new skill carries over into stepped-up verbal contacts with others.[20,23]

Articulation Defects

Omitting or substituting sounds in words results in poor articulation. Common substitutions are *th* for *s, sh, z,* and *ch:* the child says *fith* for *fish; t* or *d* for *g, k,* and *x: good* becomes *dood;* and *w* for *l* and *r: read* comes out *wead.*

Unclear speech compels the youngster to live with others' miscomprehensions and ridicule. Twice as many boys as girls have this problem.

There may be physical causes for articulation defects: hearing loss, so that individual sounds are indistinct to the child; size, shape, and motor defects in speech organs — the tongue, uvula, or palate; and deformities in the nose or larnyx, protruding teeth, or enlarged tonsils which interfere with air flow.[9]

If the child is not fluent, he sometimes makes up words which resemble those he hears and his speech is muddy. He may copy the mispronunciations of playmates, siblings, or carelessly speaking adults. If he is harshly treated, overprotected, or believes life is unfair, he may revert to helplessness and show his feelings with baby talk.

The five-year-old with articulation problems sometimes starts kindergarten with words so garbled that his teacher cannot understand him. His parents, used to the way he talks, have forgotten that his speech is unique.[23]

He can improve.

Any physical defect which interferes with articulation should be corrected to the extent possible. The deaf child should be given the special instruction he needs.

If the youngster mixes up or omits sounds from habit, one word at a time can be chosen to work on. When the child mispronounces this word, the parent says it correctly, and the youngster follows suit. Once that word is mastered, another is picked. Because every word he bungles is not corrected, the child does not become so embarrassed that he stops talking.

He also can rehearse sounds and learn to distinguish between them. Rewarding him for detecting parents' or siblings' mispronunciations encourages close attention to the sound of words.

If his speech is babyish, reflecting helplessness, he needs more independence and time with playmates, plus daily training in meeting his own needs and doing chores.[23]

Voice Disturbances

Some children have nasal or harsh voices. In others, the pitch is too high or low, the volume too loud or soft. A youngster may speak in a monotone, put peculiar breaks in sentences, or emphasize the first or last syllable of each word. His voice may tremble. He may whine.[21]

Voice disturbances can result from disease or deformity of organs lying behind the tonuge. A paralyzed or cleft palate, adenoidal growths, laryngitis, vocal cord tumors, strain from excessive screaming, or head colds cause a nasal sound or hoarseness. Kanner[9] states that respiratory control is basic to good phonation.

Central nervous system diseases can lead to monotony, slowness, slurring, and pitch changes in speaking.

Endocrine disorders are reflected in the voice.[9] Typical of these are the rough speech of the thyroid-deficient cretin and the pitch slides of the adolescent boy.

Personality and emotional make-up can be detected in voices. The aggressive youngster speaks in a loud, angry tone, attacking and accusing. The anxious, shy child mumbles, wary of attracting attention. The infantile preschooler whines, seeking comfort and indulgence.[9]

Voice disturbances can be corrected.

Physical defects should be repaired, if possible, and treatment given for conditions which affect tone, volume, and quality.

The child whose tone, pitch, or intensity is obtrusive from habit can imitate his mother's or father's more normal voice in regular, brief practice sessions.

The aggressive, fearful, or immature youngster must be managed differently so that emotion does not flood his life. But training him to speak calmly and clearly will upgrade his opinion of himself and others.[23]

Stuttering

According to Jonas,[8] there are two million stutterers in the United States. Van Riper[22] reports that 41 percent of the patients at his speech clinic over a ten-year period were stutterers.

Boys are four times more likely to stutter than girls. Stuttering is linked to left-handedness, heredity, and being a twin.[9]

No one stutters all the time. Although certain words or sounds consistently cause trouble, even these can be sung, recited with other persons, addressed to an animal or small child, or delivered in a foreign language without difficulty.[8]

Stuttering often develops between two and three years, when the child is working hard to translate his ideas into words. As he does, hesitant and repetitive speech occurs. The normal preschooler repeats 40 or 50 times in every thousand words he speaks. If his parents consider this to be stuttering, they warn him to slow down and start over. Then, fearing mistakes, he tenses and speech muscles freeze. He cannot say the word he wants to use.

Nearly every child has trouble getting the attention of his preoccupied, busy parents. Trying to do so, he talks too fast and stumbles over words.[23]

Some children, fearing rejection, are taut with strain when they try to talk to their parents. They repeat both sounds and words.

Others suffer lasting effects from a traumatic event: a family move, a fire, separation from a hospitalized or divorced parent, an encounter with a bullying playmate or snarling dog. Pervasive tension disrupts the coordination between breathing and fine muscles which smooth speech needs.

Treatment for stutterers has ranged from advice to avoid snoring to tongue slicing.[8]

Parents are the preferred therapists for the stuttering preschool child. They help by paying no attention when the child repeats words or sounds and by speaking less often and more slowly themselves. For the present, time with the child is better spent listening to music and making toys than in reading.

When the youngster speaks, the adults should stop what they are doing, look at him, and listen. Then they should answer his questions or comment on his tales.

Behavior standards should be lowered, criticism eased, and the small boy or girl given his way in minor disputes so that frantic arguing is unnecessary.[23] One child stopped stuttering in three days when his mother cut her refusals of his requests to a third of her usual daily quota.[22]

The preschooler should be sent outdoors every day to run and shout, free up muscles, and distract himself from his troubles.[20]

Most boys and girls, in time, spontaneously recover from stuttering. But until they do, they suffer intense shame and frustration. If the child still stutters when he starts kindergarten, he should work with a speech therapist so the problem can be ended as soon as possible.

Mutism

The mute child rarely, if ever, speaks. His parents are embarrassed and angry. The youngster remains socially and emotionally infantile. A variety of reasons can cause the preschooler to keep silent.

Like delayed speech, mutism may result from deafness, low intelligence, or damage to the central nervous system. But if it is emotionally based, it is termed elective.

Hayden[4] classified 68 elective mute children into four types: (1) symbiotic, in which the youngster maintained a special, submissive relationship with a caretaker, usually a dominant, verbose, jealous mother; (2) speech phobic, in which the child feared hearing his own voice and practiced ritualistic behavior; (3) reactive, in which the child withdrew as the direct result of trauma; and (4) passive-aggressive, in which the youngster used mutism as a weapon.

Six of this group became mute when they started school. For the other 62, mutism either had existed all their lives or had begun during preschool years. Fifty-six of the group were girls; twelve were boys.

All were fearful, had numerous nervous habits, and held themselves rigid, both standing and sitting. Shy and clinging away from home, they were demanding and stubborn with parents. They were immature and often cried.

Passive-aggressive mute youngsters sometimes were violent, laughed excitedly, or lacked facial expression.

Some children, especially the speech phobic, wanted to talk. Trying, they sweated and trembled. They did communicate with gestures, signs, and notes.

For many, there was a history of physical and sexual abuse. Some had once been ordered to keep a family secret; others, after punishment for sassiness, were told, "Don't you ever open your mouth again!" A few had suffered a throat or mouth injury.

Kolvin and Fundudis[11] studied 24 six- to eight-year-old mute children. Submissive and moody in social settings, at home they were aggressive and sulky, nearly always getting their own way. From an early age, twenty of them were considered shy. Ten were enuretic and four were encopretic. Electroencephalographic records indicated developmental slowness. Their mean I.Q. was 85. Nearly half of these youngsters gradually improved.

When mutism is traceable to physical problems, treatment is the same as that given the speech-delayed child.

The elective mute, lonely, inept, and frustrated, needs more contact with normally talking, cheerful, active playmates. One good friend can entice the silent preschooler to speak.

A mother and father must see to it that the child follows a regular, daily schedule of eating, sleeping, and outdoor play. Each should work, play, or read to the youngster every day. Dancing, singing, and exercising to music with his parents relaxes the small child and makes him smile.

The preschooler needs praise for obedience and for helping. He should be taught to do chores and take care of his own needs so he can gain confidence.

Emotional scenes should be short: every tantrum should lead to the child's isolation, not the adult's capitulation.

If the youngster has endured physical or sexual abuse or other emotional trauma, explanations, regrets, and reassurance must be offered. If he was directed at some previous time not to talk, the earlier order should be countermanded.

In time, with affection and discipline from parents and many chances to gain new skills and friends, the mute child will begin to speak.

REFERENCES

1. Araki, F.: (Some psychopathological observations on mutism originating in childhood.) *Japanese Journal of Child & Adolescent Psychiatry, 20*: 290, 1979.
2. Beckey, R. E.: A study of certain factors related to the retardation of speech. *Journal of Speech Disorders, 7*:223, 1942.
3. Benton, A. L.: Aphasia in children. In Trapp, E. P., and Himelstein, P., eds.: *Readings on the Exceptional Child.* New York, ACC, 1962.
4. Hayden, T. L.: Classification of elective mutism. *Journal of Child Psychiatry, 19*: 119, 1980.
5. Hurlock, E. B.: *Child Development,* 5th ed. New York, McGraw, 1972.
6. Hymes, J. L., Jr.: *The Child Under Six.* Englewood Cliffs, P-H, 1963.
7. Ilg, F. L., Ames, L. B., and Baker, S. M.: *Child Behavior.* New York, Harper, 1981.
8. Jonas, G.: *Stuttering.* New York, FS & G, 1977.
9. Kanner, L.: *Child Psychiatry,* 4th ed. Springfield, Thomas, 1972.
10. Koizumi, T., and Usuda, S.: (Developmental and biological factors on autistic children and other children with delayed speech in early infancy.) *Japanese Journal of Child & Adolescent Psychiatry, 20*: 290, 1979.
11. Kolvin, I., and Fundudis, T.: Elective mute children: Psychological development and background factors. *Journal of Child Psychology and Psychiatry, 22*: 219, 1981.
12. Langford, L. J., and Rand, H. Y.: *Guidance of the Young Child,* 2nd ed. New

York, Wiley, 1975.
13. McCarthy, D.: Language development. *Monographs of the Society for Research in Child Development, 25*: 5, 1960.
14. McDade, H. L.: A parent-child interactional model for assessing and remediating language disabilities. *British Journal of Disorders of Communication, 16*: 175, 1981.
15. McNeill, D.: The development of language. In Mussen, P., ed.: Carmichael's *Manual of Child Psychology,* 3rd ed., Vol. 1. New York, Wiley, 1970.
16. Norman-Jackson, J.: Family interactions, language development, and primary reading achievement of black children in families of low income. *Child Development, 53*: 349, 1982.
17. Peckarsky, A. K.: Maternal attitudes toward children with psychogenically delayed speech. Ph.D. thesis, New York University, 1953.
18. Smith, M. E.: Word variety as a measure of bilingualism in preschool children. *Journal of Genetic Psychology, 90*: 143, 1957.
19. Spiegel, R.: Specific problems of communication in psychiatric conditions. In Arieti, S., ed.: *American Handbook of Psychiatry,* Vol. 1. New York, Basic, 1959.
20. Spock, B.: *Baby and Child Care.* New York, Dutton, 1976.
21. Tomlinson-Keasey, C.: *Child's Eye View.* New York, St Martin, 1980.
22. VanRiper, C.: *Speech Correction,* 5th ed. Englewood Cliffs, P-H, 1972.
23. Verville, E.: *Behavior Problems of Children.* Philadelphia, Saunders, 1967.

Chapter 12

PEERS

THE opinionsof peers are a potent governor of the preschooler's self-esteem. The friendless child is likely to develop lasting emotional disorders.[11] One-third of the boys and girls referred to a child guidance clinic for various problems were described by teachers as getting along poorly with classmates.[15]

Children whose personalities and interests are similar form close friendships.[8] But preschoolers usually are limited to playing with youngsters who live in their own neighborhoods. Early unpleasant social experiences may damage self-esteem and lead to faulty perceptions of others.

The preschooler fortunate enough to have compatible, treasured friends grows in independence, cooperation, thoughtfulness, and sociability.[12,24,25] He delights in his acceptance, broadens his experiences, and gradually learns to give and take, share, cope with problems, and adjust to group rules. All of this solidifes his status with others and boosts his self-respect.[2,4,21] Suelzle[26] found that social and emotional development is related to learning capacity. The child who has friends speaks more, both when playing with them or alone.[5,6]

As the toddler grows older, idleness, on-looking, and solitary play decrease. Now he wants attention and praise from peers. Although he becomes more cooperative as he plays with others, he also becomes more assertive and competitive. Older preschoolers quarrel less often than younger ones, but their arguments last longer.[11]

97

A youngster imitates his playmates. Closeness grows as each copies the other.[9] Asher *et al.*[1] report that the most popular of 65 kindergarteners they studied knew and used a variety of social skills and strategies to get along.

Feeling comfortable in a group is never automatic nor instantaneous. The preschooler wavers from submissiveness to aggressiveness in each group he joins. The girl who is shy in nursery school one year becomes a leader there the next; the swaggering boy who tries to take charge during his first week retreats during the second. He needs time to get to know his playmates.[27]

Problems with peers include excessive or limited contacts, aggressiveness, submissiveness, or substituting an imaginary friend for a real one.

EXCESSIVE CONTACTS

Constant play with others harms the preschooler.

There may be a hundred children in his block and if he spends every moment of every day with youngsters of all ages, he's worn out from the competition and excitement. His sleeping and eating suffer. He gets little pleasure or benefit from his total immersion in a sea of children.

Some parents insist that their young boy or girl join every playing group. Turned out of the house, unpracticed in protecting himself, the preschooler is victimized by older or brutal children. Soon he fears, dislikes, and avoids all youngsters.

A social-minded mother, intent on free-and-easy contacts for her small child, sends him out to roam. He goes where he likes and returns only to eat and sleep. But wandering doesn't sharpen social skills; it only makes the youngster homesick. Instead of playing with neighbor children, he attaches himself to their mothers, seeking the interest, guidance, and comfort his own mother does not give.

The younger preschool child should play with another boy or girl only one hour at a time. Two hours is long enough for a four- or five-year-old. Playing should alternate between homes, so the youngster learns to be both host and guest and to get along with others when his mother is not within call.

Visitors should arrive and leave at the convenience of the supervising mother, but these times should be set in advance. The preschooler feels safer when he knows he is expected home at a certain hour.

Playmates should be about the same age and, more often than not, the same sex. Older or younger siblings of the host child should not be allowed to interfere with play.

LIMITED CONTACTS

Few playmates, or none at all, keep the child a social infant.

The best-liked preschoolers in nursery schools spend more time with peers and less time alone or with adults than do less popular youngsters.[7] From an early age, the child benefits from playing with a number of children, each of whom offers new ideas and challenges.

A preschooler may have no playmates because there are no children his age in the neighborhood or because he lives on a farm. But too often his contacts with other boys and girls are thoughtlessly limited by adults. His grandparents enjoy his company and monopolize his time. His parents are too busy to arrange for playmates or unwilling to supervise young visitors.

Sometimes a preschooler has only one friend. Although one is better than none, constant togetherness causes problems. Used to the unique ways of his sole companion, the youngster is startled and dismayed when he encounters the rainbow of personalities in his kindergarten class.

And, dependent on one friend for approval and companionship, the preschooler wants him to be private property. He runs off children who try to join their play and is frantic when his buddy spends time with others.

The small girl who plays only with boys or the boy whose sole friends are girls, because these are the neighborhood's available youngsters, will be in difficulty if they find no same-sex companions by three years of age. It's then that children begin to identify with their own sexes, a recognition of differences based in part on play activities.[20]

The preschooler with no companions, only one friend, or playmates entirely of the opposite sex should attend nursery school two or three times a week. He learns there both to get along with an assortment of children his age and to veer toward his appropriate sex-role. These achievements strengthen him throughout his life.

AGGRESSIVENESS

A young child attacks another to get his way or to pay back a bullying, insulting playmate. Although consistent self-control won't be reliable for years, if aggressiveness is the preschooler's only way of dealing with others, he is headed for serious, lasting trouble.

Two-year-olds get acquainted by pushing and hitting each other. Three- and four-year-olds, protecting themselves, call names and throw rocks from a safe distance. Both courage and determination grow with the child and aggressiveness continues until the age of five.[22]

Provoked aggression is reasonable; impulsive attacks are not. Kagan and Moss[16] found that physical aggression toward playmates in three-year-old children persisted until late adolescence.

Such determined belligerence is learned. Physically abused children or those dominated by older siblings and playmates mimic the violence used against them. Because the preschooler seldom can win battles against older, stronger persons, he attacks younger and weaker ones who have caused him no trouble. After his teacher scolded him on the playground, five-year-old Lyle ran up to a smaller classmate and kicked him.[27]

Some fathers and mothers encourage their preschoolers to hit. They order the child to beat up the playmate who has taken his toy or called him names. Not distinguishing between justified defense and total war, the youngster hits and kicks at random, trying to please his parents.

The indulged boy or girl, getting everything he wants from his parents, carries on with his accustomed life-style wherever he is. He attacks peers and refuses adults' orders. Soon his behavior isolates him from everyone.[3]

Antisocial attitudes are reinforced when a child complains to his parent about a playmate and the adult scolds or chases away the visitor.[28]

A boy dominated by his mother often is aggressive with peers. He tries for self-respect by bossing them as his mother bosses him.[11]

Aggressiveness toward other children can be halted. Hartup[11] reports that parents of likable boys discouraged antisocial actions. They seldom frustrated or punished their children and they encouraged them in what they tried to do. A father's affection was related to a son's popularity and liking for others.

The aggressive child's assortment of companions should be broadened; not all will back off when he attacks. The certainty that he'll be hurt if he strikes out gives him pause.

He can join a play group or nursery school where a friendly adult guides, questions, and suggests alternative actions. Preschoolers improve in self-control under this training.[11]

Parents must curb over-punishment of the child and restrict their correction to major matters. The youngster should not be subjected continually to the orders and insults of older siblings and playmates.

When he hits or kicks without provocation, the preschooler must apologize. If he repeats the offense, he should be isolated for fifteen minutes. But he should not be kept away from peers. He needs the chance to practice new ways of getting along.

As he gives up fighting, he becomes more dependent on adults. Although his whining complaints irritate his mother and father, they'll send him back to using his fists and feet if they order him not to be a baby or if they dismiss his grievances as unimportant. They should listen carefully to what he says, express mild sympathy, praise him for not striking the other youngster, and ask him how he can work out the problem.[27]

SUBMISSIVENESS

Some parents cheer when their child socks the playmate who treats him badly. But few rejoice when their preschooler hands over toys to demanding peers and remains silent when they jeer, exclude, or desert him.

Most small children, thus humiliated, are more puzzled than angered. Unused to being attacked, they don't know what to do. In time, with continued exposure to peers, they learn to say what they think, stand up for themselves, and give as good as they get.

But some sink into a habit of submissiveness.

Parents who anticipate their preschooler's every need and direct his every action produce a youngster without initiative. Kagan and Moss[16] state that passivity during the first three years of life continues as social timidity, disinterest in sports, and solitary play during the elementary school years. The quiet, unobtrusive, lacklustre child is ignored by his lively, alert peers.[23]

A mother who directs and interferes when playmates come over, who speaks for and protects her child, keeps him unsure in every social contact.[16]

Although most shy children become self-sufficient adults,[2] they lead lonely, unhappy lives as they grow up. They can be taught to like and get along with peers.

Domineering parents must disappear when the child is with playmates and let him manage as best he can. They should allow him to try his own ideas, if they're safe, and never predict he'll fail. They must neither take over for him or tell him what to do when he complains of put-downs from peers. Instead, as is best with the belligerent boy or girl, they can offer token sympathy and ask how he plans to handle matters.[27]

Variety helps. The submissive preschooler needs to be around many other people, both adults and children. He learns that everyone acts differently and gradually he approaches and becomes friends with the least fearsome.[28]

Another preschooler can be invited, with his mother, to visit for a short period of time. Later, the shy child and his mother can go to their house. Soon the youngster will be eager to play away from home on his own.

Skills boost confidence. The boy or girl can practice running, throwing, jumping, climbing, and hopping. He can learn to do chores, dress hmself, build with blocks, play board games, draw, and use wheeled toys. After Jack[14] trained submissive children to solve puzzles, remember stories, and make block designs, their assurance with other youngsters improved greatly.

If the timid child sometimes plays with younger boys and girls, he can take charge, flaunt his knowledge, and feel important.[10,28] Attending nursery school gives him practice in playing with other preschoolers in a semi-protected, encouraging setting. And his clothes should be similar to those of other boys and girls. If his mother dresses him so that he looks too old, too young, or too fancy, playmates will laugh at and avoid him.[28]

Confidence climbs when the submissive boy or girl gets daily praise for his achievements and ideas. If he's pleased with himself and sure his parents are proud of him, he moves easily into the world of peers.[27,28]

IMAGINARY PLAYMATES

Imaginary playmates are most common among three-and-one-half-year-old, intelligent children, usually girls.[18] Because youngsters of that age talk constantly, creating someone to talk to seems sensible. It has been estimated that as many as 21 percent of all children invent an imaginary playmate.[13]

Make-believe play is realistic and, of course, the preschooler is in charge of everything which happens.[13] The imaginary playmate may be a boy or girl with either an ordinary or a made-up, glamorous name.[18] The youngster orders toys and treats for his friend and glibly blames him when a mitten is missing or a glass is broken. The imaginary playmate usually disappears when the youngster starts school and real companions replace him.

Parents need not wholly accept the make-believe friend, but neither should they laugh at the pretense. It's better to know what a preschooler imagines than to force him to secrecy for fear of ridicule.

Imagining a playmate does no harm, but it does signal loneliness. Parents should arrange for their child to play with other boys and girls. If there are none in the vicinity, they can be found at church or nursery school.

Every preschooler needs real friends to talk to and play with. Imaginary ones contribute little to social know-how.

REFERENCES

1. Asher, S. R., Renshaw, P. D., and Geraci, R. L.: Children's friendships and social competence. *International Journal of Psycholoinguistics, 7*: 27, 1980.

2. Bakwin, H., and Bakwin, R. M.: *Clinical Management of Behavior Disorders in Children.* Philadelphia, Saunders, 1966.
3. DeBlois, C. S., and Stewart, M. A.: Aggressiveness and antisocial behavior in children: Their relationships to other dimensions of behavior. *Research Communications in Psychology, Psychiatry, and Behavior, 5*: 303, 1980.
4. Dreikurs, R.: *The Challenge of Child Training.* New York, Hawthorn, 1972.
5. Garvey, C., and Hogan, R.: Social speech and social interaction: Egocentrism re-visited. *Child Development, 44*: 562, 1973.
6. George, S. N., and Krantz, M.: The effects of preferred play partnership on communication adequacy. *Journal of Psychology, 109*: 245, 1981.
7. Goldman, J. A., Corsini, D. A., and DeUrioste, R.: Implications of positive and negative sociometric status for assessing the social competence of young children. *Journal of Applied Developmental Psychology, 1*: 209, 1980.
8. Goodenough, F. L.: *Developmental Psychology.* New York, Appleton-Century, 1945.
9. Grusec, J. E., and Abramovitch, R.: Imitation of peers and adults in a natural setting: A functional analysis. *Child Development, 53*: 636, 1982.
10. Hartley, R. E., Frank, L. K., and Goldenson, R. M.: *Understanding Children's Play.* New York, Columbia U Pr, 1952.
11. Hartup, W. W.: Peer interaction and social organization. In Mussen, P., ed.: Carmichael's *Manual of Child Psychology,* 3rd ed, Vol. 2. New York, Wiley, 1970.
12. Heathers, G.: Emotional dependence and independence in nursery school play. *Journal of Genetic Psychology, 87*: 37, 1955.
13. Hurlock, E. B.: *Child Development,* 5th ed. New York, McGraw, 1972.
14. Jack, L. M.: An experimental study of ascendant behavior in preschool children. *University of Iowa Studies in Child Welfare, 9*: 1934.
15. Janes, C. L., Hesselbrock, V. M., and Schechtman, J.: Clinic children with poor peer relations: Who refers them and why? *Child Psychiatry and Human Development, 2*: 113, 1980.
16. Kagan, J., and Moss, H. A.: *Birth to Maturity.* New York, Wiley, 1962.
17. la Greca, A. M.: Children's social skills: An overview. *Journal of Pediatric Psychology, 6*: 335, 1981.
18. Langford, L. M., and Rand, H. Y.: *Guidance of the Young Child,* 2nd ed. New York, Wiley, 1975.
19. McCandless, B. R.: *Children and Adolescents.* New York, HR&W, 1961.
20. McCandless, B. R., and Hoyt, J. M.: Sex, ethnicity, and play preferences of preschool children. *Journal of Abnormal and Social Psychology, 62*: 683, 1961.
21. Murphy, L.: Childhood experience in relation to personality development. In Hunt, J. McV., ed.: *Personality and the Behavior Disorders.* New York, Ronald Pr, 1944.
22. Murphy, L.: Coping devices and defense mechanisms in relation to autonomous ego functions. *Bulletin of the Menninger Clinic, 24*: 144, 1960.
23. Sorokin, P. A., and Gove, D. S.: Notes on the friendly and antagonistic behavior of nursery school children. In Sorokin, P. A., ed.: *Explorationsin Altruis-*

tic Love and Behavior. Boston, Beacon Pr, 1950.

24. Stith, M., and Connor, R.: Dependency and helpfulness in young children. *Child Development, 33*: 15, 1962.

25. Stott, L. H., and Ball, R. S.: Consistency and change in ascendance-submission in the social interaction of children. *Child Development, 28*: 259, 1957.

26. Suelzle, M.: The structuring of friendship formation among two- to five-year-old children enrolled in full day care. *Research in the Interweave of Social Roles, 2*: 51, 1981.

27. Verville, E.: *Behavior Problems of Children.* Philadelphia, Saunders, 1967.

28. Zimbardo, P. G., and Radl, S.: *The Shy Child.* Garden City, Doubleday, 1982.

Chapter 13

TENSION HABITS

TENSION habits trouble and embarrass parents. Relatives, friends, and strangers frown on the child's behavior and order him to stop. Thumbsucking, rocking and head-banging, nail-biting, masturbation, tics, and hair-pulling are common.

THUMBSUCKING

Traisman and Traisman[26] state that 46 percent of 2,650 infants they studied were thumb- or finger suckers, with no difference in frequency between boys and girls. Honzik and McKee[11] found more sucking in girls.

Because he needs food, the infant is strongly motivated to suck during his early months. Later, sucking is associated with objects and events other than feeding.[24]

Many children soothe themselves to sleep by sucking their thumbs and stroking their cheeks with a favorite blanket. Between 18 and 21 months, when the toddler stands on the sidelines watching others play, he is likely to suck his thumb. As he develops courage and joins playmates, day sucking decreases, then ends, usually between three and five years.

Although some investigators connect prolonged thumbsucking to insufficient sucking during infancy,[10,28] Sears and Wise[22] report no increase among 80 children cup-fed since birth or early infancy.

Steady pressure against teeth can move them, but most dentists believe no permanent damage occurs if sucking ends before permanent teeth erupt. Sillman[23] states that inherited mouth structure is a more important factor in tooth alignment than early thumbsucking.

Treatment of thumbsucking ranges from scolding and shaming to coating the thumb with bitter-tasting medicine to mechanically restraining the hand.[20] But humiliating and forcing tend to prolong the habit.[23] More reasonable methods work better.

A pacifier can replace the thumb during infancy; most children give it up between one and two years. The toddler can be distracted with a variety of toys and activities.[27] By three years, busy with playmates and projects, he sucks in the daytime only when he is quiet, watching television or listening to a story.

If the youngster often sucks his thumb when he is four, his parents should train him to stop. Otherwise, next year's kindergarten classmates will mock him and he'll think school is no place for him to be.

Because both his mouth and thumb are stimulated by sucking, the child is being asked to give up a double pleasure. A reward for the pain of sacrifice is only fair.[27] Grand prizes for total abstinence — promising the youngster his first bicycle if he keeps his thumb out of his mouth for six months — are useless. No small child can instantly and permanently drop a habit.

But small rewards for short periods of success produce steady gains. If the preschooler keeps his thumb out of his mouth for four hours, he gets a nickel; when he has six nickels, he can buy a candy bar or ice cream cone. If he forgets and fails, and he will, his lapse is merely a misstep, not a disastrous, final plunge to failure. He can try again at once.[27]

Azrin and Nunn[2] taught parents to record thumbsucking, note situations in which it occurred, and tell the child, when he started to put his thumb into his mouth, to place his hands at his sides or clench his fists instead. Praised for success, the youngsters learned quickly.

If the child sucks only while watching TV or hearing stories, the parent can turn off the set or close the book as soon as the thumb goes into the mouth. The cut-off signals the preschooler to remove his thumb and soon he remembers by himself to keep it out. Praise strengthens and speeds learning.[4,14]

If bedtime sucking continues, it's no cause for alarm. Usually it ends when the child's beloved blanket has worn to a two-inch scrap.[27]

ROCKING AND HEAD-BANGING

Rocking or head-banging occurred in 15-20 percent of an unselected group of preschoolers studied by Lourie.[16] Head-rolling sometimes starts as early as two months, head-banging between five and eleven months, and rocking when the child moves from one developmental stage to another: *e.g.*, from sitting to standing. These habits rarely develop after two years of age. They usually cease by five years.[5] Most rocking and head-banging occur prior to sleep and are carried on from standing, sitting, kneeling, and prone positions.

The newborn infant, with a nervous system not yet tuned to his new environment, is over-sensitive to stimulation. Accustomed in the womb to the steady beat of his mother's heart and to the slow motion of her walking, he tries to re-create former peacefulness with monotonous sounds and rhythmic movements.

The older child comforts himself with rocking and head-banging when he is lonely or bored, has been scolded, or has failed in what he tried to do.

DeLissovoy[7] reports more otitis media among 15 head-banging preschoolers than among 15 control children. Pain of which adults are unaware may cause the child to hit his head.

To help the rocker or head-banger, a physical examination is needed. If there is infection or nervous system damage, treatment can begin.

Rocking the child, giving him private attention, limiting correction, and rewarding control all help.[18]

If he continues rocking or head-banging after the age of three, he needs either more variety in his life or more protection from overstimulation. Recording the events of the preschooler's usual day alerts parents to needed changes.[27]

NAIL-BITING

Nail-biting is both persistent and common. Sometimes it runs in families, with both adults and every child chewing on nails.[13]

Generally it occurs in tense, excitable youngsters. Kanner[13] reports that, among nail-biters he studied, 27 percent were restless, 23 percent cried out, walked, or grit their teeth while sleeping, 19 percent had tics, and 50 percent engaged in various body manipulations. Some children, mostly girls, also bite their toenails.

Nail-biting usually starts when the child is four. Thirty percent of all children chew their nails by the age of six.[5]

Scolding changes nothing. Enlisting the child in a self-improvement campaign often does. A professional manicure, combined with regular use of nail polish and manicure tools, can start the youngster in a new direction.

Bakwin and Bakwin[5] suggest that the nail-biter carry a nail file to use on rough edges before they entice him to chew them off. He also can stick adhesive tape on his nails as a reminder not to bite them. Chewing gum during exciting shows or games prevents him from chewing his nails.

Freeman *et al.*[9] report that a six-year-old girl was re-trained by holding her hands to her sides for one minute each time she started to bite her nails. She also was praised and rewarded for abstaining.

MASTURBATION

Parents and teachers abhor masturbation in a child. Sears *et al.*[21] state that only 18 percent of 379 mothers of five-year-olds considered masturbation the natural result of curiosity. Nearly half believed it to be wrong or harmful. Parents who object strongly to masturbation scold, slap the child's hand, and predict he'll go insane if he keeps it up.

The toddler examines his genitals, when he is undressed, with the same interest with which he studies his navel. Because sex organs usually are covered, exploring them is an attractive novelty. And, watching himself urinate, he is fascinated by this unusually productive area of his body.

A three-year-old boy, newly aware of sex differences, may think girls are mutilated and, to protect his genitals, he holds them.[24] A four-year-old automatically grabs his genitals when he's excited or wants to stop imminent urination. More than half of all children who masturbate begin before they reach five years of age.

Exploring children may chance on the pleasant sensation of genital manipulation and try to recapture it. They rub on pillows stuffed between their legs or squeeze their thighs together. Small girls shove buttons and hairpins into their vaginas.[13]

Infection or chapping causes itching and burning. Tight clothing rubs. The preschooler tries to ease the discomfort by squeezing or massaging his genitals.[27]

When the small child masturbates regularly, his parents should first find out whether he has an infection or his clothing is too snug. They can remedy these problems.

The masturbating infant or toddler can be distracted with a toy and if his clothing is replaced promptly after toileting, he seldom acquires the habit of genital play.

The three-year-old needs to know why there are body differences between boys and girls and be assured that visible genitalia are never removed.

The older preschool child can be told, each time he handles his genitals, that this is impolite.[27] Because most masturbation is thoughtless, having the child put his hands at his sides for a minute whenever he starts to masturbate soon trains him out of the practice.[8]

TICS

Tics are involuntary, persisting small muscle contractions. Appearing many times daily, they sometimes last for weeks. Throat-clearing, sniffing, eye-blinking, and dry coughing have been observed in two-year-olds.

Although the problem is more common in the elementary school child, Kanner[13] reports that 15 percent of a group of two- to four-year-olds he studied had tics. Zausmer[29] notes that there were twice as many boys as girls in a group of 96 tiquers he treated and that a high proportion of their parents also had tics. Abe and Oda[1] found a link to heredity.

A sensitive, dutiful child may develop tics when he is criticized, believes he has failed, or often is restricted in his activities or plans. Angry and troubled, he suppresses his feelings and his tension erupts in twitches and spasms.[13,24]

Any small muscle movement originating from physical irritation may develop into an enduring tic. The child with chronic sinusitis may blink, twitch his nose, and jerk his mouth.[6] If he has a cold, he often coughs and clears his throat. Tight clothing causes him to shrug or shake.

The tiquer needs a physical examination and treatment for any chronic illness. The fit of his clothing should be checked.

Mansdorf and Friedman[17] describe elimination of eye-blinking in a child taught to notice and then control it.

Parents should understand that their preschooler is tense from trying to please them and upset when they criticize him. They can learn to overlook errors, permit freedom, and recognize success and obedience. A more relaxed home atmosphere and a less crowded day for adults and child alike will help.

HAIR-PULLING

Hair-pulling, or trichotillomania, announces serious emotional problems.[13] It develops between 18 months and five years and is three times more common in girls than in boys.[5]

Yanking on his hair, the child hurts himself and ruins his looks. He does so because he feels angry, defeated, and unloved. Often his home is chaotic, his parents are unstable emotionally, and he is subjected to and witnesses violence.[15,19,25,27]

Four-year-old Courtney pulled out handfuls of hair as she sucked her thumb. She also hit her mother, called her names, and screamed at playmates, behavior which was never corrected. The mother also yelled and hit. Her anxious daughter copied her.[27]

Hair-pulling sometimes starts when the scalp is inflamed or infected. Or it can begin as aimless hair-twisting.

To stop the habit, hair can be cut short but should not be shaved off completely. If the youngster looks worse than ever, he'll consider the baldness as punishment and resume yanking as soon as he can. But if a boy has an attractive short cut and a girl's hair is curled and bedecked with bows, the hair-puller is less likely to savage his new and handsome image.

The wild emotion surrounding him must end. Adults must submerge anger and abandon violence as ways of dealing with frustrations. They need to train the child to control his own temper, isolating him for tantrums, refusing demands made in anger, and teaching him to obey reasonable parental requests. When his mother and father no longer indulge in or permit furious behavior, the child's anxiety ceases.[27]

Affection and private time with parents can replace the preschooler's habit of gaining attention by hair-pulling.

Lester[15] describes a seven-year-old girl who had pulled out her hair since she was 18 months old. The oldest of four children, burdened with chores and a critical mother, she was tense, competitive, and lonely. A few months after her mother began to spend time alone with her each night at bedtime, talking and comforting, her hair-pulling became negligible.

REFERENCES

1. Abe, K., and Oda, N.: Follow-up study of childhood tiquers. *Biological Psychiatry, 13*: 629, 1978.
2. Azrin, N. H., and Nunn, R. G.: Habit reversal: a method of eliminating nervous habits and tics. *Behaviour Research and Therapy, 11*: 619, 1973.
3. Azrin, N. H., Nunn, R. G., and Frantz-Renshaw, S.: Habit reversal treatment of thumbsucking. *Behaviour Research and Therapy, 18*: 395, 1980.
4. Baer, D. M.: Laboratory control of thumbsucking by withdrawal and representation of reinforcement. *Journal of the Experimental Analysis of Behavior, 5*: 525, 1962.
5. Bakwin, H., and Bakwin, R. M.: *Clinical Management of Behavior Disorders in Children.* Philadelphia, Saunders, 1966.
6. Brown, E. E.: Tics (habit spasms) secondary to sinusitis. *Archives of Pediatrics, 74*: 39, 1957.
7. DeLissovoy, V.: Head banging in early childhood: A suggested cause. *Journal of Genetic Psychology, 102*: 109, 1963.
8. Ferguson, L. N., and Rekers, G. A.: Non-aversive intervention in public

childhood masturbation: A case study. *Journal of Sex Research, 15*: 213, 1979.
 9. Freeman, B. J., Graham, V., and Ritvo, E. R.: Reduction of self-destructive behavior by over-correction. *Psychological Reports, 37*: 446, 1975.
10. Gandler, A. L.: Nature and implications of thumbsucking; a review. *Archives of Pediatrics, 69*: 291, 1952.
11. Honzik, M. P., and McKee, J. P.: Sex difference in thumbsucking. *Journal of Pediatrics, 61*: 726, 1962.
12. Ilg, F. L., Ames, L. B., and Baker, S. M.: *Child Behavior.* New York, Har-Row, 1981.
13. Kanner, L.: *Child Psychiatry,* 4th ed. Springfield, Thomas, 1972.
14. Kauffman, J. M., and Scranton, T. R.: Parent control of thumbsucking in the home. *Child Study Journal, 4*: 1, 1974.
15. Lester, E. P.: Brief psychotherapies in child psychiatry. *Canadian Psychiatric Association Journal, 13*: 301, 1968.
16. Lourie, R. S.: The role of rhythmic patterns in childhood. *American Journal of Psychiatry, 105*: 653, 1949.
17. Mansdorf, I. J., and Friedman, S.: Sensory feedback training to eliminate eye tics: A study in self-control. *Behavior Theapist, 3*: 23, 1980.
18. Prytula, R. E., Joyner, K. B., and Schnelle, J. F.: Utilizing the school to control head-banging behavior of a child at home. *Psychological Reports, 48*: 887, 1981.
19. Reinelt, A., and Breiter, M.: (Therapy of a case of trichotillomania.) *Praxis der Kinderpsychologie und Kinderpsychiatrie, 29*: 169, 1980.
20. Schaefer, C. E., and Millman, H. L.: *Therapies for Children.* San Francisco, Jossey-Bass, 1977.
21. Sears, R. R., Maccoby, E. E., and Levin, H.: *Patterns of Child-rearing.* Evanston, Row, Peterson & Co., 1957.
22. Sears, R. R., and Wise, G. W.: Relation of cup-feeding in infancy to thumbsucking and the oral drive. *American Journal of Orthopsychiatry, 20*: 123, 1950.
23. Sillman, J. H.: Serial study of occlusion from birth to three years. *American Journal of Orthodontics, 26*: 207, 1940.
24. Spock, B.: *Baby and Child Care.* New York, Dutton, 1976.
25. Toback, C., and Rajkumar, S.: The emotional disturbance underlying alopecia areata, alopecia totalis, and trichotillomania. *Child Psychiatry and Human Development, 10*: 114, 1979.
26. Traisman, A. S., and Traisman, H. S.: Thumb- and finger-sucking: A study of 2,650 infants and children. *Journal of Pediatrics, 53*: 566, 1958.
27. Verville, E.: *Behavior Problems of Children.* Philadelphia, Saunders, 1967.
28. Yarrow, L. J.: The relationship between nutritive sucking experiences in infancy and non-nutritive sucking in childhood. *Journal of Genetic Psychology, 84*: 149, 1954.
29. Zausmer, D. M.: The treatment of tics in childhood: A review and follow-up study. *Archives of Diseases of Childhood, 29*: 537, 1954.

Chapter 14

WITHDRAWAL

WITHDRAWING is the preschooler's way of protecting himself from unpleasant, challenging, or devastating situations. Because he is inexperienced, unskilled, and quite small, such behavior is both sensible and normal.

Sometimes retreat is obvious: the child hastily hides his arm behind him when the nurse and her needle appear, or he vanishes behind the drapes as dinner guests descend on him.

Concealment may be contrived. A three-year-old girl, approaching a horde of adults and children at a company picnic, transformed herself into a retarded youngster of whom nothing need be expected: she stuck a finger in her mouth, turned her feet inward, and, pigeon-toed, slowly made her way to the awesome gathering.[27]

Other children disguise fear with frenzy: they yank at their parents, knock over and climb on furniture, run, and yell. The adults, not recognizing panic, scold and threaten without effect.[25]

Withdrawal reactions include crying, regression, lying, fear, anxiety, and autism.

CRYING

A child's crying bothers and frustrates parents. They order the youngster to stop. He seldom can or does, and if the adult gets an-

114

grier, he hits and slaps the child. Small boys and girls have been beaten to death for crying.

But the infant or toddler has no way other than crying to communicate distress and ask for help. The older preschooler is able to talk about what happens and is more skilled at managing trouble. Normally, the child cries less as he matures.

If the three-, four-, or five-year-old cries at every unpleasantness — his parents are going out, a playmate argues with him, he must go to bed, he can't have more popcorn — his tears reflect self-pity.

When crying wins solicitous attention or overturns a parent's decision, the youngster quickly learns to use it as a weapon.

To help the young boy or girl stop automatic crying, a parent should neither see, hear, nor mention the tears. Instead, he can repeat the ruling which brought on the crying and add a one-sentence explanation.

Then he should change the subject. He can ask the child a question — "Did we have oatmeal for breakfast this morning?"; request his opinion — "Do you think it will rain today?"; or invite him to join in weeding the garden or playing the piano. With this total dismissal of his woeful state, the child finds that tears over minor disappointments are wasted.

When crying is reasonable — the child has gashed his knee or a playmate has run off with his favorite truck — a parent still should avoid mentioning tears.

He can say, "That must hurt! Let's bandage it," or "Too bad. What are you going to do about getting your truck back?"

The preschooler turns his attention to fixing what's wrong and away from weeping over it.

REGRESSION

An unhappy, lonely child may revert to thumbsucking, whining, wetting himself, and crying, actions he long ago out-grew.

Regression often begins with the arrival of a new baby brother or sister. Distressed by the fleeting attention of parents, the youngster tries to attract them by imitating the baby. He demands bottles and diapers for himself. He forgets how to brush his teeth and pick up his toys.

A preschooler starting nursery school or kindergarten can be overwhelmed by the noisy crowd of children and the orders of strange adults. He doesn't like school, so he cries, tries to follow his mother home, and won't join games or listen to stories.[5] He hides under a table or grabs toys from classmates, actions more common in toddlers.

The hospitalized child usually backslides when he returns home. He sucks his thumb, masturbates, rocks, and refuses to talk.[2] He demands help with eating, toileting, dressing, and playing. Clinging to his mother, he orders her visitor to go home.

Fatigue causes regression. The youngster who is dragged around all day and half the night or who is constantly with other children and adults gets too little rest and privacy. Trying to escape incessant stimulation, he retreats to infancy.[27]

The child can be taught to act his age.

Parents who hand him bottles, put him in diapers, wait on him, or sleep with him strengthen his feelings of helplessness. Instead, they need to play and work with him regularly each day and encourage him to do all he can for himself. When they are confident that he can act in a grown-up way and show it by treating him as an equal, he'll switch back to his former competency.

New experiences can devastate the small child and he should be well prepared for them. He needs to be told what he will see, who will be there, what will happen, and what he is to do. This holds true for starting school, going to the doctor, living with a new baby sibling, attending a party, or making visitors welcome. With accurate knowledge and prior rehearsal, he will not be defeated by what he must face.

If he's worn out from over-crowded days and nights, he needs to stay home more. For awhile, adults other than his parents should disappear from his life and he should be scheduled for more rest and solitary play time.[27]

LYING

A parent is angry and insulted when his son or daughter lies. It's an undeserved break in trust. Furthermore, the mother or father thinks the youngster considers him to be stupid and gullible. In lengthy sessions which leave lasting scars of ill-feeling, the adult demands that the deceptive child admit the truth.

But the preschooler is not trying to humiliate anyone; he's trying to protect himself. He automatically denies guilt when confronted by a furious parent. He escapes the troubling present by wishing the past away, sometimes blaming his misdeed on others.[17] That he is not dedicated to lying is apparent when his mother beguiles him into truth-telling by casually asking, "Show me how you cut the drapes."[27]

Some falsehoods reflect a fuzzy distinction between reality and make-believe. The young child is certain that what he sees on television and what he hears from others (lions prowl the basement and Santa Claus squeezes down chimneys) is true. Thus his own stories about riding the dragon in the back yard and dispatching the bear in his bedroom do not seem strange to him. Besides, if he can catch the attention of busy adults and feel like a hero with grand tales, what could be more fun on a dull day?

Many young children lie in imitation of their parents. Hearing his father instruct his mother to say he's not home when the boss calls, listening to his mother tell the door-to-door salesman that she's just bought a new vacuum cleaner, he too experiments with deception.

To steer the preschooler toward truthfulness, adults must forego tall tales, exaggerations, and lying. A double standard makes no sense to the youngster.

Occasional fanciful tales can be accepted for what they are and topped by a play-acting parent, thus noting that story-telling is a game. But if make-believe studs the child's conversation, something is wrong. He may be over-excited. Fewer contacts with older children and no television will help. Or, he may create startling stories to brighten a boring life. If so, he'll stop when he plays with other children, visits the zoo, watches an air show, attends church school, and dances with his mother.

If his tales are designed to attract attention and gain status, he needs the private time of one or both parents daily. They and his older brothers and sisters should listen when he speaks and include him in what they do.

Any child who bravely admits a misdeed should be praised for doing so. Telling the truth in such a situation is not easy and a pat on the back testifies to the youngster's honor. It's more natural for the young child to lie and this should be expected.

Parents confuse the boy or girl when they say they are not punishing him for putting sand in the gas tank but for lying about it. With no idea what his parents want or will overlook, his wobbly concepts of right and wrong collapse completely.[27]

The agony of obtaining a confession is not worth its price. If the parent knows the child is guilty, he should say so and set the penalty for the misbehavior without further talk. Penalties should be mild, brief, and reasonable, so the preschooler is not pushed into lying to save himself from brutal punishment.

FEAR

Fear can protect. The youngster who is unafraid risks injury when he pulls the tail of the strange dog, fishes broken glass from the garbage can, or zooms his tricycle into the street. From an early age he must be taught caution, a wariness based on fear of harm. For most youngsters, this develops as he does.

Fear of strangers may appear as early as four months. It becomes acute at eight and twelve months. Burying his head, the infant whimpers when the smiling but unfamiliar adult talks to and tickles him.[14]

At 18 months, the toddler panics when his parents try to leave him at a nursery or with a sitter. His screams often thwart their plans.

When he is two, noises he does not recognize — sirens, thunder, telephone rings, flushing toilets — all produce fear.[12] Unexpected sights frighten. A small girl walking outdoors suddenly began to cry and cling to her mother. Her own dark, mysteriously moving shadow had scared her. Two-year-olds develop lingering fears from watching the sudden movements and leering close-ups of cartoon figures on television.[27]

Much to the distress of parents, the child's fears multiply as he grows older and becomes more alert. He backs away from barking dogs, huge cranes, and thundering trains. He breathes faster when he hears about witches, an all-seeing God, drownings, murders, car accidents, and wars.[16] Hagman[13] reports that between two and six years children are most afraid of doctors, dogs, storms, and darkness. The possibility of death, either a parent's or his own, frightens the five-year-old.

Separation from a parent is scary. If his mother leaves home to enter a hospital or care for a relative, the child may show a variety of fears while she is gone and refuse to let her out of his sight when she returns. Divorce, with its permanent loss of one parent, causes the preschooler to fear that the remaining parent also will desert him.

A young child knows so little about the workings of the world that he expects danger when there is none. He refuses to wade into the lake; he screams to be taken off the swing; he runs from a crawling caterpillar; and he imagines wild beasts and evil monsters are hiding under his bed or behind his closet door.

He believes what he hears. One father jokingly commented to his small daughter on a windy day, "Be careful. The wind might blow you away." For weeks, the child tensely gauged the strength of every breeze.[27]

Fear can be taught. If the preschooler's mother shudders during storms or his father laughs uneasily about a dental appointment, the youngster shrieks at lightning and screams when he must visit the dentist. And if his parents let him take his toy gun to bed or leave his ceiling light blazing at night to ward off burglars he fears, he is sure the danger is real.

Direct experience with fear-producing events leaves a lasting impression.

> Adam C. would not come straight home when his kindergarten class was dismissed. Instead, he walked blocks out of his way. Sometimes he stopped at a strange house and asked the adult who came to the door to take him home.
>
> Adam's parents fought all the time. Each had threatened to leave the family. His mother spent her days visiting around the neighborhood with her two younger children and often was not home when Adam came from school. Once, when he was hours late, she had whipped him hard.
>
> Never knowing whether he'd be beaten or deserted when he got home, Adam postponed the dreaded moment and enlisted an adult escort for protection.

When his mother understood why her son was afraid to come home, she began meeting him at school and walking with him. A week later, she met him half way, and a week after that, she watched for him at the corner near their house. Once Adam was home, she sent the younger children off and spent 30 minutes alone with him, sharing a snack and listening to his tales of school.

The parents stopped quarreling and the mother disciplined herself to a system of regular meals and bedtimes for the children. Within a few weeks, Adam not only lost his fear of coming home, he also began to do better work at school.[27]

Ridicule and forcing won't build a frightened child's courage, but they are ways many parents try.[14,16] There are better ones to manage fearfulness.

The infant and toddler need protection from what they fear. Strangers can be kept at a distance, the television set turned off, and older children forbidden to tell stories of kidnappers and ghosts.

A night light and open door help the small child who is afraid of the dark. If his mother has been gone, the family has moved, or his parents are separated and he fears being abandoned, he needs extra private time with one or both adults. They should stay home with him more than usual for a few weeks.[27]

An older preschooler can be accustomed gradually to what he fears.[16,18] If it's going into the lake, the youngster should decide for himself when he's ready to stick his toes in the water. On his next visit, remembering that the lapping wavelets did not hurt him, he'll wade in up to his knees. In time, he will happily crawl, splash, and float in the water.

Watching a fearless child entices courageous behavior in a frightened one. Adelson and Goldfried[1] report that a three-year-old girl, alarmed in the dentist's office, watched the examination of an unafraid four-year-old. Finished, the older girl jumped down from the chair smiling and got a nickel from the dentist. When the three-year-old's turn came, she acted exactly as the older youngster had. The investigators suggest that a film of a cheerful, confident child going through the procedures in the dentist's or doctor's office might be shown to youngsters in the waiting room.

Training the small boy or girl in skills which enable him to function by himself is the surest way to eradicate fear. The child can practice what to say to visitors. He can rehearse with his mother what the visit to the doctor or dentist will be like. If he must enter the hospital, he can play the part of doctor and nurse, using a doll as a stand-in for himself. His father can teach him how to talk to the dog bounding toward him, how to pump while swinging, and how to count the seconds between the flash of lightning and the boom of thunder.

When the preschooler worries about death or accidents, or if he is disturbed by deformed or strange-acting people, talking over his ideas, giving him facts and reasons, and reassuring him will help.

ANXIETY

Anxiety is a generalized, pervasive fear reaction which develops from insecurity. It is not associated with a specific event or object. Usually it occurs in a child who has no close relationship with a caring adult. Restlessness, mannerisms, speech disorders, sleeping and eating problems, and overdependency are behaviors which may reflect underlying anxiety.

The insecure child tends to play alone, seldom tried to join peers, cries often, and seems apprehensive most of the time.[15] Bender[3] describes the child deprived of parenting as infantile in behavior, clinging, passively dependent, and unable to tolerate demands, disappointments, or separation.

Despert[8] studied 78 two- to five-year-olds and found that anxiety was twice as common in boys as in girls. It also was twice as frequent in children with an unfavorable birth history, and occurred six times more often in youngsters from broken homes than in those from intact homes.

Kanner[17] notes that children separated from their mothers and sent to the country for safety during World War II were more anxious there than during bombing they experienced while remaining in the city with their mothers. This held true even though some mothers were cross and punitive.

Droske[9] observes that hospitalized children continue to be anxious after they return home. They make increased demands for attention, strongly object to temporary separation, and are troubled with sleep disorders.

Anxiety in children bewilders parents and they often react to it by punishing.[25] Their disapproval only makes the preschooler more tense.

The anxious child needs daily personal and pleasant contact with one or both parents. Adults should not argue in the youngster's presence nor indulge in erratic emotional tirades against neighbors, bosses, or relatives when he is listening.

Parents should do their best to explain any worrisome event which upsets the child.

They can train him to dress himself and get his own drinks, to run faster, speak better, and be friendlier. As he grows steadily more competent, he finds security within himself.

The anxious child also feels more secure if his days are predictable: getting up and going to bed, playing, working, and eating should come at the same time each day. If his parents always enforce a few necessary rules, the boy or girl knows that they are both concerned and reliable.

AUTISM

Autism, first described by Kanner[17] in 1943, is extreme withdrawal from human contact. The autistic child refuses to look at or communicate with people. He prefers to be alone, occupying himself for hours with toys or other objects. Angrily pushing away the adult's hand, he rejects attempts to take away his playthings or interfere with what he is doing. He is visibly upset when his belongings are moved or his furniture rearranged.

The older child sometimes mimics phrases used by adults or recites long memorized passages and lists of numbers. He may recall minute details of events occurring months or years earlier. His words seldom have meaning.[27] Autistic youngsters do better on nonverbal than verbal parts of intelligence tests.

Faretra[11] notes that the disorder is more common in boys than girls, in ratios as high as eight to one, and that physical function is undeveloped: muscles are flaccid, respiration is poorly patterned, vasomotor and autonomic systems are unstable, and sleeping and waking are erratic. The children are small for their ages and look immature.

Sankar[24] reports that biochemical changes and vestibular stimulation in the autistic child cause feelings of body instability.

Central nervous system damage or malfunction is indicated by the youngster's inability to communicate, his need for restricted stimulation,[26] his quick irritability,[23] and abnormalities in electroencephalograph tracings.[11]

Ney[20] posits that the autistic child is hypersensitive to sound. Human noises frighten instead of soothe him and he withdraws to protect himself from the pain of sound. Autistic children allowed to select the volume of a continuously playing record kept the sound low.

Because the child isolates himself from people and sound, he is fascinated by other kinds of stimuli: lights, patterns, textures, and motion. He focuses on these, watching, tracing, feeling, and mimicking over and over.

He drives his parents away by covering his ears and hiding his head when they speak to him. Angry at his rejection, depressed by their failure to reach him, they give up and leave him alone. But without them, he learns nothing, cannot speak, and sinks into irreversible retardation.

Phillips[22] points out that most autistic children not only are boys, but first-born boys. He believes that the youngster's determination to shut out others and to have his way discourages inexperienced and indecisive parents, who then cease all attempt to contact and control the child.

Eisenberg[10] studied 100 fathers of autistic children and found 85 of them to be detached, humorless, obsessive, and perfectionistic. In other studies, parents have been described as persons of high intelligence, more interested in solitary than social pursuits, and cold and formalistic both within and without the family.[17] These traits may have been present before the birth of the autistic child or they may represent the adults' painful reaction to their strange, rejecting youngster. The fact that normal children are born into these families suggests that the problem is primarily physical, though complicated by the helplessness of parents to deal with it.

Because the autistic child seldom speaks, he sometimes is credited with great wisdom. He is so sure of what he wants — no interruption or disturbance — that he is thought to know more than do his parents about what is best for himself. He doesn't. Lonely and helpless, bewildered by an unreliable, malfunctioning body, deprived of guidance and affection, the youngster desperately needs prompt and expert training.

Lovatt[19] reports on the progress of several autistic children, each of whom was given a private playroom with one teacher for two hours daily, four days a week. At first the teacher followed the child's lead. Then she gradually began to set rules. After a time, the youngster was moved for short periods into a nursery with normally-playing children. All of these autistic children entered kindergarten at the age of five or six. Although some had a difficult initial adjustment, several were doing well two or three years later.

Cohen[7] used behavior modification techniques, modeling, and stimulus control to decrease echolalia and increase naming and telegraphic speech in an autistic four-year-old girl.

Cobrinik[6] achieved promising results with autistic children using the Dixon Responsive Environmental instrument, or "Talking Typewriter." Programmed personal computers may prove to be one tool for breaking the communication logjam.

Oppenheim[21] advises the use of intrusion, control, structure, and variety in teaching the autistic child. He must be able to get across his ideas and learn from others and he must also relate to and depend on people, not solely on himself. Parents should not accept his limited version of their life together.

Whether or not he wants his mother's companionship, he needs it for regular periods each day. She can read simple stories, name pictured and real objects and people, play records, dance and sing with him. A few quick hugs and kisses and a cheerful attitude will help.

The autistic youngster must not be allowed to go off by himself when the family is eating or cleaning the house. He needs to be with them, doing what they do. His furious refusals should be ignored and he should be required to obey family rules. When the child no longer bears total responsibility for his life, some of his anxiety will disappear.

A regular playmate of his own age is someone he can imitate. As he does so, his interests, skills, and human contacts broaden.[27]

Speech therapists, child psychologists, and teachers of the deaf know useful techniques which can aid parents in freeing the child from his lonely isolation.

REFERENCES

1. Adelson, R., and Goldfried, M. R.: Modeling and the fearful child patient. *Journal of Dentistry for Children, 37*: 34, 1970.
2. Bakwin, H., and Bakwin, R. M.: *Clinical Management of Behavior Disorders in Children.* Philadelphia, Saunders, 1966.
3. Bender, L.: *Aggression, Hostility, and Anxiety in Children.* Springfield, Thomas, 1953.
4. Bender, L.: *Psychopathology of Children with Organic Brain Disorders.* Springfield, Thomas, 1956.
5. Blehar, M.: Anxious attachment and defensive reactions associated with day care. *Child Development, 45*: 683, 1974.
6. Cobrinik, L.: Programmed learning in the treatment of severely disturbed children: The role of motor patterning. *Acta Paedopsychiatrica, 39*: 11, 1972.
7. Cohen, M.: Development of language behavior in an autistic child using total communication. *Exceptional Children, 47*: 379, 1981.
8. Despert, J. L.: Anxiety, phobias, and fears in young children. *Nervous Child, 5*: 8, 1946.
9. Droske, S. C.: Children's behavioral changes following hospitalization — have we prepared the parents? *Journal of the Association for the Care of Children in Hospitals, 7*: 3, 1978.
10. Eisenberg, L.: The fathers of autistic children. *American Journal of Orthopsychiatry, 27*: 715, 1957.
11. Faretra, G.: Lauretta Bender on autism: A review. *Child Psychiatry and Human Development, 10*: 118, 1979.
12. Gesell, A., and Ilg, F. L.: *The Child from Five to Ten.* New York, Harper, 1946.
13. Hagman, E. R.: A study of fears of children of preschool age. *Journal of Experimental Education, 1*: 110, 1932.
14. Hurlock, E.: *Child Development,* 5th ed. New York, McGraw, 1972.
15. Jersild, A. T.: Emotional development. In Carmichael, L., ed.: *Manual of Child Psychology.* New York, Wiley, 1946.
16. Jersild, A. T., and Holmes, F. B.: Methods of overcoming children's fears. *Journal of Psychology, 1*: 75, 1935.
17. Kanner, L.: *Child Psychiatry,* 4th ed. Springfield, Thomas, 1972.
18. Leitenberg, H., and Callahan, E. J.: Reinforced practice and reduction of different kinds of fears in adults and children. *Behaviour Research and Therapy, 11*: 19, 1973.
19. Lovatt, M.: Autistic children in a day nursery. *Children, 9*: 103, 1962.
20. Ney, P. G.: A psychopathogenesis of autism. *Child Psychiatry and Human Development, 9*: 195, 1979.

21. Oppenheim, R. C.: *Effective Teaching Methods for Autistic Children.* Springfield, Thomas, 1974.
22. Phillips, E. L.: Contributions to a learning-theory account of childhood autism. In Trapp, E. P., and Himelstein, P., eds.: *Readings on the Exceptional Child.* New York, ACC, 1962.
23. Rimland, B.: *Infantile Autism.* New York, ACC, 1964.
24. Sankar, D. V.: A summary of thirty different biochemical tests in childhood schizophrenia. In Sankar, D. V., ed.: *Schizophrenia: Current Concepts and Research.* Hicksville, PJD Pubns, 1969.
25. Thompson, G. G.: *Child Psychology,* 2nd ed. Cambridge, HM, 1962.
26. Vaillant, G. E.: Twins discordant for early infantile autism. *Archives of General Psychiatry, 9:* 163, 1963.
27. Verville, E.: *Behavior Problems of Children.* Philadelphia, Saunders, 1967.

Chapter 15

AGGRESSION

PARENTS are outraged when their child strikes them. They are alarmed when he threatens their control. But if he shoves the playmate who grabbed his balloon, they are proud that he defended himself.

A preschooler cannot reason with or command respect from anyone. But he can pinch the baby when he is jealous. He can yell, hit, kick, and call names when he is angry. He can deliver a stout "No!" to his mother and father when it suits him. He can steal, run away, and ruin clothes and furniture.

By the time he is two, he fights back often, his spunkiness hooked into his drive for independence. [29] He rejects dancing to another's tune; he refuses slavery.

As he reaches four years, his furious assaults wane. Instead of hitting the companion who takes his truck, he shouts, "That's mine. Give it back."

When his mother orders him to hang up his jacket, he abandons "I won't!" for a mild "Okay." Leaving his jacket exactly where it is, he placidly zooms his airplane back and forth across the living room sky.

The four- or five-year-old who still uses fists and feet to make his point lags behind age-mates in self-control. He stays aggressive until he is ten years old. [19]

There are reasons why attacks persist.

127

The child is damaged when his mother is cool toward him. Siegal and Francis[27] report that rule violations in five-year-olds are related to lack of identification with the mother. Jones[18] states that attacks on other children by 21-month-olds are related to indifference of the mother when the child needs comforting: *e.g.*, he cries after a fall and she walks away.

Physical problems or neurological abnormalities keep the youngster irritable[4] and his behavior becomes impulsive and destructive. Angered by disobedience and uproar, his parents criticize and punish him dozens of times every day. The unhappy child, rejected and reviled, strikes out in every direction.

Young boys whose families are poor and those whose fathers do not live at home are over-aggressive.[14,26] A father who cannot easily feed, house, and clothe his family is ashamed and discouraged. A mother who must support and rear her youngsters alone is tired and edgy. The adults, resentful and self-pitying, lash out at offspring. The small child mimics his parents' physical and verbal attacks.

Learning how to act, preschoolers copy all aggressive behavior. They repeat the insults and fighting they see on television.[32] They swagger and yell after hearing parents quarrel.[22] They push and grab when they see other children do so, especially if hostility goes unpunished.[2]

Young boys are more aggressive than girls. Boys attack physically and directly; girls snub and slur, sneak toys, and entice away friends.[13,23,26]

Aggression in the preschool child emerges as destructiveness, running away, negativism, stealing, and behavior stemming from jealousy and anger.

DESTRUCTIVENESS

Small children and destructiveness mix in the same cauldron. Preschool boys and girls cut drapes, scribble on walls, and hammer dents in coffee tables. Usually the damage is the sequel to an experiment. A youngster applies what he holds — scissors, pencil, hammer — to what is handy: drapes, wall, table.

Or he spies a new object and, curious about its properties, he pushes, bangs, throws, tears, or pounds it. Three preschoolers playing in a garage noticed a sack of cement mix and soon they were kicking it vigorously, delighted with the clouds of dust they created. It took hours to clean the cement particles from their hair, eyes, and clothing. The garage never again was the same.[34]

A young child is both awkward and in a hurry, so he yanks off buttons, drops dishes, and overwinds springs on his toys. He cannot predict outcomes,[20] so he cheerfully rips apart pillows and plunges his teddy bear into the toilet.

Sometimes he means to wreck things. Sneered at by his older sister, four-year-old Alan ripped off the arms of her favorite doll. Sent to her room, rebellious three-year-old Megan swept all the toys off shelves, tore books, pulled clothes from hangers, and smashed a dresser lamp.

Accidentally or for reason, young children cause damage and sensible parents protect themselves. They buy inexpensive furnishings, clothing, and toys. They put away what they do not use daily and keep rooms bare. They stow scissors and hammers, crayons and paint out of reach, to be used only under adult supervision. They check often on playing children and block grand destructive sprees.

A three-, four-, or five-year-old child should try to repair what he damages. He can scrub a crayoned wall with soap and water. He can straighten and reset trampled flowers. He can sweep up pieces of a broken glass. He also can work to earn money: with it he pays part of the cost of replacing his brother's smashed model airplane or his sister's ruined doll dress.

Although he cannot restore the damaged object to its original condition, the attempt teaches him that destructiveness carries a penalty. As he learns, he will try to be more careful and self-controlled.[35]

RUNNING AWAY

Many curious preschoolers leave their yards and wander off to see the world. Four-year-old Kenneth mounted his tricycle, rode for hours, and crossed several busy streets. Three-year-old Dixie hiked two miles to a shopping center nearly every day.[35] Two-year-old

Billy, who visited a park with his parents on Sunday, set off to find it on Monday. Exploring can be such fun that a small child regularly slips away when his parents are not looking.

Sometimes a thoughtless parent encourages running away.

The mother of a two-year-old girl retrieved her from a neighbor's kitchen after an absence of several hours.

"Isn't it wonderful?" she mused. "Carrie is getting acquainted with the whole world."

Some youngsters, angry with parents after punishment, take off in revenge. They hide behind a trash can in the alley or present themselves to a friend's mother as a new member of her family.

Preschoolers must be taught to stay home. They are too young to travel alone. They cannot cope with distant places, immoral strangers, and traffic.

A two-year-old can play outdoors by himself, but he must be watched continually through a window and stopped at once if he strays from his yard.

The three- or four-year-old can walk or peddle around his block or visit a nearby friend's home, but only with permission. Whenever the youngster leaves his own house, he should know when he is due back.

The child who runs off, even once, should stay inside for a few days except when his mother can be outdoors with him. Maternal guarding in public embarrasses him and the next time he wants to leave, he is likely to ask permission.

NEGATIVISM

Before he is six months old, the infant energetically thwarts adult plans. He rolls over as his mother diapers him; he bats away the cup she offers. As a toddler, he knocks over the lamp his father ordered him to stay away from. When he is two, "No!" is his conversational centerpiece and he spouts resistance each time he is told to come to lunch, pick up his toys, eat his cereal, or sit on the potty. By three, his refusals are more reasoned. They also are more firm.

He is not being deliberately obnoxious. But he wants independence, so he objects to control.

Parents who worry about negativism sometimes panic. Over and over, they scold and spank the resisting child. He responds, not with docile obedience, but with louder shrieks and speedier exits. A battle starts which can last for years.

Other parents, afraid of combat and averse to racket, back off when the youngster objects. They give up on diapering, feeding, or training and let the child do as he pleases. Astonished at winning the war when he intended only to lodge a protest, the preschooler adopts negativism as a way of life.

Negativism should be treated as a mirage. The adult, making no comment, always should finish what he starts. Without apology, explanation, or argument, he can carry or haul the objecting child to wherever he wants him. When a parent never hears the feisty, "No!", refusals taper off.

Experienced parents avoid announcements.

"It's time for your nap," automatically produces objection. Holding the child's hand and walking him to his crib, undressing and lifting him in seldom does.

The small boy or girl has less need to stand up for himself when parents ease up on criticism. If they are forever after him — he messes at the table, puts his clothes on backwards, wets on the rug, garbles his words — someone must preserve his dignity and he takes on the chore.

And he will be more pliable if it's not two against one. Either his mother or his father, not both, should take charge at any given time.[28]

As he learns how to do more by himself and is truly independent, the daily deluge of unwelcome parental commands becomes a tolerable trickle. And when he finds that no matter what he says or does, daily routine never varies, his negativism gradually fades.

STEALING

The one- or two-year-old preschooler is not stealing when he takes what belongs to someone else. At his age, ethical reasoning remains unborn.[20] Although he knows that "hands off" applies to certain things, he does not know why. And if his brother and sister help themselves to his rag doll or pull toy, he thinks nothing of heading for home with a playmate's fire engine.

An older preschooler vaguely understands that he ought not to take money from his parents' dresser. But, wanting a candy bar, he scoops up the cash and runs to the corner store.

Some small children grasp the idea of exchange but not of value. Teagarden[30] writes about a four-year-old girl who bought candy with pennies she took from a visitor's purse. Scolded for stealing money, she insisted that pennies weren't money. Her father, every day, picked out the pennies from his change and gave them to her. She believed that pennies were discards, useless to adults. A two-year-old grabbed a handful of buttons from his mother's sewing supplies and tried, in vain, to trade them for a cone from the ice-cream vendor.

A small child raids his mother's jewelry box and stuffs a sparkling necklace under his pillow to admire later. He takes his big sister's book with its pretty pictures and stows it under his bed. He comes home from the store with an unpaid-for package of gum in his pocket.

He takes things because they attract him and because he correctly assumes that asking guarantees refusal. But his careless hiding of his collection testifies to his belief that moving what he likes to a handier spot is of no major importance.[35]

Many mothers and fathers are shocked when a child steals. They tell him he is a disgrace to the family and surely will wind up in jail. Five-year-old Chris stole everything in sight. His parents had labelled him a thief when he was two and he played the part.

A child learns about others' property rights if his own are respected. There should be a family rule that everyone, parents included, must get the owner's permission to use anything.

When permission is denied, adults must honor the decision. If a four-year-old is playing with his dozen plastic cowboys and Indians and his two-year-old brother wants one, the older child must not be forced, coaxed, or shamed into handing one over. When he has sole right to say what is done with toys, clothes, or equipment he owns, he can understand that others have the same right. When he shares — and usually he will — he's truly generous because the decision to give is his own.

Adults trying to teach a sticky-fingered preschooler to ask rather than to take should grant every request possible. If he wants candy at the store, they should buy it. If he's intrigued by his father's pipe, he can be given it briefly to hold and study. When he learns that asking works, he'll no longer need to take what he wants. Going along with the child's every wish needn't be continued forever. It's a teaching device for re-training a youngster who steals persistently.

When a child has taken candy or a water pistol from a store, he must return it to a clerk and apologize. What he stole should never be bought for him. If it is, he'll conclude that the way to get what he wants is first to take it.

A youngster learns that everything in stores must be paid for if his mother lets him hand the clerk money for purchases. Once he understands what money is for, his parents' cash should be kept out of sight so he is not tempted to help himself.

But he needs to practice buying what he wants with his own money. He can work — set the table, feed the dog, dust, pick up trash in the yard — and discover that before money is spent, it is earned.[35]

JEALOUSY

Jealousy in children is common and should be expected. It is no fatal disease; parents need not fall apart with pity for the jealous boy or girl.

Some mothers and fathers of a second baby try to make their older child feel better by insisting that the infant is a nuisance and by neglecting to feed or change him when he cries. This peculiar behavior makes the first-born wonder if his parents consider him a nuisance too.

A new baby can alter drastically the first child's belief in his own worthiness. His parents are the most important people in his life and, with their complete attention, he is closely bound to them in a joyful trio. Suddenly there is a second child and everything changes. His mother, his father, his grandparents, the neighbors, and his playmates are fascinated with the newcomer. No one notices him; no one cares about what he says or does. He's out of the picture. Someone else has seized his place.

Kendrick and Dunn[21] note a marked decrease in maternal playfulness after the birth of a second child. Dunn *et al.*[8] report that a third of a group of 40 first-borns they studied regressed severely after a younger sibling was born, but the rest became more mature. Previously moody children turned demanding, developed sleep problems, and isolated themselves.

Feelings of abandonment are stronger at certain ages. A one-year-old is too young to notice much difference in others' actions toward him. A two-year-old, struggling for independence but still needing near-total care, may attack his parents when they admire and care for the new baby.

Older preschoolers can and do harm the intruder.[17] Squeezing the baby hard, four-year-old Steven insisted that he was only loving his little brother. Some children drag infant siblings from bassinets and drop them on the floor. Others shove them out windows and assault them with matches, knives, and scissors. Hurting the baby does not make the jealous child happier. Instead, feeling guilty, he becomes flighty, destructive, and angry.

Sometimes a younger child is jealous of an older one. The first-born, managed anxiously by unskilled parents, gets what he demands and escapes correction or punishment. The younger child, reared more normally and held to higher standards, believes his mother and father like the older youngster better.[35]

The preschooler may be jealous when his parents show affection toward each other.[20] While they embrace, he hugs his daddy's legs and begs a kiss from his mother. If loving is the activity of the moment, he dislikes being odd man out.

Jealousy need be neither severe nor lasting. The preschool child expecting a baby sister or brother should see a newborn and understand that infants cry and need hours of daily care. Too often the youngster is told that the baby is being ordered especially for him as a playmate. As he checks the size and talents of the newcomer, his sense of betrayal is keen.

If sleeping and room arrangements will differ when the baby arrives, changes should be made several months ahead.[28] If the preschooler will spend some mornings in nursery school to ease the burden on his mother, he should start long before the infant is due. A young child should know well the person who will care for him while his mother is in the hospital, and when she and the baby come home, his own routine should stay as nearly the same as possible.

Trause[33] found that one- to three-and-one-half-year-olds allowed to visit their mothers an hour each day in the hospital were more responsive to both mothers and newborn siblings when they returned home.

The older boy or girl must never be allowed to hurt the baby. Usually the jealous child announces what he plans to do, hoping to be stopped.

When he makes his move, his mother needs to say firmly, "Perhaps you don't like little Tommy all the time, but you may not hurt him."

When the preschooler suggests taking the baby back to the hospital or dropping him in the trash, the distressed adults should not react with the hoary reproof that he ought to love the little one. He does not. Right now he cannot and guilt floods over him.

He should not be allowed to suck on a bottle or don diapers when he begs to do so. This only proves to him that his parents value babyish traits and he clings to infant trappings.

The jealous child thinks he is unloved and unappreciated.[7] To convince him otherwise, parents can spend time alone with him daily, arrange family excursions without the baby, listen when he talks, and clap when he turns a somersault or rides his trike fast. When visitors come to admire the new infant, the older child can put their coats in the bedroom and pass the plate of cookies, earning conversation and a smile from them. Once a youngster is convinced he is not inferior or less preferred, he welcomes the infant into the family, takes charge of him, and brags to everyone about him.

Jealousy sometimes does not appear until the baby can walk and begins to help himself to his big brother's toys. The older child hits the marauding toddler and then is scolded or spanked by parents for brutality. Such inequity leads him to hate the protected little one. A hook on the door or a lock on the toy chest solves the problem.[28]

When a younger child is jealous of an older one, parents need to check on whether they play favorites. A week or two of recording how they handle rule-breaking and conflicts between themselves and each child tells a mother and father if they treat one youngster more gently than another. If they are unfair, they can change. If they are not, they can review their diary of events with the jealous child to scotch his protests.

The small child needs to share in his parents' loving. Shoving him away with, "I'll tell you when I'm ready to give you some sugar," degrades him. When he wants a hug, he should get it.

ANGER

A small child's anger is helpful, Jersild[17] writes, when it highlights irritation or injustice which needs correction. But if it creates more problems for the child, does not suit the circumstances, or is aimed at blameless persons or objects, anger is harmful.

Goodenough,[10] in her classic study, *Anger in Young Children*, reports that tantrums normally peak when the child is 18 months old and decline sharply after that. But some preschoolers stay angry for years. This happens when the child is surrounded by people — many older brothers and sisters, frequent visitors, or extra adults living with the family — or his parents are critical and discipline is erratic, or he suffers from chronic physical problems: hunger, fatigue, constipation, or illness.

The young child who is kept from exploring or not allowed to finish what he starts gets angry. If his parents rarely hug or kiss him and if they are careless about his safety or health, his temper flares.[2] Parents who explode at each other set off explosions in their young children.[20]

Loneliness leads to anger. Vandersall and Wiener[34] describe firesetting in boys deprived of support and control by parents.

A tiny infant shows anger by holding his breath, sometimes until he turns blue. Older, he hits his head on the wall, screams, or throws himself on the floor, pounding and kicking. A two-year-old strikes his tormentors, but a four-year-old hollers from a safe distance, "You stinkin' doo-do!" and runs away fast.

If a child throws tantrums on and off all day, life is painful both for him and his mother. He is exhausted; she is furious. As long as the angry child gets attention — good or bad — and wins his way with tantrums, he continues them. They become habit, his way of reacting to or controlling events.

Ryan K., five years old, was the third of five children. Many times every day he had stormy tantrums. He wet the bed at night and, since starting kindergarten, also wet during the day. His intelligence was average, but at school he avoided classmates and sometimes hid behind a door.

He had only one friend, a boy who always played at Ryan's house. The parents had gone along with the child's tantrums and wetting, hoping he would grow out of them.

When Ryan was first brought to the clinic, he screamed in rage at being left with the psychologist. The second time he stayed alone, but talked non-stop. He exaggerated, acted, and laughed loudly. Tests suggested that he was anxious because his busy parents did not control him and because he had little practice at managing away from home without them. Also, he was lonely and jealous of his two younger sisters.

Mrs. K. began to play with Ryan, just the two of them, once each day, which gave him the private attention he craved. She sent him to his room when he threw a tantrum, which told him that she would control him when he could not control himself. She arranged for him to play at other children's homes, so he could practice getting along on his own. She began re-training for day wetting, taking him to the bathroom every two hours. No longer was he allowed to creep into bed with her and his father when he wet at night. If he wanted to sleep in a dry bed, he had to change his sheet.

Ryan's temper outbursts disappeared within a few weeks and soon he was playing happily with his classmates.[35]

To change a furious child into a more reasonable one, parents must learn what makes him angry. Does he blow up late in the day because he is tired? Is it when many people hound him with orders? Or does it happen if bullying playmates take his toys and laugh at him? Is he out of control when parents hurry him and force him to fit into their schedules? Or does he get angry because no one plays with or listens to him? These are scenes adults can banish from his life.

Parents need to monitor their own behavior. They induce anger outbursts when they spank the preschooler hard and often or call him a baby, a pest, and a bad boy. One mother whipped her two small girls weekly whether they deserved it or not, "just to keep them in line."

An angry young child may not be able to end his kicking and screaming by himself. Hare-Mustin[12] reports that tantrums ceased in an overprotected four-year-old boy told when and where he could have them. The security of parental control was what he needed to quell his anxiety.

A mother and father also help by their response to the child's anger. If the adult tosses the furious small child in the air, he no longer can thresh about and pound his fists. As parent cheerfulness chases away the memory of what upset him, the youngster's crying switches to laughter.

When he is too heavy for this kind of distraction, isolating him speeds recovery from temper spells. A parent either can walk off, leaving the child kicking in the kitchen, or banish him to his room with permission to come out when he is quiet. Alone, he cannot fight with or maneuver anyone. Both parent and child gain cool-down time.

Later they cn talk about what angered him. Then the adult can explain or compromise. Although parents should never give the child his way to stop a tantrum, once his is calm, his opinions should be heard.

Relentless name-calling or hitting of his mother and father must be stopped. The preschooler allowed to attack his parents becomes the teenager who abuses or kills them. A small child who assaults adults verbally or physically should apologize.[5] After he has said he is sorry, whether or not he appears to be, the parent should forgive and forget. The adult will want to lecture the disrespectful young-ster, but this only heats up flickering rage in both parent and child. Instead, he should suggest a game or walk. Activity banishes the in-cident from memory.

Persistent and excessive anger ends when the young child neither is constantly attacked by others not permitted to win his way with temper.

REFERENCES

1. Ammons, C. H., and Ammons, R. B.: Aggression in doll-play: Interviews of two- to six-year-old white males. *Journal of Genetic Psychology, 82*: 205, 1953.
2. Bandura, A., Ross, D., and Ross, S. A.: Vicarious reinforcement and imita-tive learning. *Journal of Abnormal and Social Psychology, 67*: 601, 1963.
3. Bankart, C. P., and Anderson, C. C.: Short-term effects of prosocial televi-sion viewing on play of preschool boys and girls. *Psychological Reports, 44*: 935,

1979.

4. Bender, L.: *Aggression, Hostility, and Anxiety in Children.* Springfield, Thomas, 1953.

5. Caldwell, B. M.: Aggression and hostility in young children. *Young Children, 32*: 4, 1977.

6. Church, J.: *Understanding Your Child from Birth to Three.* New York, Random, 1973.

7. Dreikurs, R.: *The Challenge of Child Training.* New York, Hawthorn, 1972.

8. Dunn, J., Kendrick, C., and MacNamee, R.: The reaction of first-born children to the birth of a sibling: Mothers' reports. *Journal of Child Psychology and Psychiatry, 22*; 1, 1981.

9. Feshbach, N., and Feshbach, S.: Children's aggression. In Hartup, W. W., ed.: *The Young Child.* Reviews of Research, Vol. 2. Washington, D. C., National Association for the Education of Young Children, 1972.

10. Goodenough, F. L.: *Anger in Young Children.* Minneapolis, U of Minn Pr, 1931.

11. Gordon, J. E., and Cohn, F.: Effect of fantasy arrousal of affiliation drive on doll play aggression. *Journal of Abnormal and Social Psychology, 66*: 301, 1963.

12. Hare-Mustin, R. T.: Treatment of temper tantrums by a paradoxical intention. *Family Process, 14*: 481, 1975.

13. Hartup, W. W., and Himeno, Y.: Social isolation vs. interaction with adults in relation to aggression in preschool children. *Journal of Abnormal and Social Psychology, 59*: 17, 1959.

14. Hetherington, M., and Deur, J.: The effects of father absence on child development. In Hartup, W. W., ed.: *The Young Child.* Reviews of Research, Vol. 2. Washington, D. C., National Association for the Education of Young Children, 1972.

15. Hurlock, E.: *Child Development,* 5th ed. New York, McGraw, 1972.

16. Jersild, A. T.: *Child Psychology,* 7th ed. Englewood Cliffs, P-H, 1975.

17. Jersild, A. T.: Emotional development. In Carmichael, L., ed.: *Manual of Child Psychology.* New York, Wiley, 1946.

18. Jones, N. B., Ferreira, M. C., Brown M. F., and MacDonald, L.: Aggression, crying and physical contact in one- to three-year-old children. *Aggressive Behavior, 5*: 121, 1979.

19. Kagan, J., and Moss, H.: *Birth to Maturity.* New York, Wiley, 1962.

20. Kanner, L.: *Child Psychiatry,* 4th ed. Springfield, Thomas, 1972.

21. Kendrick, C., and Dunn, J.: Caring for a second baby: Effects on interaction between mother and first-born. *Developmental Psychology, 16*: 303, 1980.

22. Larder, D. L.: Effect of aggressive story content on nonverbal play behavior. *Psychological Reports, 11*: 14, 1962.

23. McKee, J. P., and Leader, F.: The relationship of socio-economic status and aggression to the competitive behavior of pre-school children. *Child Development, 26*: 135, 1955.

24. Parke, R. D.: Some effects of punishment on children's behavior. In Hartup, W. W., ed.: *The Young Child.* Reviews of Research. Vol. 2. Washington, D. C., National Association for the Education of Young Children, 1972.

25. Santrock, J. W., Smith, P. C., and Bourbeau, P. E.: Effects of social comparison on aggression and regression in groups of young children. *Child Development, 47*: 831, 1976.

26. Sears, P. S.: Doll play aggression in normal young children: Influence of sex, age, sibling status, father's absence. *Psychological Monographs, 65*: 1951.

27. Siegal, M., and Francis, R.: Parent-child relations and cognitive approaches to the development of moral judgement and behaviour. *British Journal of Psychology, 73*: 285, 1982.

28. Spock, B.: *Baby and Child Care.* New York, Dutton, 1976.

29. Sroufe, L. A., Socioemotional development. In Osofsky, J. D., ed.: *Handbook of Infant Development.* New York, Wiley, 1979.

30. Teagarden, F. M.: *Child Psychology for Professional Workers.* New York, P-H, 1940.

31. Thompson, G. G.: *Child Psychology,* 2nd ed. Cambridge, HM, 1962.

32. Tomlinson-Keasey, C.: *Child's Eye view.* New York, St Martin, 1980.

33. Trause, M. A.: Separation for childbirth: The effect on the sibling. *Child Psychiatry & Human Development, 12*: 32, 1981.

34. Vandersall, T. A., and Wiener, J. M.: Children who set fires. *Archives of General Psychiatry, 22*: 63, 1970.

35. Verville, E.: *Behavior Problems of Children.* Philadelphia, Saunders, 1967.

Chapter 16

HANDICAPS

A HANDICAPPED child is a shock to his parents. Their dreams of pride in him and joy in his rearing change to nightmares. Sometimes they blame themselves for genetic defects; sometimes they believe God is punishing them.[78]

Their initial feelings of loss, anger, self-pity, and guilt do not disappear. For years, uncertainties, conflicts, and problems shadow the mother and father. For some parents, there is chronic sorrow.[49] For others, exhaustion and anger lead to abuse of the child.[42]

But most manage. In one study 69, percent of the mothers stated that their handicapped youngsters didn't insist on constant attention, were easy to handle, and were happy.[33]

Feelings affect rearing methods. Pity produces overprotection;[44] the child grows up demanding and dissatisfied. Hopelessness leads to neglect; the youngster becomes depressed and resentful. Shame promotes ridicule and isolation; the boy or girl grows up aggressive and anxious. If parents refuse to accept the existence of the handicap, they goad and dominate without let-up and the failing child loses all confidence.[86] But some studies suggest that parents rear their handicapped child exactly as they would if he were sound and whole.[7,33]

Frustrated because their activities and experiences are restricted,[87] isolated from peers and unable to compete with them, handicapped boys and girls tend to be unstable and self-centered.[22]

But they want to be independent, successful, and well-liked.

They need to be thought of as children, not disasters. With public education mandated for every handicapped youngster,[69,85] instruction for parents available in books and group meetings, and well-trained specialists on hand to teach him, his future has never been brighter.

Physical problems — diabetes, asthma, leukemia, ulcers, bone deformities and defects in the heart, kidneys, or liver — cause suffering and disruption in the family. But sometimes these can be treated so that the child functions most of the time at near-normal capacity.

Permanently handicapping are mental retardation, brain damage, blindness, and deafness.

MENTAL RETARDATION

An accurate count of mentally retarded preschoolers is difficult to make,[38] but 5 percent of school pupils and 3 percent of the general population are retarded.[24]

Although the severely or moderately retarded young child is easily recognized, diagnosis of the mildly retarded boy or girl can be difficult. Findings sometimes are uncertain because of environmental influences, physical defects, and negativism of the preschooler during testing.

Etiology

There are more than 200 different causes of mental retardation. Damage can occur during the prenatal, paranatal, or postnatal period.[48]

Prenatal

INFECTIONS. Syphilis or toxoplasmosis may be transmitted by the mother. Pneumonia, influenza, and rubella in the mother may produce brain lesions in the fetus.

METABOLIC DEFECTS. Disorders in the metabolism of carbohydrates (galactosemia), proteins (phenylketonuria), or fats (Tay-

Sachs disease and Frölich's syndrome) can cause mental deficiency if diet changes are not made soon after birth.[70]

ENDOCRINE DISORDERS. Diabetes or thyroid problems of the mother may affect the fetus. Hypothyroidism in the infant stunts growth and intelligence. Prompt dosage with desiccated thyroid improves both conditions.[74]

BRAIN ABNORMALITIES. Porencephaly (lack of brain substance) and microcephaly (a small brain with simplified convolutions) cause retardation. Hydrocephaly is enlargement of the brain by an accumulation of one to five quarts of cerebral spinal fluid.[45] If detected before birth, hydrocephaly can be relieved by intrauterine surgery.

TRAUMA. Accidents, maternal convulsions, or premature rupture of membranes or placenta may cause tears and uterine bleeding with subsequent anoxia.[76]

TOXICOSIS. Alcohol, nicotine, and other drugs taken in excess by the mother are damaging. Radiation injures the fetus, so physicians now use sound scans for prenatal inspections and dentists shield X-rayed women with a lead-lined apron.

An extra chromosome is present in the mongoloid (Down's syndrome) child. This happens most often when the mother is older. Senescence in the endocrine system, lesions of the uterus, problems with the union of sperm and egg, and other disabilities related to aging may occur.[38]

Incompatibility of Rh factors of the blood systems of mother and unborn child can cause lesions in the basal ganglia. Transfusions at birth prevent retardation.[38]

INHERITANCE. Bakwin and Bakwin[5] state that 98 percent of retardation is caused by genetic endowment. When both parents are retarded, 90 percent of their children are below average in intelligence. Inherited defect always is mild, never severe.

Paranatal

The infant may suffer anoxia during delivery. Precipitate or prolonged delivery, Caesarean section, spasm, breech, or a maternal pelvis too small for the baby block oxygen flow. Gonorrheal infection, maternal hypertension, fetal hemorrhage, or excessive anesthesia damage the child. Any premature or postmature birth carries risk to the infant.[76]

Postnatal

ENCEPHALITIS. A virus associated with measles, scarlet fever, influenza, or chicken pox can cause encephalitis.[38] Immunizations now protect more youngsters from childhood diseases and subsequent dangers.

TRAUMA. Children fall frequently. If the accident damages his brain, the youngster develops headaches and turns irritable. Aphasia, paralysis, and intellectual deterioration may follow.[45] Traffic accidents result in blows to the head. Several states now require restraints for small children riding in cars. Child abuse is increasing: beating and slapping youngsters about the head injures the brain.

TOXIC AGENTS. Although lead-based paint is no longer used, it remains on the walls of older houses and on inherited cribs and toys. Gnawing it, small children are poisoned. A nursing baby may ingest toxic substances from his mother's milk or from powder or ointment on her breasts. If enough poison accumulates, the child develops headaches, convulsions, paralysis, and retardation.[45]

NEGLECT. Mild retardation occurs in youngsters reared in institutions, ignored or left alone by parents, physically abused, or given little social, verbal, or intellectual stimulation.[81]

The Head Start program, which offers personal contacts, learning experiences, and good physical care to preschoolers from poor families, has turned neglected boys and girls into alert, active children of normal intelligence.

Description

Mildly Retarded

Seventy-five percent of the intellectually deficient are classed as mildly retarded. With an intelligence quotient between 55 and 75, they function at half to three-quarters of normal capacity. Many, as adults, support themselves, marry, and raise families.

PHYSICAL. The mildly retarded child is one to four months behind in sitting, standing, and walking. Usually he is short and slight.[50] He tires easily,[1] and his fine and gross motor movements are awkward.

He also may have visual defects (strabismus, myopia, cateract), hearing problems, balance difficulties, or abnormalities of the face, mouth, nose, jaw, and teeth. There may be metabolic, endocrine, cardiovascular, gastrointestinal, respiratory, and genito-urinary system disorders.[65] Because of these defects, the child may lack tolerance to heat and cold and have problems with bladder and bowel control, speech, and running. Retarded boys and girls are exhausted by constant stimulation.[67]

Some mildly retarded youngsters do not differ in appearance from normal children. Their features are regular; their size and physical coordination are average. Spared from instant rejection, they may be considered lazy or peculiar by friends, teachers, and parents because their judgment, memory, and learning skills do not match their looks.

Schools, both public and private, now provide physical training for the retarded child. Many are coached in one or two of a dozen track, field, and game events for competition in the Special Olympics. Over 4,000 retarded athletes from every state in the Union and fifty countries participated in the 15th Special Olympics Games at Baton Rouge, Louisiana, in 1983. A million retardates take part in year-round athletic programs.

SPEECH. Because speech is symbolic, it is difficult for the retarded child to use. He starts talking later than average, his vocabulary is limited, and often his articulation is poor.

But some older youngsters, especially those whose retardation developed from social-emotional factors or other postnatal events, talk continually and have adequate vocabularies.

The retarded boy or girl needs to be able to relate his experiences and feelings, to report his needs, and to ask questions. If he cannot communicate to this extent, he is constantly frustrated and sometimes endangered.

With training, the child can improve his articulation and increase his vocabulary.[86] Giving him close attention when he speaks encourages him to try more often.

SOCIAL. The mildly retarded preschooler who competes with more able children in his neighborhood has a hard time of it. Often he is labelled, ridiculed, and left behind. Some parents order their children to stay away from him. Not until he enters a special nursery or public school class can he find friends among those of his own ability.[36,86]

Sometimes his own family isolates and taunts him. Retaliating, he grabs, hits, pushes, and screams, behavior which boosts his unpopularity at home and sets habits which ostracize him from outsiders.

Because his socialization is delayed, the retarded child doubts his acceptability. He seeks a friendly response from others by offering gifts and compliments to acquaintances and talking to strangers about his personal problems.

Early in his life, the retarded child should have playmates, preferably younger children whose abilities more nearly match his own. Siblings and parents should include him in some of their activities. They must refrain from teasing him for his inadequacies lest he grow up resenting everyone and certain that no one will ever like him.

EMOTIONAL. The child's emotional behavior is linked to the physical, intellectual, and social facets of his life. His failures anger him. He cannot make his parents understand what he wants. No one approves of him or seeks him out.

His self-acceptance is related to the stability of family life during his preschool years.[86] Adult retardates who were institutionalized before they were five years old admitted that they often cheated, swore, and fought. Those who lived longer at home before entering an institution and who later moved into the community thought more of themselves and were more self-controlled.[30]

As does every child, the retarded boy or girl needs acceptance and affection. He should be given many tasks at which he can succeed and he should get the same attention as do other members of the family.

INTELLECTUAL. Public schools must educate every handicapped child. Currently, controversy is heated over the government mandate to teach the child in the "least restrictive environment."[69] This is called "mainstreaming" and means that the retarded youngster attends classes with boys and girls of normal intelligence. Teachers and many parents oppose this law, pointing out the inordinate effort needed to teach the slow-learning youngster in a regular class and the devastating comparisons he suffers daily.

Compromises are being worked out. In many schools, the retarded child takes music, art, and physical education with normal boys and girls, but he goes to a resource room for academic subjects. Because youngsters with speech or learning disabilities also get special training in resource rooms, stigma for the retarded youngster is not extreme.[36]

After nine or more years of instruction, the mildly retarded youngster may be able to read, write, spell, and do arithmetic at the fourth or fifth grade level.

Adults can help the preschooler by steady efforts to build vocabulary, encourage creativity, and provide a variety of experiences for him to recall and describe.

Moderately Retarded

Twenty percent of the intellectually deficient are classed as moderately retarded. With an I.Q. between 25 and 50, they function at one-fourth to one-half of normal capacity. As adults, most live with parents or in group homes with a supervisor. They work at routine jobs, sometimes in sheltered workshops.

PHYSICAL. Growth is stunted, with some investigators reporting that two-thirds of moderately retarded youngsters are below the 17th percentile in height and three-fourths are below it in weight.[50] Vision and hearing deficits occur. Lacrosse,[51] who accurately tested anfrainedutionalized group, found hearing impairment in only 16 percent an improvement over the 30-60 percent commonly reported.

SPEECH. The child may not speak at all. If he does, his vocabulary is small, his sentences short, and his articulation so poor he rarely is understood. Often he uses single words, does not answer questions, and feels angry and isolated because he cannot make his wants and thoughts known.

But speech varies. Rosenberg *et al.*[75] report less socializing between retardates whose verbal ability differs. For optimum socialization and learning, children of similar speaking ability should be grouped together.

SOCIAL. The moderately-retarded boy or girl has little chance for friends in the neighborhood because he cannot keep up with normal youngsters. Because of his limited capacity to care for himself, he sometimes is treated as a pet. The mongoloid child, cheerful and adaptable, usually is liked by others.

EMOTIONAL. The moderately retarded child shows less aggression and anger than the mildly retarded youngster, perhaps because he doesn't understand the meaning of names he is called. He does recognize both angry and approving facial expressions and voice tones and reacts appropriately to each.

INTELLECTUAL. Academically, the child rarely gets beyond kindergarten or first grade level.[12] He is taught words needed for safety or information (*Exit, Stop, Danger, Boys, Girls*) and symbols used on road signs and in buildings.

In class he learns to cook, clean, iron, and use simple tools. He acquires social skills as he joins classmates in welcoming, entertaining, and feeding adult guests. If he is taught to obey, to be considerate, and to finish what he starts, he meets others' expectations and gets along well with them.

Severely Retarded

Five percent of the intellectually deficient are classed as severely retarded. With an I.Q. below 25, they must be cared for as long as they live.

The maximum mental age the severely retarded child will reach is three years and often he does not attain the competency of a one-year-old. He may never be able to sit, stand, or walk. He uses, at most, two or three words. Life expectancy is short.

As he grows older and heavier, the physical burden of caring for him at home becomes too great and ordinarily he is placed in an institution. There, with steady, repetitive training and special equipment, many severely retarded boys and girls learn to feed themselves and to move from their beds and wheelchairs to the toilet.[40] Tension habits, such as head-banging and masturbation, decrease as they become more self-sufficient.

McKinney and Keele[59] found that 24 severely retarded boys given special attention by mildly retarded women in the same institution talked more and managed better on their own than they had before.

The Retardate's Family

Feelings

Even when they have long suspected it, the verdict that their child is retarded devastates a mother and father. They correctly predict upset lives, destroyed hopes, and drained physical and financial resources.[36]

Guilt smothers them. They caused the child's defect: an uncle is retarded, there was an attempted abortion, the mother drinks and smokes. Resenting the burden the youngster imposes, they are ashamed of their anger and self-pity.

Marriages are tested. The mother, weighted with the child's care, envies the father's daily escape to his job. She is furious when he defends the youngster in conflicts and fails to appreciate, comfort, and support her.

Sometimes a father feels degraded and refuses to have anything to do with his imperfect son or daughter. One parent favors institutionalization; the other objects.

More often than not, parents grow sturdy and adjust to their unexpected, unwanted duties. Life must go on. They learn to manage efficiently both day-to-day care and crises which never end.

Siblings and Grandparents

Parents often ask the diagnosing psychologist what effect the retarded youngster will have on the family's other boys and girls.

Nearly always, siblings regard the handicapped child exactly as the parents do. If the adults ridicule, isolate, and scorn him, so do his brothers and sisters. But if the mother and father include him in family activities, require him to obey rules and do chores, give him affection and attention, and train siblings to help with teaching, brothers and sisters benefit from his presence.[31]

Grandparents can help or hurt. If they spew a torrent of advice, pound the alphabet into the child to make him "normal," threaten never again to speak to the parents should they institutionalize the youngster, or ignore him, they compound parental troubles.

What they can do is hug, talk to, and play with the child and teach him practical skills in short and limited doses. A pressured mother and father feel better when their own parents admire and encourage them as they handle their complex, trying task.

Aid for the Parents

The mother and father of a retarded youngster need not go it alone. Help is available, both for them and for their child.

For years, parents of retarded boys and girls have banded together to compare experiences and obtain adequate facilities and teachers for their youngsters. Since education of the handicapped now is required of public school systems, extraordinary personal effort no longer is crucial. But parents who work with each other and with the schools become more knowledgeable and competent.

Discussion groups prepare parents to accept the retarded child's weaknesses and strengths, to explain these to friends and relatives, to provide for his medical, educational, and recreational needs, and to give him as much love, but no more, than they give other children in the family. Mothers in such groups value their youngsters more than do those without this training.[79]

A Pilot Parent program started in Omaha, Nebraska, in 1974 has aided over 500 families with retarded children. The parents of newly-diagnosed mental retardates are assigned a trained parent who has a child of similar retardation level, age, and family background. The Pilot Parent talks with them about what they can expect of their boy or girl, how to rear him, and what community facilities are available. They are encouraged to keep their goals reasonable and to enjoy their child.[61]

Family atmosphere lightens when adults learn how to look after their retarded child. A four-unit parent-training program to teach preschool retarded youngsters self-care skills produced marked spurts in ability.[34]

Retarded children in nursery school decreased habitual disruptive and undesirable behaviors when they were taught with reward tokens and simple punishments.[4,8]

Hayden and Haring[32] describe a program for Down's syndrome children at the University of Washington. Its intent is to improve the child's gross and fine motor coordination, social skills, communication, cognition, and competence in self-help. During infancy, the child and his parent come for once-weekly instruction. When he is older, the youngster attends a training class four times a week. Results are dramatic. By kindergarten age, many of these moderately retarded children are performing nearly up to age norms.

Some investigators report increased interest, concentration, and vocabulary in retarded children exposed to music. This includes simple rhythmic games and instrument-playing, dancing, and listening.[6]

Books for parents give detailed instruction on caring for and teaching the retarded child.[65,67] Step-by-step training at home and school motivates the young child to achieve, decreases distractability, calms him emotionally, and sharpens his social abilities.[2,89]

BRAIN DAMAGE

Major damage to the central nervous system of the fetus or neonate causes epilepsy or cerebral palsy; minor impairment disturbs perceptual, social, emotional, and learning function. Three to ten percent of American newborns suffer from some degree of impairment to the central nervous system because of pre- or perinatal trauma or infection.[42]

Epilepsy

Abnormal electroencephalographic tracings occur in the epileptic, whose seizures result from disturbance in electro-chemical action of his brain. Five in every thousand persons under 21 years of age have the disorder.

Etiology

A child may be predisposed to epilepsy. Persons whose attacks begin before the age of one year have four times as many epileptic relatives as those who suffer no seizures until after age 30. The child of an epileptic has one chance in 70 of developing seizures.[53]

Infection, trauma, malnutrition, and prenatal injury are etiological factors. Problems with the endocrine system, drug use, kidney disease, and allergies have been related to the disorder. Kanner[45] states that epilepsy results from generalized dysrhythmic, inadequate physiological functioning. Seizures increase with fatigue, malnutrition, and emotional instability.[15,20]

Description

There are three types of seizures, *grand mal, petit mal,* and *psychomotor.*

In the *grand mal* attack, the child loses consciousness, falls, and suffers a tonic spasm of the entire body. Within sixty seconds, rigidity is replaced by clonic convulsions which last from one to three minutes. Gargling noises, involuntary defecation and urination, heightened pulse rate and temperature, salivation, and pupils unresponsive to light accompany the convulsions. After the attack, of which he has no memory, the child falls into a deep sleep.[45] Prognosis is poor if *grand mal* seizures develop before the age of two.[55]

The *petit mal* attack consists of a short, blank stare, followed by a pause in awareness and action. There may be a few seconds of rhythmic motion. The child may have several attacks daily, many unnoticed by adults. *Petit mal* attacks begin between four and eight years, seldom last into adulthood, and are more common in children than *grand mal* seizures.[55]

The psychomotor seizure is rare in children. It lasts for two or three minutes and consists of odd behavior such as tearing paper or making sucking noises.[20]

The epileptic boy or girl has limited ability to tolerate stress and seizures tend to occur when he is emotionally upset.

He may or may not be retarded. In some cases, retardation results from the same brain defect which causes epilepsy.[45]

Treatment

Dilantin® is the drug most often prescribed. At first it is given daily, but later the dosage can be reduced gradually and in some cases, eventually eliminated. Seizures can be almost completely controlled with its use, although parents and child often fail to understand the need for years of medication when seizures are rare or non-existent.

If a seizure does occur, adults must remove nearby hard or sharp objects and insert a handkerchief between the child's teeth to protect him from hurting himself as he threshes about.

At present, physicians impose little or no restriction on the epileptic child's activity.[52]

Strange and superstitious ideas about epilepsy persist. The child fears death, his parents feel shame, and teachers, relatives, and friends dread witnessing a seizure. All need complete information about the cause and course of the disorder. Calmness, both in accepting the epilepsy and in home life, keeps the youngster from worrying unduly about the problem.[45]

Cerebral Palsy

Cerebral palsy is a disturbance of muscle function caused by brain damage. One cerebral palsied child is born every 53 minutes in the United States. There are 990,000 cerebral palsied children and adults in this country.[39]

Etiology

Defective development in the midline of the brain causes cerebral palsy. Other damaging agents are hemorrhage in premature infants, birth injury, kernicterus, infection, and encephalitis. One-third of a group of athetoid children were jaundiced at birth. Many others did not breathe for several minutes after birth.[18]

Description

Spastic paralysis results from hyperirritability to stimulation and subsequent severe, persisting muscle contraction. The brain's cortex or pyramidal system is damaged.

In *athetosis,* there are involuntary muscle contractions which appear as twisting movements extending in waves down the arms or legs. Motion may be slight or so extreme that the trunk and limbs are thrown about. The basal ganglia are damaged.

Less common conditions are *flaccid paralysis,* in which the muscle does not respond to stimulation; *congenital tremor,* present at birth or soon thereafter; and *ataxia,* the inability to produce voluntary movement.

Mental retardation occurs in 27-50% of cerebral palsied children. Speech problems, impaired vision, and defective hearing are common. Visual-motor coordination is poor.[66] Height and weight are below normal.[63] Studies show that between 14 and 75 percent of all cerebral palsied children suffer from seizures.

Treatment

Finnie[25] writes on how to train the young cerebral palsied child to develop movement and to dress and feed himself. She suggests techniques for toilet training, bathing, and management of sleep and play.

Kastein[46] describes sipping, blowing, sucking, and tongue movement exercises which coax the cerebral palsied preschooler to master speech.

Nursery school helps. The youngster can make friends, manipulate materials, and join in group activities. Motivation to learn increases there, followed by improved physical and social growth.[35] Appropriately chosen materials and methods improve the child's balance and his fine and gross motor skills.[72]

At home, parents who assist the child to learn help him and themselves.[77]

Because the child has major problems with receiving and responding to stimulation, his intelligence is difficult to gauge. It's best to assume that he has normal intelligence and rear him with the goal of independent adulthood. Some cerebral palsied children grow up to graduate from college and become counselors, writers, or teachers. With less formal education, others earn money in sheltered workshops or establish their own businesses.

Some cerebral palsied children attend regular classes in public school; some have their own class and teacher. Equipment such as page turners, standing tables, pencil-holding devices, and special typewriters enables youngsters to learn. Boys and girls with limited manual control can use their toes to type and to feed and dress themselves.[19]

Minimal Brain Dysfunction

Signs of minimal brain dysfunction exist during preschool years, but often the disorder is undetected until the child enters school. Estimates suggest that 7.5 million children under age 18, more boys than girls, are affected.[16,21]

Etiology

It is believed the problem is caused by damage — faulty electro-chemical function, lesions, or slowed development — in cortical areas adjacent to those responsible for vision, hearing, speech, and motor function. Neural impulses are blocked so that stimulus and response do not merge smoothly or consistently. In a group of 75 children born to mothers when they were 35 or older, 18 percent suffered minimal brain dysfunction.[29]

Description

LEARNING. Although his intelligence is normal or even superior, the youngster may function poorly in learning.

He may be troubled by perceptual-motor disability. If so, he cannot synthesize parts into a whole: to him, the letters *d, b,* and *p* each consist of a line and a circle. He cannot distinguish one from another.[27]

He is unable to block out peripheral stimuli in order to attend solely to what's important: *e.g.,* he studies the freckle on his hand while his teacher announces workbook instructions.

He perseverates. He fills his paper with circles when his teacher says to draw three. It takes more energy than he can muster either to stop what he has begun or to shift to a new activity.

He cannot make the muscles of his body work right. As a young child, he clings to his mother's legs for support and cannot right himself when he falls.[62] In school, he cannot write legibly or in a straight line.

Because he can neither generalize nor remember,[62,83] he does not learn from experience. His world is a parade of nonsense events[86] livened with fantasy.[9]

BEHAVIOR. Often his behavior is uninhibited. Distractible and active, he constantly interferes, talks, moves, and interrupts. He is disobedient and argumentative, acts impulsively, and frequently endangers himself. He may turn violent at minor provocation and frenzied without good cause.[10] Accumulated nervous impulses which suddenly discharge may be responsible for such explosions.[83]

Or, in contrast, the youngster may be over-inhibited. He restricts his playing to a few toys, isolates himself from his family, and does not respond to attempts to entertain or stimulate him.[73]

Socially, the child has serious trouble because he does not fit in. Sometimes he tries to copy the clowning and joking of playmates, but what he does seems artificial and inappropriate. He seeks friends with lavish compliments bestowed on adult and child alike and offers to help anyone he sees with whatever he is doing.

The impulsive and disobedient youngster, who hurts other boys and girls or isolates himself, is disliked. Because he is confused and inept, he needs more comfort than most children, so he hangs on his parents and complains. Most of the time he feels totally alone and quickly attacks anyone who criticizes him.

Treatment

Diagnosis of minimal brain dysfunction in the preschooler often is missed. Brutten *et al.*[16] describe an uncontrollable two-and-one-half-year-old girl whose wild, impulsive, aggressive actions turned her parents' attention away from the fact that both her speech and muscular coordination were below her age level. After she was given speech therapy, perceptual-motor training, and medication, her behavior calmed and her skills improved.

The preschooler benefits from a simple, regimented daily life with less-than-normal stimulation and few surprises. Because he often confuses sounds and misunderstands words, instructions should be clarified with demonstrations.

If he cannot get across his ideas and worries, speech therapy, with exercises at home and time to talk with parents, will help.

He needs to play alone every day and he requires much more rest than the ordinary child. Music relaxes him. He must be rehearsed in what to say and do in every new situation and most old ones.

He should play with other children for limited periods of time and under clear, consistently-enforced rules. If he hurts another child, he should apologize and do something kind for his victim. When he plays outdoors, he needs supervision so that he doesn't run off or hurt himself with dangerous experiments.[86]

Better self-control can be taught. A new rule should be stated often and practiced rigidly. When the youngster breaks a rule, isolation or an extra chore are the best punishments. Yelling and whipping don't improve memory or control; they only convince the child that he is disliked.

The boy or girl should be taught to do simple chores well and not allowed to escape them because he balks or his work is sloppy.

Life is confusing, so he stays dependent on adults for years. But it's better for him to seek their help than to believe he must defend himself from real and imagined threats.

Ritalin and similar stimulant drugs are believed to help the minimally brain-damaged youngster by easing passage of neurons across synapses. In one study, 60 percent of medicated children were calmer and easier to manage, although there were temporary side effects of restless sleep and decreased appetite.[56] But because hundreds of thousands of youngsters are given stimulant drugs, questions are being raised about their automatic and indiscriminate use. Many investigators urge that re-education be tried before drugs are prescribed.[14,28,43,56,88]

Once in school, the child with minimal brain dysfunction needs identification of his specific problems and tutoring by learning disabilities specialists. The pediatric neurologist, optometrist, reading expert, speech therapist, psychiatrist, and psychologist all can contribute to the understanding and treatment of his difficulties.[80]

BLINDNESS

A child is considered legally blind if his visual acuity is 20/200 or less in the better eye after correction. He needs a sight-saving class if his vision is 20/70 or less in the better eye after correction.

About one in 8,000 children must learn Braille;[41] two in 1,000 are partially sighted. Forty-six percent of the visually impaired were born blind; 38 percent became blind in their first year of life.[5]

Etiology

Disease produces half of all blindness. Measles, scarlet fever, typhoid fever, smallpox, diphtheria, and meningitis cause 15 percent; eye diseases, such as interstitial keratitis, trachoma, and cataract cause 35 percent.

Accidents are responsible for 15-25 percent of blindness, with the incidence five times greater in boys than girls.

Poisons or tumors may damage the optic nerve or visual cortical centers.

Children born to closely related parents are ten times more likely to be blind than those of non-related parents.[3]

Description

Blind children differ physically from sighted ones. Neurological abnormalities occur, less sleep is common, and growth is steady, rather than in spurts like that of the normal child.[37] Hospitalization is more frequent and prolonged.

A blind child's psychological difficulties often develop from the rearing he receives and the attitude of others toward him. If he is frustrated, he becomes intolerant; if he is isolated, he becomes helpless. He cannot share fully in what others do, so he tends to withdraw from people. They, uneasy about his sightlessness, keep their distance.

Without human contacts, he entertains himself with fantasy. Imagined sound and movement can become more real than actual experiences. He develops habits known as "blindisms": rocking, rubbing his fists into his eyes, whirling, and nodding his head.[26] When little else stimulates him, these movements do.

The more he keeps to himself, the less he speaks. Instead of talking normally, he parrots others' phrases or TV commercials.

Because he seldom plays with other boys and girls, he never learns to adapt to their ways or defend himself. Lack of initiative is characteristic of some blind children,[57] but others are described as suggestible, easily encouraged, and liking to play practical jokes.[11] Some sightless boys and girls, believing themselves inferior, are aggressive, angry, and demanding with others.

Treatment

Blind children show a normal range of intelligence, but they may be retarded educationally by as much as three years. Slow learning occurs if the child enters school at a later-than-normal age, if special equipment and teachers are not available, or if the child is so dependent or withdrawn that he pays no attention to instruction.[26]

Parents of the blind preschooler can get him off to a good start. During his infancy, they can move and talk to him often. They can tie toys to strings near him and help him reach and hit them. When the child is old enough to crawl or walk, they can entice him to do so by ringing a bell and guiding him with a light touch.[17]

Kastein *et al.*[47] give detailed instructions on what to expect and how to teach the child from infancy through his fifth year. They point out that the blind child must depend on his memory to get along. Adults need to explain events, describe objects, and have the child repeat what they say.

The youngster can learn to wash his face and brush his teeth, to comb his hair by feeling the part, and to dress himself with colors cued by patches of different materials on clothing. The boy or girl should put his belongings away on the same shelves or in the same drawers each time, set the table and make his bed, feeling his way. Playing with a pegboard prepares him to learn Braille. With training and practice, he can cook, skate, open doors with a key, button his jacket, and go from one place to another out of doors.

As soon as he is old enough, he should attend a regular nursery school. He also needs playmates in the neighborhood. Norris *et al.*[68] found, in a five-year study of 259 blind preschoolers, that the blind youngster can become as self-sufficient as the sighted one. If he is trained to independence from an early age, the blind child can attend kindergarten with sighted boys and girls.[82]

One blind child, given the chance, tackled life with vigor.

> Jane W., six years old and blind since birth, had a violent temper, rarely spoke, and was not toilet trained. An only child, Jane was rocked to sleep, fed, dressed, and moaned over by her distraught parents.
>
> When an intelligence examination indicated that Jane had normal ability to learn and her parents were given a realistic appraisal of what her future could be, they began to toilet train her and encourage her to feed and dress herself.
>
> She was enrolled in a public school class for visually handicapped children, where her teacher corrected both her learning errors and her tantrums. During her first school year, Jane learned to use a Braille-writer and answer her teacher's questions. She was delighted both with her achievements and her classmates.[86]

DEAFNESS

It is estimated that 0.7 percent of the school population has impaired hearing.[5] Their problems range from profound deafness (hearing loss which exceeds 60 decibels) to imperfect hearing, for which the child may need a hearing aid.

Etiology

Half of the hearing impaired are believed to have inherited the defect. Prenatal and paranatal conditions such as maternal rubella, asphyxia, and metabolic disorders account for another 17 percent. The rest are victims of postnatal early infectious disease, especially meningitis.

Premature infants are susceptible to abscesses and infections of the middle ear.

Description

Hearing loss can be suspected if the infant does not react to sounds as most babies do. Under three months of age, the infant jumps at loud noises. At four months, he moves his eyes or wriggles when his mother speaks and his own sounds increase in number and variety.

Too often, a hearing problem remains undetected. The passive baby is labelled retarded; the silent toddler, stubborn. Not until the child is three or four years old does someone suggest checking his hearing with an audiometer. By then, he lags far behind his peers in social development, learning, and communication.

As an infant, the child feels, but cannot hear, his own sounds. Older, trying unsuccessfully to guess what his parents are saying to him, he learns little from their teaching efforts.

He thinks without words, so his own messages are few, short, and repetitive. They are accompanied by shouts and grunts as he attempts to make others understand.

Because the child cannot follow group conversation easily and must strain to hear, he soon tunes out others' speech.[23] Gradually he no longer attempts social contacts and they become of little importance to him. He leads a life of fantasy, depends on his parents, and settles into a never-ending round of sleeping, eating, enuresis, and temper.[64]

Deaf-blind children live with added complications. Their sleep patterns are unusual; they cannot chew and swallow; and some are so over-sensitive to tactile stimulation they cannot stand clothing. Irregular biological function causes poor bladder and bowel control. Meager communication between child and adults leads to discipline problems and delayed social, emotional, and cognitive growth.[58]

Treatment

The deaf child bewilders and thwarts his parents and they despair at his slow progress. But because he is deaf, it is vital that he learn to communicate and take his place in the family and the community.

Infants under one year of age, fitted with hearing aids, can be taught to respond to sounds and to develop vocabularies. Parents should speak directly to the child, name objects, and constantly relate words to events. Any effort the child makes to speak should be accepted as adequate.

The John Tracy Clinic publishes correspondence courses in instruction of deaf babies and preschoolers. Parents learn to understand their child and train him in listening, lip reading, and using his other senses.*

The young deaf child needs playmates. He can attend a nursery school for hearing children and practice normal give-and-take with peers. As he handles toys, tries crayons and scissors, marches, and plays drop-the-handkerchief with other boys and girls, he joins his own generation.[54]

A mother and father benefit from attending discussions with other parents of deaf youngsters. In some groups they can learn about the mechanics of hearing, what an auditory examination tells, how to care for hearing aids, and what to do to help the youngster speak more and grow independent.[71] Working together, they can educate the public and promote needed legislation.

Many deaf boys and girls must be taught in a residential facility

---

*The courses, in English and Spanish, can be obtained by parents free of charge from the clinic at 806 W. Adams Blvd, Los Angeles, California, 90007.

away from their homes. Parents should visit the school, meet the teachers, observe the classes, and inspect the living quarters. Although separation is difficult, the child's education must not be delayed or neglected. Older children who are taught during their first years in residential schools often return to their home communities and to regular classes when they reach junior high school level.

His mother and father are the handicapped child's primary therapists. Working with teachers and other parents, setting short and long-term goals, they can help the youngster both to function adequately and to enjoy and appreciate life.[84]

REFERENCES

1. Abraham, W.: *The Slow Learner.* New York, The Center for Applied Research in Education, Inc., 1964.
2. Andrews, R. J., and Apelt, W. C.: The role of the special school in the integration of mentally retarded children into the community. *Australian Journal of Mental Retardation, 2*: 54, 1972.
3. Baker, H. J.: *Introduction to Exceptional Children.* New York, Macmillan, 1953.
4. Baker, J. G., Stanish, B., and Fraser, B.: Comparative effects of a token economy in nursery school. *Mental Retardation, 10*: 16, 1972.
5. Bakwin, H., and Bakwin, R. M.: *Clinical Management of Behavior Disorders in Children,* 3rd ed. Philadelphia, Saunders, 1966.
6. Barber, E.: Music therapy with retarded children. *Australian Journal of Mental Retardation, 2*: 210, 1973.
7. Barsch, R. H.: *The Parent of the Handicapped Child.* Springfield, Thomas, 1968.
8. Becker, J. V., Turner, S. M., and Sajwaj, T. E.: Multiple behavioral effects of the use of lemon juice with a ruminating toddler-age child. *Behavior Modification, 2*: 267, 1978.
9. Bender, L.: *Aggression, Hostility, and Anxiety in Children.* Springfield, Thomas, 1953.
10. Bender, L.: *Psychopathology of Children with Organic Brain Disorders.* Springfield, Thomas, 1956.
11. Benton, P.C.: The emotional aspects of visual handicaps. *The Sight-Saving Review, 21*: 23, 1951.
12. Benton, P. C., McHale, J., and Whitmore, L.: Habilitation of mentally retarded. *The Journal,* Oklahoma State Medical Association, June, 1958.
13. Blanco, R. F.: *Prescriptions for Children with Learning and Adjustment Problems,* 2nd ed. Springfield, Thomas, 1982.

14. Bower, K. B., and Mercer, C. D.: Hyperactivity: etiology and intervention techniques. *The Journal of School Health, 45*: 195, 1975.

15. Broida, D. C.: Psychosocial aspects of epilepsy in children and youth. In Cruickshank, W. M., ed.: *Psychology of Exceptional Children and Youth.* Englewood Cliffs, P-H, 1955.

16. Brutten, M., Richardson, S. O., and Mangel, C.: *Something's Wrong with My Child.* New York, HarBraceJ, 1973.

17. Burlingham, D.: Some notes on the development of the blind. *Psychoanalytic Study of the Child, 16*: 121, 1961.

18. Churchill, J.: Current research in chronic neurologic diseases of children. *Merrill-Palmer Quarterly, 9*: 95, 1963.

19. Clements, S. D., and Peters, J. E.: Minimal brain dysfunction in the school age child: Diagnosis and treatment. *Archives of General Psychiatry, 6*: 185, 1962.

20. Connor, F. P.: The education of children with chronic medical problems. In Cruickshank, W. M., and Johnson, G. O., eds.: *Education of Exceptional Children and Youth.* Englewood Cliffs, P-H, 1958.

21. Daryn, E.: Problems of children with "diffuse brain damage": Clinical observations on a developmental disturbance. *Archives of General Psychiatry, 4*: 299, 1961.

22. Delorme-Schoof, F. and Précourt, P.: (Study of the social adaptation of handicapped and normal children in a daycare environment.) *Apprentissage et Socialisation, 5*: 32, 1982.

23. Ewing, I. R., and Ewing, A. W. G.: *New Opportunities for Deaf Children.* London, U of London Pr, 1958.

24. *Farrell, M. J., Chipman, E. E., and Brazier, M. F.: Training and education of the mentally retarded. In Frampton, M., and Gall, E. D., eds.: Special Education for the Exceptional.* Boston, Porter Sargent, 1956.

25. Finnie, N. R.: *Handling the Young Cerebral Palsied Child at Home.* New York, Dutton, 1970.

26. Frampton, M., Hoard, S. Kerney, E., and Mitchell, P.: The blind. In Frampton, M., and Gall, E. D., eds.: *Special Education for the Exceptional.* Boston, Porter Sargent, 1955.

27. Frostig, M.: Visual perception in the brain-injured child. *American Journal of Orthopsychiatry, 33*: 665, 1963.

28. Gardner, W. I.: *Children with Learning and Behavior Problems.* Boston, Allyn, 1974.

29. Gilberg, C., Rasmussen, P., and Wahlström, J.: (Neuropsychiatric problems among children born to older mothers.) *Acta Paedopsychiatrica, 46*: 57, 1980.

30. Gorlow, L., Butler, A., and Guthrie, G. M.: Personality differences between institutionalized and noninstitutionalized retardate females. *American Journal of Mental Deficiency, 67*: 543, 1963.

31. Graliker, B. V., Fishler, K., and Koch, R.: Teenage reaction to a mentally retarded sibling. *American Journal of Mental Deficiency, 66*: 838, 1962.
32. Hayden, A. H., and Haring, N. G.: Programs for Down's syndrome children at the University of Washington. In Tjossem, T., ed.: *Intervention Strategies for Risk Infants and Young Children.* Baltimore, Univ Park, 1976.
33. Hewett, S., Newson, J., and Newson, E.: *The Family and the Handicapped Child.* Chicago, Aldine, 1970.
34. Hofmeister, A. M., and Latham, G.: Development and validation of a mediated package for training parents of preschool mentally retarded children. *Improving Human Performance, 1*: 3, 1972.
35. Holden, R. H.: Motivation, adjustment, and anxiety of cerebral-palsied children. In Trapp, E. P., and Himelstein, P., eds.: *Readings on the Exeptional Child.* New York, ACC, 1962.
36. Ingalls, R. P.: *Mental Retardation.* New York, Wiley, 1978.
37. Jan, J. E., Freeman, R. D., Scott, E. P.: *Visual Impairment in Children and Adolescents.* New York, Grune, 1977.
38. Jervis, G. A.: The mental deficiencies. In Arieti, S., ed.: *American Handbook of Psychiatry,* Vol. 2. New York, Basic, 1959.
39. Joel, G. S.: *So Your Child Has Cerebral Palsy.* Albuquerque, U of NM Pr, 1975.
40. Johnson, E. W., Gove, R., and Ostermeier, B.: The value of functional training in severely disabled institutionalized brain damaged children. *American Journal of Mental Deficiency, 67*: 860, 1963.
41. Jones, J. W.: The blind child in school. *School Life,* February-March, 1961.
42. Kagan, J.: Overview: Perspectives on human infancy. In Osofsky, J. D., ed.: *Handbook of Infant Development.* New York, Wiley, 1979.
43. Kalverboer, A. F., vanPraag, H. M., and Mendlewicz, J.: *Minimal Brain Dysfunction: Fact or Fiction.* Basel, Karger, 1978.
44. Kammerer, R. C.: An exploratory psychological study of crippled children. *Psychological Record, 4*: 47, 1940.
45. Kanner, L.: *Child Psychiatry,* 4th ed. Springfield, Thomas, 1972.
46. Kastein, S.: Speech hygiene guidance for parents of children with cerebral palsy. In Michal-Smith, H., and Kastein, S.: *The Special Child.* Seattle, New School for the Special Child, Inc., 1962.
47. Kastein, S., Spaulding, I., and Scharf, B.: *Raising the Young Blind Child.* New York, Human Sci Pr, 1980.
48. Kopp, C. B., and Parmelee, A. H.: Prenatal and perinatal influences on infant behavior. In Osofsky, J. D., ed.: *Handbook of Infant Development.* New York, Wiley, 1979.
249. Kornblum, H., and Anderson, B.: "Acceptance" reassessed — a point of view. *Child Psychiatry and Human Development, 12*: 171, 1982.
50. Kugel, R. B., and Mohr, J.: Mental retardation and physical growth. *Ameri-*

can Journal of Mental Deficiency, 68: 41, 1963.

51. LaCrosse, E. L., and Bidlake, H.: A method to test the hearing of mentally retarded children. *Volta Review, 66*: 27, 1964.

52. Lagos, J. C.: *Seizures, Epilepsy, and Your Child.* New York, Har-row, 1974.

53. Lennox, W. G.: The epileptic child. In Michal-Smith, H., ed.: *Pediatric Problems in Clinical Practice.* New York, Grune, 1954.

54. Lieberth, A. K.: Functional speech therapy for the deaf child. In Sims, D. G., Walter, G. G., Whitehead, R. L., eds.: *Deafness and Communication.* Baltimore, Williams & Wilkins, 1982.

55. Livingston, S.: *Comprehensive Management of Epilepsy in Infancy, Childhood, and Adolescence.* Springfield, Thomas, 1972.

56. Loney, J., and Ordona, T. T.: Using cerebral stimulants to treat MBD. *American Journal of Orthopsychiatry, 45*: 564, 1975.

57. McAndrew, H.: Rigidity and isolation. A study of the deaf and the blind. In Trapp, E. P., and Himelstein, P., eds.: *Readings on the Exceptional Child.* New York, ACC, 1962.

58. McInnes, J. M., and Treffry, J. A.: *Deaf-Blind Infants and Children: A Developmental Guide.* Toronto, U of Toronto Pr, 1982.

59. McKinney, J. P., and Keele, T.: Effects of increased mothering on the behavior of severely retarded boys. *American Journal of Mental Deficiency, 67*: 556, 1963.

60. Menolascino, F. J., and Coleman, R.: The Pilot Parent program: Helping handicapped children through their parents. *Child Psychiatry and Human Development, 11*: 41, 1980.

61. Menolascino, F. J., and Eaton, L. F.: Future trends in mental retardation. *Child Psychiatry and Human Development, 10*: 156, 1980.

62. Michal-Smith, H., and Morgenstern, M.: Psychodynamics of the brain-injured child and its implication in habilitation. In Michal-Smith, H., and Kastein, S.: *The Special Child.* Seattle, New School for the Special Child, Inc., 1962.

63. Mitchell, R. G.: The growth and development of children with cerebral palsy. *Cerebral Palsy Review, 22*: 3, 1961.

64. Myklebust, H. R.: Towards a new understanding of the deaf child. In Frampton, M., and Gall, E. D., eds.: *Special Education for the Exceptional.* Boston, Porter Sargent, 1955.

65. Nichtern, S.: *Helping the Retarded Child.* New York, G & D, 1974.

66. Nielsen, H. H.: (Visual-motor functioning of cerebral palsied and normal children.) *Nordisk Psykologi, 14*: 43, 1962.

67. Nissen, G.: (On the effects of stimulus flooding on mentally retarded children.) *Praxis der Kinderpsychologie und Kinderpsychiatrie, 22*: 195, 1973.

68. Norris, J., Spaulding, P. J., and Brodie, F. H.: *Blindness in Children.* Chicago,

U of Chicago Pr, 1957.
69. Orlansky, M. D.: The deaf-blind and the severely-profoundly handicapped; an emerging relationship. In Walsh,S. R., and Holzberg, R., eds.: *Understanding and Educating the Deaf-Blind/Severely and Profoundly Handicapped.* Springfield, Thomas, 1981.
70. Pfundt, T. R.: A consideration of the etiology of mental health retardation. *The Journal.* Oklahoma State Medical Association, June, 1958.
71. Pollack, D.: *Educational Audiology for the Limited Hearing Infant.* Springfield, Thomas, 1970.
72. Reger, R.: *Preschool Programming of Children with Disabilities.* Springfield, Thomas, 1974.
73. Rimland, B.: *Infantile Autism.* New York, ACC, 1963.
74. Robinson, H. B., and Robinson, N. M.: *The Mentally Retarded Child.* New York, McGraw, 1965.
75. Rosenberg, S., Spradlin, J., and Mabel, S.: Interaction among retarded children as a function of their relative language skills. *Journal of Abnormal and Social Psychology, 63*: 402, 1961.
76. Russell, G. R., and Endres, R. K.: The physician's responsibility in mental retardation. *The Journal,* Oklahoma State Medical Association, June, 1958.
77. Safford, P. L., and Arbitman, D. C.: *Developmental Intervention With Young Physically Handicapped Children.* Springfield, Thomas, 1975.
78. Schechter, M. D.: The orthopedically handicapped child: Emotional reactions. *Archives of General Psychiatry, 4*: 247, 1961.
79. Siegel, B., Sheridan, K., and Sheridan, E. P.: Group psychotherapy: Its effects on mothers who rate social performance of retardates. *American Journal of Psychiatry, 127*: 1215, 1971.
80. Solan, H. A., ed.: *The Treatment and Management of Children With Learning Disabilities.* Springfield, Thomas, 1982.
81. Stott, D. H.: Abnormal mothering as a cause of mental subnormality: II. Case studies and conclusions. *Journal of Child Psychology and Psychiatry, 3*: 133, 1962.
82. Stratton, J.: *The Blind Child in the Regular Kindergarten.* Springfield, Thomas, 1977.
83. Strauss, A. A., and Kephart, N. C.: *Psychopathology and Education of the Brain-injured Child,* Vol. 2. New York, Grune, 1955.
84. Timm, M. A., and Rule, S.: A cost-effective, parent-implemented program for young handicapped children. *Early Child Development & Care, 7*: 147, 1981.
85. Trapp, E. P., and Himelstein, P., eds.: *Readings on the Exceptional Child.* New York, ACC, 1962.
86. Verville, E.: *Behavior Problems of Children.* Philadelphia, Saunders, 1967.
87. Wall, W. D.: The psychology of the handicapped child in relation to his fam-

ily. *Journal of Education and Psychology, 14*: 4, 1956.
88. Weithorn, C. J., and Ross, R.: Stimulant drugs for hyperactivity: Some additional disturbing questions. *American Journal of Orthopsychiatry, 46*: 168, 1976.
89. Zigler, E. F.: The retarded child as a whole person. In Routh, D. K., ed.: *The Experimental Psychology of Mental Retardation*. Chicago, Aldine, 1973.

Part III.
DIAGNOSIS

Chapter 17

PAPERWORK

THE preschooler arrives at your office door with problems no one has been able to solve. If you are to do better, you'll need to collect every scrap of information you can find. You must learn about the structure, background, and characteristics of his family. You must find out what physicians, teachers, and social workers know about the child and his parents.

Paperwork yields handsome rewards.

FAMILY HISTORY FORM

Every family is a complex mix of people, jobs, values, and attitudes. It can take dozens of interview hours to unravel the tangle. An easier way to get information is to ask the parents, when they first come in, to fill out a Family History form.

They'll be glad to. Pen in hand and task set, their discomfort at being in your office fades. They can deal first with facts, only later with the dread duty of reciting failures with their child.

Scan their answers for a quick overview of the family. Then ask about obscure matters. Because you are seeking clarification of data they have noted, they will not regard your questions as intrusive or irrelevant to the youngster's problems.

171

A one-page form serves the purpose. Questionnaires which run two to four pages and include columns of symptoms to ponder and check weary the parents and cause resentment. If they must put down on paper everything they know, they reason, what's the point of coming in to talk?

A form has been filled out by the parents of Teresa, age five, referred for nightmares, temper tantrums, lying, and bedwetting (see Appendix A).

Reading the form, you know that Teresa has just turned five and has moved at least once: she was born in Kansas but now lives in Texas. Both parents work and she is not in school, so someone other than her mother and father looks after her for part of the day.

You can assume that Teresa's parents care for her because they take her to a pediatrician. They have confidence in him. He referred them to you and here they are.

If you are familiar with different neighborhoods in your city, you can guess from the family's address something about their socio-economic status and values. These may be similar to those of neighbors, whose children, in all likelihood, are playmates of your small client.

Because they are Baptists in a southern state, chances are that the family attends services regularly. It's possible that Teresa has heard dramatic preaching about the consequences of evil thoughts and actions.

You know that both parents have been married before. The stepfather, who has adopted Teresa, is 50, but his wife is only 28. The child's natural father, 30, is a traveling salesman about whom little is presently known.

Both parents work at physically demanding occupations. They may be exhausted at day's end and as a result, short-tempered. Because she is a waitress, the wife and mother probably prepares no more than one meal a day at home. Someone else does the cooking for the family.

You learn that Teresa has a full brother, two years older, who is keeping up with his age-group in school. She also has a baby half-sister, born last year two days before her own birthday. And there are two step-siblings, offspring of the adoptive father. They are adults, 24 and 22 years old, not much younger than their stepmother. One or both do not live with their father's new family.

Someone else does: a grandmother. At sixty, she is Mrs. Barnes' mother, only ten years older than her son-in-law.

Without appearing to pry, you can learn more about the facts they have recorded.

Ask if this is the second marriage for each (it may be the third or fourth). Was Mr. Barnes widowed or divorced and when?

Why and when did he decide to adopt his wife's two children? As he replies, Mrs. Barnes may add something about Teresa's natural father and the circumstances of their break-up.

If you comment on the fact that baby Lana was born two days before Teresa's birthday, you may get a report on the five-year-old's behavior then and now toward her half-sister.

The whereabouts and occupations of Mr. Barnes' son and daughter can be determined. Do either or both ever stay with the couple? Are they fully self-supporting or are they a drain on the family's income?

You can inquire how long Mrs. Barnes' mother has been living with them and why.

Keep your questions objective and brief. Accept whatever answer you get. After the three of you are better acquainted and the parents trust you to make no judgments, then you can ask how their jobs affect them and their children, how long their courtship was, how every member of their extensive family hurts or helps the others, if the natural father still is in the picture, whether they attend midweek as well as Sunday morning and evening church services, and if the grandmother has her own friends.

RELEASE FORMS

At the end of your interview with the parents, ask them if they have any objection to your getting in touch with professional people they have mentioned: a physician, teacher, or social worker. Explain that you need all the information you can get.

Rarely do parents refuse permission. They are after answers and want to help in every way they can.

You must have their written authorization to obtain information about their child from other professionals. Have one of the parents sign a release form for each person or agency you plan to write.

Ask if there's been contact with any other professional or agency not mentioned during your discussion. Get a release for hospital birth records if you're wondering about normality of development or central nervous system function.

Keep copies of the releases in your files. Send the originals, with a covering letter, to those persons from whom you are requesting information (see Appendix B).

After a release form for each individual or agency has been signed and witnessed, ask if it's all right for you, once your study is complete, to send these professional people a summary of your findings. Tell the parents that working with the youngster's physician, teacher, or speech therapist speeds results. Again, there is seldom objection.

You keep this release form (see Appendix C).

Covering Letters

To obtain more than bare-bones replies from physicians and teachers, write your covering letter in question form.

Physicians

State in the opening paragraph that you are enclosing written permission from Mrs. William Barnes to obtain information about her daughter, Teresa, born April 12, 1979.

Then ask:

Is this child above or below normal in height and weight?

Is she more sickly or accident-prone than the average child?

Does she have difficulties with vision, hearing, central nervous system function, gross or fine motor coordination?

Has she had surgery?

Does she suffer from any chronic physical handicap?

Do you have knowledge of the family situation which will aid in understanding the problems of the child?

Enclose a stamped, self-addressed envelope. Invite the doctor to write his answers on your letter, if this will save him time, or to phone. End the letter with thanks for his help.

With this approach, chances are good that he'll send at once for the child's chart, scribble answers, and put the letter in your envelope for mailing. Or he may pick up the phone and call you, wanting to get acquainted and work with you in straightening out the child's difficulties.

But if you send only the release form with a one-sentence request for information, your letter may lie for days hidden in a pile on his receptionist's desk. After you place a reminder call two weeks later, you'll get a Xeroxed copy of the child's office appointments.

Schools

Most five-year-olds you'll see are in kindergarten. They may have been referred by the school. A teacher, working with the child daily, can give an objective description of the child's behavior and progress.

The covering letter should help the teacher assess the child socially, emotionally, and developmentally. Include questions like these:

Does John get along better when he is working or playing?

Does he get along better when he is alone or doing something with classmates?

Does he respond better to praise or punishment?

How much of each is needed to establish control?

What makes him angry?

What frightens him?

What makes him unhappy?

What makes him happy?

Is emotional expression extreme, moderate, or mild?

Is emotional experession brief, temporary, or prolonged?

Is speech rare, occasional, or constant?

What is your estimate of John's capacity to learn?

What are his strengths?

His weaknesses?

What do you believe to be the reasons for his difficulties at school? (if the school referred him)

Do you have knowledge of the family situation which will aid in understanding the problems of this child?

A kindergarten teacher may work with fifty children each day. If you ask her to sit down and try to think how one youngster behaves, you'll get much less information — and that more emotionally based — than if you direct her memory with specific questions.

As you did with the physician, include a stamped, self-addressed envelope and invite the teacher to write her answers on your letter.

Some elementary schools have a guidance counselor. In this case, address your request for information to the counselor. She will confer with the teacher and get answers back to you.

Many elementary school principals require that all transfers of information about pupils funnel through their offices. Find out if you should write to the principal, not the teacher. It's a bonus when you know administrative staff and involve them in plans for the child.

Address requests for help from teachers at nursery schools or day care centers to the director. Later, when you have facts and recommendations to share, you can meet with the teacher and the counselor, principal, or director.

Agencies, Clinics, and Hospitals

In a covering letter to an agency, clinic, or hospital, you need not ask specific questions. Almost without exceptions, welfare agencies, the courts, child guidance centers, speech clinics, and hospitals will send you a copy of their detailed reports on the family and the child.

Hospital records are brief, but reports from other agencies often are three to four single-spaced pages. They describe in detail past events in the family's life, test findings, treatment or management procedures, results, and prognosis.

Appendix A

FAMILY HISTORY FORM

FAMILY HISTORY

Date _Nov. 19, 1954_ Name of Child _Teresa Barnes_

Birthdate _April 12, 1929_ Birthplace _Manhattan, Kansas_

School _Davis_ Grade ___ Referred by _Dr. Curry_

Parents or Guardians

Name _William and Alice Cheney_ Tel. (home) _631-6368_

Address _7491 Second Ave._ Tel. (bus.) _795-5750_

Austin, Texas _530-1691_

Physician _Dr. David Curry_ Religion _Baptist_

Father Name	Birthdate	Occupation	Employer	Step or adoptive?
James McCowan	11-2-33	mfg. rep.	?	
William Cheney	3-9-34	Carpenter	union constr.	Pres.

Mother Name	Birthdate	Occupation	Employer	Step or Adoptive?
Alice Barnes	7-3-55	waitress	Holiday Inn	

Both parents living? _yes_ Separated or divorced? _Divorced_

First marriage for father? _no_ For mother? _no_

Brothers and Sisters Name	Birthdate	School	Grade	Step, half, adoptive?
Jerry Barnes	10-1-57	Preview	2	
Tom Cheney	4-10-83			half
Joan Barnes	1-8-60			step
Marion Primm	2-17-62			step

Are all brothers and sisters living at home? _no_

Other persons living in the home _JoAnn Walker_

Age _60_ Relationship to child _grandmother_

177

Appendix B

PERMISSION FORM TO OBTAIN INFORMATION FROM OTHER PROFESSIONALS

Release Authorization

I hereby authorize the Family Counseling Center to obtain information concerning my child, _Teresa Barnes_ from:

schools _____

physicians _Dr. David Curry_____

agencies, clinics, hospitals _____

_____

Date _May 19, 1984_____ Signed _Alice Barnes_____

Witnessed: _Joseph R. Jones, Ph.D._ Relationship _mother_

Appendix C

PERMISSION FORM TO RELEASE INFORMATION TO OTHER PROFESSIONALS

<u>Permission To Release Information</u>

I hereby authorize the Family Counseling Center to release
information about my child, ___*Teresa Barnes*___,
(name)
to physicians, school personnel, or other professional
persons who, in the judgment of the Family Counseling Center
staff, can be of assistance to the child. I do not wish
information released to _____.

Date *May 19, 1984*_____ Signed: *Alice Barnes*_____

Witnessed: *Joseph R. Jones, Ph.D.* Relationship: *mother*

Chapter 18

INTERVIEWING THE PARENTS

PARENTS are your colleagues, your prime information source. They share with the child hundreds of thousands of joyous, irritating, boring, proud, and agonizing experiences. They know both the past and the present. Much of the past they forget; much of the present they ignore. Your job is to dredge from their memories those events which have led to their seeking help now.

Count on at least 90 minutes for the interview. You need a vast array of facts to make your diagnosis accurate.

THE PARENTS

Guilt

Parents enter the psychologist's office ashamed and angry.

The mother announces, "Our folks say we're too hard on Scott."

The father says, "We must be doing something wrong."

The mother confesses to yelling and spanking hard. She wards off your disapproval with, "I know I shouldn't."

Respect their honesty. Few among us admit error and it is never easy. Show no shock. Assign no blame. Treat them as honorable, intelligent, baffled people who need information.

Child-rearing consumes hundreds of hours, requires management of incident after incident of temper and tears, and demands endless sacrifices of time, freedom, and money. Admire parents for what they try to do rather than condemn them for lapses in judgment or control. With your diagnosis, conclusions, and guidance, they will do better.[4]

Address them as "Mr. Thompson" and "Mrs. Thompson," not with an overly-familiar, undignified "Bill" and "Shirley," or worse — an impersonal, humiliating "Dad" and "Mother." Treat them as serious, competent adults and they will act that way.

Fathers Versus Mothers

Often parents disagree about what is wrong and what to do. Fathers believe mothers are too tender; mothers believe fathers are too harsh. The child's problems divide them. A side benefit of your aid is closing the gap in their marriage.

A man is devastated by imperfection in his child. If his four-year-old Scott cannot speak clearly, dress and feed himself, or follow directions, the father denies the youngster's clearly laggard progress by assuring himself and everyone else, "He's just a late bloomer."

If his five-year-old Cindy, bullying and dictating, screams her way through every day, he insists, "She'll grow out of it."

When a nursery school teacher or pediatrician urges testing and special training for the atypical youngster, the father bristles.

"No one tells me how to bring up my child!" he roars.

Then he removes the youngster from school or finds another doctor.

Expect a father to be leary of psychologists, to have come under duress, and to talk sparingly during the interview. Many men arrange to be absent.

It will be the mother who calls for an appointment. She explains that her husband cannot take off work to come with her. (He has shouted that he will NOT go to some shrink to discuss his son.)

Tell her that it is vital for her husband to be there. Each parent sees the child differently; each has unique experiences with him. The father's information and ideas are required for a complete, accurate picture. Also, a secondhand report from his wife on what the psychologist does or says is unreliable and narrow. The father himself must hear and question what is said. Nor should the father be left out of plans for helping his child. Both parents are needed to set matters straight.

If, at the last minute, you are told that a business trip or boss's demand prevents the father from keeping the appointment, make another one. Or set a time for him to come alone.

Variety in Parents

There are different sorts of parents: twenty-year-olds and forty-year-olds, Ph.D.'s and school drop-outs, welfare recipients and the moneyed. They work as lawyers, teachers, carpenters, policemen, custodians, journalists. Age, background, and occupation mold their thoughts and actions.[18]

But parents seeking help for a preschool child have a common quality: they're trying hard to do their best. A mother and father want their child to behave well, to learn easily, to be kind and cheerful. But parents vary in their ability to guide sons and daughters toward these wispy, elusive goals.

Some read widely. Parents of preschoolers buy most of the child-care books and from them they learn how to encourage speech, handle temper tantrums, and cope with jealousy. But they forget what they read, or they lack the stamina and determination to persist with planned attack on a problem.

Others who try to learn are flustered by the books' disagreements. Some experts advise showing the child who's boss; others insist on unflagging tolerance; a few recommend actions which strike parents as unnatural: ignore a screaming, kicking child; fix a bottle for a jealous five-year-old.

Some parents never read and flounder through the days in desperate hopelessness.

Reassure them. Boost their knowledge; bolster their confidence. Tell them that problems with children are the rule, not the exception.[16] During each of his growing-up years, every child is garnished with four or five reversible sins. Remind them of earlier child-rearing troubles which have disappeared with time and attention.

A mother and father who expect rocks and ruts in the road do not collapse helplessly. If you teach them how problems are born and why they remain glued to their lives, what motivates children of different ages, and how re-training works, they can learn to master any difficulty.

INTERVIEW MECHANICS

Note-taking

Write as you listen. As you pick up your pen, explain to the parents that you must write what they tell you: your memory will not serve. They will not object.

Your scribbling while they talk gives them time to remember and your sometimes averted glance gives them courage to volunteer facts and feelings they might otherwise hide. Also, a written record alerts you to omissions in the story.

Getting the Facts

Start easily and keep going the same way. Looking at both parents, ask them to tell you what troubles them about Scott and Cindy.

Nearly always the mother, not the father, will begin. As she names each problem, delve deeper by asking how often it occurs (three or a dozen times daily, weekly, or monthly), how long it has been going on (six months, two years, always), when it happens (when given an order, while playing with sister, at bedtime), and what they do about it.

"We've tried everything," the mother will say, "spanking, ignoring, sending him to his room, taking away TV, grounding. Nothing works."

Remember that they are talking to you because nothing has worked, so make no comment on their techniques or inconsistencies. Later, when you have facts to back your recommendations, you can persuade them to better methods.

As the mother's version ends, follow up by questioning the father. Is he worried about this same behavior? Does he have additional information?

Then probe for more problems, switching from one parent to the other. Most mothers and fathers are relieved to talk over their distress with a knowledgeable outsider who, they believe, can tell them what to do. As they mention facts and hint at causes, follow their leads.

Following Leads

Her four-year-old son stutters, a mother reports, and adds, "It's worse when he's not feeling well."

Ask how often the boy is sick and what diseases he has had. Veer into the pregnancy and delivery; then find out the ages at which he walked, talked, and was toilet-trained.

A father says that his two-year-old daughter won't eat and, at the table, "She seems so tired."

Find out when the child goes to bed and how soundly she sleeps, how long her nap lasts, whether she plays outside daily, and how many hours she watches television.

A mother complains that her five-year-old daughter pushes and hits a two-year-old brother who tries to join in when she plays with her dolls.

Discover how much time the children spend together and if the older is forced to play with the younger. Does each play alone with his own friends? How do the adults react when their daughter bothers them while they are talking or reading?

His three-year-old son is messy at meals and the father is disgusted.

Inquire about other problems at the table. Does the child dawdle or gulp his food? Is he finicky? What happens if he dislikes what he is served? What and how often does he eat between meals and who decides that?

A mother announces that her three-year-old daughter cries when she has trouble with playmates.

Ask the age and sex of the other children and how often, how long, where, and what they play. Does the little girl cry over other kinds of trouble? Does she attack or retreat? Does she sometimes handle problems in ways other than crying?

Whenever he talks on the phone, a father reports, his four-year-old son pesters him with questions.

Find out if the child interrupts whenever the father is busy, how much time the two spend alone with each other, what they do, and who suggests that they get together.

A mother is unhappy because her two-year-old son erupts with, "No!" whenever she wants him to come to lunch, sit on the potty, or put on his sweater.

"It's automatic, as though he's decided ahead of time to make me mad."

Discover whether he refuses if his father or big sister delivers the order and what he does without resisting.

Her five-year-old daughter insists on "helping" when dinner guests are coming, a mother protests, but won't set the table, fetch in the milk, or make her bed when asked to do so.

Learn what daily chores are expected of the child, how well they are done, and what comments the parents make at the time. Does the little girl earn money by working? What does she do with it? Which jobs does she like and dislike?

Following leads, you can get most of the facts you need. When neither parent can think of anything more to say, compliment them on the completeness of their information, check your notes against your list of required data, and add that you have only a few more questions to ask.

REQUIRED INFORMATION

Pregnancy and Birth

Difficulties during the pregnancy, a lengthy or precipitous birth, and abnormal birth weight and length give clues about possible physical or neurological damage which affects the child's behavior or development. The premature child may take months, even years, to catch up, even though he arrived only four to six weeks ahead of schedule.[12]

Early Adjustment

If their infant nursed poorly, slept little, and cried constantly after they brought him home from the hospital, the mother and father led a hard life. Discover whether they picked him up each time he cried during the first months. If they sometimes let him cry, was it for long or short periods, and why? Was he held for hours daily?

A child rescued the instant he whimpers never learns to wait for food or comfort. Because he need not entertain himself when attention is postponed, he fails to observe lights, sounds, and objects. If he is held constantly, he becomes irritable and jumpy. He learns neither independence nor self-control.

Initial feelings of antagonism, anxiety, or helplessness spawned during these early months may linger, directing the parents' management of the child for years.

But if the mother and father overcame disturbing early adjustment problems, they are proud of themselves and their baby and continue to handle problems with confidence.[1]

Development

Ask when the child walked, talked, and was toilet trained to learn whether development was normal, slow, or advanced. Inquire about training methods, which can range from casual to overpowering. Sometimes a mother spends hours in the bathroom every day for a year, reading and singing to her child to entice him to remain on the potty.[15]

If the child arrives at these major milestones — getting about on his own two feet, translating his thoughts into words, civilizing his evacuation of wastes — easily and quickly, his parents are delighted. But if he attains them only after a huge investment of time and effort by everyone, parents and child are discouraged about themselves and unhappy with one another.

Health

Check on illnesses the child has had. Is he sick often or rarely and is recovery speedy or slow? When do the parents call the doctor and what do they think of his help? Is the sick child put to bed or does he run about as usual?

The frequently ill youngster depends on adult service and direction. He is slow to learn to dress himself and do chores. He shows little initiative and, isolated from playmates, he falls behind in social know-how. If his parents are indifferent to illness and he gets poor care, he recovers slowly and remains tired and cross.

Does the child have many accidents? If so, probably he experiments with danger: he climbs on roofs, plays in traffic, and turns on his father's power equipment. Find out if he risks injury because he is unsupervised or because he is uncontrolled, either by the adults or himself.

Repeated accidents suggest impulsiveness, a failure to anticipate danger and to learn self-discipline. Such heedlessness may be caused by central nervous system damage, by careless and sporadic teaching and supervision by parents, or by anxiety based on the youngster's fear of either severe punishment or the loss of his parents.

Mothers and fathers can judge coordination. If their child is clumsy, he regularly spills food, knocks over his milk glass, walks into doors, trips over his own feet, and loses his grip while swinging and sliding. When such mishaps are common, assume that the youngster lives with trouble. Every accident reaps a scolding and the preschooler believes he is stupid.

But if he is well coordinated — managing crayons skillfully, throwing a ball accurately, running smoothly, climbing surely, handling buttons and zippers easily, and pouring orange juice without a splash — he avoids ridicule, earns praise, and is pleased with himself.

Sleep

Inquire how much the child sleeps and what the bedtime routine is. Does he nap or, if he is three or older, rest in the afternoon? Are the parents firm or lax about nap and bedtimes? Where does the child sleep and does he share a room or bed with siblings or adults?

Problems with sleep can lead to daily fights between parent and child or to the youngster's calling the tune about where and when he sleeps. Nightly bedding down with parents or a grandparent postpones independence. Insufficient, erratic sleep heats up a child's temper and interferes everyday with learning, playing, and eating.

A preschooler who rests after lunch and goes to bed early every night, sleeping alone, gets along better with family and friends because he is rested and because there is order in his life. He also learns to be self-sufficient, entertaining himself during rest time and falling asleep by himself at night.

Eating

Learn how often and what the child eats. Does he put away huge amounts or pick at his food? Do parents prod him to eat? Does he snack between meals, on what, and when? Does he refuse food at mealtime, then demand it once the dishes are cleared away? Does he want special food prepared just for himself? Does he raid the refrigerator and what does he take? Where does he eat — at the table with his family, in the living room in front of the TV, in his room, in the kitchen while passing through? Are meals on time and must he be there? Is breakfast early and dinner late because both parents work?

The child who eats at odd hours or exists on potato chips and pop is quick to anger and often depressed. It is hard for him to concentrate, remember, or finish what he starts. If he feeds himself when and how he chooses and seldom sits down with his family, he is lonely and anxious. He tries bizarre or disruptive behavior to win attention from neglectful parents.

The finicky child who gives orders about what and when he will eat rules his mother and father. Their obedience frightens him, so he defies them often, trying to force them to take charge of him.[13]

The youngster who is pushed to eat more than he needs gets fat. Unable to keep up with playmates, he is taunted and left behind. Unhappy with himself, he turns aggressive.

The preschooler who gets nutritious meals and snacks at regular times functions well. If little notice is given to complaints or to what he leaves on his plate, he never uses food to control adults. Eating with his parents and siblings, he is reminded daily that he belongs to a family. Mealtime, even though it is studded with sibling irritations and lessons on manners, also lets him in on adult discussions of fascinating subjects he otherwise would miss.

Independence

Ask if the one-year-old feeds himself and if the three-year-old dresses himself and takes care of his toilet needs. Parents often reply that the child *can*, but usually doesn't, a sign that they take over out of impatience with his awkwardness or slowness.

When the child cannot open a door, put on a boot, get a toy from a shelf, or persuade a playmate to stop calling names, does he run for help or work things out himself? Does he want his mother and father to wait on him? How persistent is he in trying again after he fails to put on his socks or climb a tree?

The preschooler whose parents do for him what he can do for himself is sure that he is still a baby who can manage nothing alone. If adults promptly lend a hand when he cannot reach a glass or button his coat, he soon stops trying to do anything. He has instant servants; he also has no skills and is sure that he is useless.[2]

The proud, confident child is allowed to practice feeding and dressing himself and try whatever he believes he can do. The drive to independence is inborn. Squelching it makes everyone miserable, sometimes for a lifetime.[7]

Responsibility

Question the parents about the child's ability to work. What are his daily chores? Is he able and willing to run errands or fetch objects? How often is he asked to help? Does he earn money by working and what happens to the money?

A preschooler wants to join his mother and father in their work in the house and yard. Copying them makes him feel grown-up.

But, trying for independence, he dislikes orders. He objects when told he *must* help. If he succeeds in escaping work, he tries to evade all adult direction, both at home and at school. When adults sometimes insist that he do chores and other times give up because he resists, the child often dodges work by deception: he insists that he has done the dusting or he promises he'll do it right away. He hasn't and he doesn't.

If the young child is held to regular chores and earns money which he spends both on himself and others, he learns to be responsible and generous. Knowing he can handle a variety of daily tasks, he feels good about himself.

Play

Discover whether the child plays most of the time alone, with his parents, his siblings, or other children. What age and sex are his playmates? What do they play, how long, and how often? What toys does the child have and which ones does he like best? Is he original or imitative in play? How long does he play outdoors every day? How much television does he watch and when does he watch it?

The preschooler who plays alone day after day often is content and imaginative, but he misses out on normal social growth. Later, at school, he differs from his classmates and cannot mingle easily with them.

If his constant companions are older or younger than he or of the opposite sex, he cannot get along well with children his own age and sex.[7] If he has too many playmates or plays too long, he is worn out from competing with peers and striving to impress them. Also, when no one can play, he is uneasy and lost, incapable of entertaining himself.

Parents complain that their youngster does not play with his toys. Instead, he throws and scatters them and they fear he has a short attention span. A preschooler mishandles toys when there are too many. With no more than six available at a given time, he plays steadily with each.[15]

The small child who rarely is sent or taken outside to play sleeps and eats poorly. Tired and bored, he shows little initiative.[13]

Television-watching promotes lethargy: the overdosed youngster rarely experiments, explores, or thinks. Sitting still for hours daily, with eyes, ears, and emotions bombarded, the preschooler's health is damaged. And television can frighten, fostering nightmares, uneasy sleep, and jumpiness.[17]

Small children who enjoy and learn from playing are those who play outside for several hours daily, spend an hour three times weekly with one or two friends their own age and sex, and seldom or never watch television.

Relationships with Others

Friends

Find out if the preschooler is aggressive or shy with playmates, if he's a leader or a follower. Is he jealous when another child plays with a friend of his? Is he deserted by playmates and why? Does he share ideas and equipment, obey game rules, and avoid fights? Does he like to be with other children?

Learning how to get along with people outside the family starts early and is a lifetime project. The youngster's first contacts with others strike him as either pleasant or scary. They steer him toward liking and cooperating with outsiders or disliking and fearing them. Age and experience make him braver.

Social give-and-take is easier or harder depending on how he feels about himself. If he is pleased with what he knows and can do, he welcomes the chance to try himself with others and to learn from them. If he is unsure and critical of himself, he dreads the challenges and rebuffs of peers. What he thinks of himself faithfully mirrors what his parents think of him.

Siblings

Find out who is the preschooler's favorite sibling and why, who the least-liked and why. Does he pester older brothers and sisters or bully younger ones? Does he get automatic aid from parents when he complains of siblings' treatment? Or is he the one scolded and held responsible for trouble?

When you learn how parents handle problems between offspring, you discover much about the family atmosphere.[10]

Brothers and sisters do fight. Each is useful to the other because of it. If parents don't interfere, the children make up quickly. The preschooler with siblings is better able to cope with people and problems than is the child who never endures the irritations and putdowns dumped on him by brothers and sisters.

Father

Learn how much care the father gives the preschooler. Does he teach the child how to manage zippers, use a straw, climb a fence, brush his teeth? How much time do they share? Does the father read bedtime stories, let the youngster help with weeding, and take him to the hardware store? Is it the father or child who first suggests that they get together? What do they think of each other and what does each demand of the other?

The preschooler who spends little or no time with his father is robbed of his chance to discover how a man differs in behavior and thinking from a woman. Also, with no father to serve as a model, he may shy away from the difficult or disagreeable, try hard to please everyone, and habitually avoid other children, men, and male activities.

A father who spends little time with his child feels strange around him. Not knowing what to say or do, he finds excuses to stay away from him. Some men resent a first-born youngster for destroying the private and exclusive marital bond. A father unwilling to share his wife with his child gets back at him by ridiculing, punishing, and shoving him away when he tries for affection or companionship. Treated this way by a parent he counts on for closeness, the son or daughter feels betrayed and worthless.

If a father shares the care of his young child, teaches him skills, and plays and works with him, the youngster grows in sureness, independence, and pride. He values his father's approval more than his mother's because it is more difficult to win.[11]

Mother

Inquire how much time alone the mother and child spend together. Are these solely care-taking hours, or do the two also play and work together? Which of them initiates contacts? What do they think of each other and what demands do they make on each other?

Do the parents go out together without the child? Is the mother careless about choosing an adequate sitter? Or does she refuse ever to hire a sitter? Does she leave the child alone to look after himself?

After they have fed and bathed the child and provided him with clean sheets and clothes, some mothers call it quits. Their contacts with him are all business and they never take time to discover what the youngster is really like and what he can do.

Or, in contrast, a mother becomes her preschooler's constant companion. She neglects her husband, other children, friends, and her own need for diversion and privacy. Mother and child, together for hours every day, become irritated and dictatorial with each other.

A few mothers never give the youngster the chance to adapt to a substitute caretaker. He is taken along shopping, to movies, to parties, and on visits. Or, the chosen sitter is flighty and unreliable, an adult or teenager who ignores his charge, abuses him, or risks his safety. Sometimes a small boy or girl is left alone at home. Fires and accidents kill these neglected children every year.

A child respects his mother if she sees to his physical needs and also plays and works with him an hour or two each day. If she saves time for the other members of her family, for friends and activities away from home, and for herself, he welcomes the chance to be with her and she enjoys being with him.

Emotion

Fear

Ask what the youngster is afraid of and what the parents do about it.

If they laugh at his fears or force him to do what he dreads, he turns away from them. His uncertainty builds and soon he is afraid of every new person, place, or activity.

But if his mother and father reassure him, encourage him gradually to approach or do what frightens him, and shield him from unnecessary fears (television, horror stories, gloom and pessimism), he will master his worries as best he can for his age.[8]

Anger

Find out what makes the child angry and how often he gets that way. Does he throw full-blown tantrums — screaming, kicking, and holding his breath? How do the parents handle tantrums?

Nearly every child becomes angry over what someone says, forces him to do, or refuses to let him do. The preschooler who never shows temper either is developing slowly or is dedicated to avoiding trouble.

Parents who damp their child's anger by never crossing him teach him to rule with temper.

Those who send their furious youngster off to be alone until he feels better and never let tantrums dictate their decisions direct him toward self-control.[10]

Jealousy

Is the preschooler jealous of a sibling? How does he show it? How do parents feel about jealousy and what do they do?

If parents are over-sympathetic and permit the jealous child to harm either a younger or older rival, they teach him that hurt feelings justify any behavior. He learns to resent and attack anyone who displeases him.

Extra attention and praise from parents root out jealousy.[13]

Crying and Whining

Check on how often the child cries and what he cries about. Is crying — or whining if he is older — his usual response to problems? Does crying make things better for him?

Scolding or pitying the weeping youngster heightens and prolongs his misery.

Parents help the young child bear his burdens stoically if they never mention his tears or petulant tone but merely ask what is troubling him and what he plans to do about it.[15]

Affection

Discover whether the child seeks hugs and kisses from his parents. Does he show affection toward people outside the family? With whom is he most affectionate? Least? Is he generous? Sympathetic?

The child who continually kisses his mother or asks if she loves him believes that he is unloved, usually because he is often and severely criticized.

Or, the preschooler may rebuff anyone who tries to touch him. His behavior devastates his mother and father, who often react with anger and avoidance.[1] A child's rejection of parents is abnormal and suggests that he is the victim of central nervous system damage, physical abuse, or neglect.

Most preschoolers like to cuddle and want a hug and kiss when they are injured or disappointed. They often are generous and they symnpathize with a parent who is distraught, ill, or sad.[15]

Learning Ability

Question the parents about what the child can do well. How clearly and often does he speak? How accurately does he understand what people say to him? Does he listen quietly to stories and records? Can he cut with scissors and use paste correctly? Does he work jigsaw puzzles? How good is his memory, his drawing ability, his imagination?

A three-year-old who seldom speaks, does not remember where his coat is hung, cannot manage the kindergarten tools of scissors, paste, and crayons, and is uninterested in stories and unable to concentrate on handwork or puzzles is not learning normally.

Some parents neglect their preschooler's intellectual growth. They never read to him or work puzzles, sing, or create toys with him. Brushing off his questions, they speak only to give orders. They never take him to the zoo or airport. He has no scissors or crayons with which to practice cutting and drawing.

When he starts kindergarten, everything he is asked to do is new to him. Sure that he will fail, he refuses to try and soon he is far behind his classmates.

Another mother and father work too hard at stretching their youngster's intelligence. They coach him in the alphabet, drill him in counting, require him to copy letters, and teach him poems to recite for guests. Pushing parents dull a child's eagerness for knowledge. Learning, for him, is drudgery.

The child whose parents support his interests, talk with him and answer questions, read to him, play games, give him varied toys, and take him to see whatever the community offers can think, remember, question, explore, and learn.[7]

Family Events

Activities

Ask what the family does together and how often they share work and play. Does everyone take a turn at choosing activities, including the preschooler? Does he like family excursions and games?

In some homes everyone trots out a different door. At no time is everyone together doing chores, having fun, or talking over mutual problems. If he can, the preschooler in such a family attaches himself to one person. If he cannot, he grows up lonely and unnoticed, certain that no one cares what happens to him.

The small child who plants a garden, watches a parade, plays ball, and decorates the Christmas tree with his family knows that being one of this busy bunch is both joy and comfort.

Rules

Check on rules. Parents dislike the term, but if the preschooler must come to lunch at noon, be in bed at seven, stay out of the street, and eat nothing within an hour of mealtime, he is subject to rules.

A mother and father who can think of no family rules probably run their home haphazardly. They give little thought to what is best for the child.

Rules which guard the health and protect the rights of the family's members relieve and strengthen the youngster.

Tragedies and Crises

Discover if there has been a death in the family within the child's memory, if a parent or siblng has been hospitalized with serious illness, if there has been a fire or an auto accident.

Such tragedies and crises disturb the preschooler. Fears crop up which last for many months.

The youngster's anxiety is more acute if his parents are shaken by these troubles for a long period of time. If they show steadiness and optimism, his own worries lessen.

The Child's Day

Learn what happens to the child from the moment he gets up until he falls asleep at night. Is a schedule followed? With whom does he spend his time? What play and work activities fill his day?

The preschooler who gets up when he chooses and wanders through an unpredictable day is more easily defeated and disturbed, more tired and angry than the youngster held to a schedule.

When the small child lives within a stable time framework of daily events, his failures and fight upset him less.

Other Caretakers

Does the child go to nursery school or a day care center? How often and for how long? What happens there? Does a sitter look after him during the week? At her home or his? With other children or alone? Is the sitter rigid, helpful, punishing, conciliatory, careless?

Small children have been seriously harmed by being placed in the care of adults who are ineffective, emotionally disturbed, or who dislike boys and girls. A preschooler resents being left in the care of other adults. He thinks his parents are tired of him; he worries that his mother and father will vanish forever; he is distressed by strange food and new rules for behavior. In a crowd of children he is homesick and lonely.

But sometimes working parents are too busy and tired to notice their child's changing needs and to give adequate training and protection. Then a cheerful, friendly, firm substitute caretaker helps the youngster grow up well.

Discipline

Because parents are embarrassed by their emotional storms over disobedience, the touchy subject of discipline should be left till last.

Find out for what misbehavior they punish, what they do, and whether it helps. Does the child behave better or worse than other children his age? Do they reward obedience? How? Do they agree on discipline?

A preschooler devotes much of his life to learning what is expected of him. He wants to please. But memory fails, instructions and warnings never cease, and orders from his father, his mother, his big brother, the neighbors, his teacher, and his sitter clash. Besides, he has his pride to consider.

The young child who is scolded and spanked continually becomes anxious. Always expecting punishment, he is jumpy because he never knows when it will come. He is afraid he's so bad that his parents will get rid of him. Often unsure about what he is supposed to do, he experiments: he jumps on the couch or tramps through the flower bed to find out if the adults really mean that he must *never* do those things.

Vigilant parents physically retrain a small child from doing what harms him: dashing into the street, grabbing the hot pan off the stove, poking his finger into a socket. When he runs off, they catch him, turn him around, and point him in the right direction. If he yanks the cat's tail, they show him how to stroke the pet. When he tears a book's pages, they have him practice turning them slowly.

Taught in these ways, the child becomes neither anxious nor defiant. Gradually, he learns what is expected of him and he does it.

His Assets

Listing all that is wrong with their child, baring home secrets, admitting punishment or neglect, the parents are wounded by the end of the interview. That's the time to ask what the child's best qualities are. As they shift to happier ideas, they re-discover that their little one is a person of some talent and charm.

A few mothers and fathers, down on the child and distressed by parenthood, can think of nothing good to say about their youngster. But they'll remember your question. When they reach home, they'll notice that their preschooler is glad to see them, he eats his dinner quickly, he points out that tomatoes are red and lettuce is green, and he lets his little brother play with his truck. This clear evidence of sound character and good intelligence cheers them. He is not a total nothing, so they are not miserable failures.

Reviewing the child's past and present life with you reminds them of the hundreds of happenings in their family history. No longer will they focus solely and forlornly on the problems which brought them to you. They will begin to consider causes and effects, to hope that they can rid themselves of worry and conflict. Already, they feel better.

REFERENCES

1. Bell, R. Q., and Harper, L. V.: *Child Effects on Adults*. Lincoln, U of Nebr Pr, 1980.
2. Cameron, J. R.: Parental treatment, children's temperament, and the risk of childhood behavioral problems: I. Relationships between parental characteristics and changes in children's temperament over time. In Chess, S., and Thomas, A., eds.: *Annual Progress in Child Psychiatry and Child Development*. New York, Brunner-Mazel, 1978.
3. Church, J.: *Understanding Your Child from Birth to Three*. New York, Random, 1973.
4. Donofrio, A. F.: Parent education vs. child psychotherapy. *Psychology in the Schools, 13*: 176, 1976.
5. Gorden, R. L.: *Interviewing*. Homewood, Dorsey, 1980.
6. Hartup, W. W., ed.: *The Young Child*. Reviews of Research, Vol. 2. Washington, D. C., National Association for the Education of Young Children, 1972.
7. Hurlock, E. B.: *Child Development*, 5th ed. New York, McGraw-Hill, 1972.
8. Jersild, A. T.: *Child Psychology*, 7th ed. Englewood Cliffs, P-H, 1975.
9. Kagan, J., and Moss, H.: *Birth to Maturity*. New York, Wiley, 1962.
10. Kanner, L.: *Child Psychiatry*, 4th ed. Springfield, Thomas, 1972.
11. Lamb, M. R., ed.: *The Role of the Father in Child Development*, 2nd ed. New York, Wiley, 1982.
12. Osofsky, J. D., ed.: *Handbook of Infant Development*. New York, Wiley, 1979.
13. Spock, B.: *Baby and Child Care*. New York, Dutton, 1976.
14. Thompson, G. G.: *Child Psychology*, 2nd ed. Cambridge, HM, 1962.
15. Verville, E.: *Behavior Problems of Children*. Philadelphia, Saunders, 1967.
16. Welding, G.: (The prevalence of behavior problems in preschool children.) *Zeitschrift für Kinder- und Jugendpsychiatrie, 5*: 299, 1977.
17. Winn, M.: *The Plug-In Drug*. New York, Viking, 1977.
18. Zegiob, L. E., and Forehand, R.: Maternal interactive behavior as a function of race, socioeconomic status, and sex of the child. *Child Development, 46*: 564, 1975.

Chapter 19

EXAMINATION OF THE CHILD

CHILDREN, like parents, come in many sizes, shapes, and characters. Some will scream, run, hit, and throw things, convincing you in ten seconds that you've chosen the wrong field. Others will charm you with their determination to win you to lifelong friendship.

With most, it's you who must charm. If you're cheerful, confident, courteous, and handy with compliments, youngsters will chatter and grin with friends over the exciting time they spent with you.

You need not always examine the child. Calm parents who ask what to do about thumbsucking, jealousy, dawdling at meals, or resistance to bedtime want information. There's no reason to turn an average preschooler inside out to learn why he dislikes his younger brother or hates to go to bed.

Explain to the mother and father what is happening. Tell them what to do. In two weeks, see them again or have them call to let you know if there's improvement. If they've followed your directions, there will be.

REASONS FOR EXAMINATION

If the child is to be adopted or is the principal in custody suit, if his development lags or he has multiple problems, examination provides answers to vital questions.

200

Adoption

An infant scheduled for adoption needs evaluation. You can test him for development and record the daily behavior his foster mother describes. Your summary gives the adoption agency facts to pass on to prospective parents.

Custody

In these troubled times of incessant divorce, children are the victims of custody suits. You may be asked to check a youngster and report to the judge your opinion about which parental home offers him the best chance for using his talents and steadying his emotions. To make this judgment, you must study the child and his mother and father thoroughly.

Development

A child also must be evaluated if he is not developing normally. Perhaps he is four years old, but he does not speak, he is not trained, and he does not feed or dress himself.

You must use all the tests, observation, and information from others you can get to determine if he is retarded, emotionally disturbed, neglected, mismanaged, or suffering from physical damage. Only when you know what is wrong can you decide what to do.

Multiple Problems

Examination of the child also is needed if there are multiple, long-lasting problems. If this is the case, the parents may be deeply discouraged with themselves and their preschooler. They dislike him because he makes them feel inadequate; they clash over handling him; family life has been smashed.

You cannot help distraught, angry parents in one interview. They will dismiss your sound recommendations as instant solutions unsuited to their complex situation. Before they will listen, you must convince them that you know their child better than anyone else ever has, that you understand why he acts as he does, and that you can guide them in changing his behavior.

After they have reviewed for you all they can recall about their preschooler and you have observed and tested him, they will accept you as an expert armed with knowledge about *their* son or daughter. Then they will try your suggestions, report in regularly for more, and even join a class in child management.

PLANNING THE EXAMINATION

The Child

For a preschool child, an hour's examination is long enough. He will tire after that, lose interest, and not do his best. Plan for the hour to include the tests and observations you consider important. If there are too many, schedule the youngster for a return visit.

A second visit has its advantages. This time he knows you, the testing room, and what is expected of him. He'll do better, talk more, and play naturally.

Sometimes a child won't come near you. After a lengthy struggle for cooperation, you dub him untestable and give up. Don't. Learning what a difficult child is capable of doing makes all the difference in how he is managed and what plans are made for his education.

If you cannot test a youngster because he has backed into a corner and is trying to kick you, retreat. Coax him out by putting a truck or doll in the middle of the floor. If you keep your distance, he may emerge from hiding to play with the toy.

Later, when he's calmer, try rolling a ball to him. When he rolls it back, you've made contact.

Chances are he'll need to come two or three times just to play and get acquainted before you can entice him to the testing table. Then he may or may not answer questions and follow your directions. Stay with it. He needs your help.

Parent Assistance

Usually the parent is not involved in the actual examination, but sometimes he needs to be. If he can provide information and coax performance, the results are more comprehensive and accurate.

Information

A mother can describe actions which the examiner cannot observe himself. Does the youngster feed himself, run errands, pull off his socks, climb stairs? She knows.

A quick way to gauge the child's behavioral development is to review with the parents the items of the *Vineland Adaptive Behavior Scales,* revised in 1984. The test consists of a series of questions about activities and abilities from birth to adulthood. The answers set the child's age level in communication, daily living skills, socialization, and motor skills. Maladaptive behavior is indicated.

But you'll need that grain of salt. Song and Jones[13] studied the maturation of 150 children between the ages of two weeks and thirty-six months. On the Vineland Scale, their social age consistently was higher than their chronological age, especially for the second year of life. This suggests that parents tend to report youngsters' feats which occur rarely, or even just once. The scale is meant to chart consistent, regular behavior.

To avoid this problem, Fadely and Hosler[4] devised a check-list of behavior which parents can use at home. Watching their preschooler in action, adults with slippery memories will neither exaggerate nor guess. The *Fadely-Hosler System Survey* measures general health and the physical, social, pesonality, cognitive, and language development of two- to six-year-olds.

Motivation

The presence of the parent of the very young child (infancy to two years) can make the difference between accurate assessment of the youngster's abilities and disaster.

A baby or toddler left with a stranger may be overwhelmed by fear and loneliness. He wants his mother. He distrusts the unknown, grinning, huge person who offers toys and gives orders. He shoves away the outstretched hand. He sticks his thumb in his mouth. He cries.

Eighteen-month-old Maria, shy and resistive, emerged from an intelligence test session with a score which branded her borderline retarded. Twenty years later she was elected to Phi Beta Kappa.

Not only is the presence of the parent comforting to a small child, the adult's help in wheedling a response often is needed. You point to a line-up of small objects in front of the child and say, "Give me the doggy." The youngster leans back in his chair and stares at you.

His mother says, "Kevin, give me the doggy."

Kevin promptly and proudly hands it over. You've discovered that he knows a dog from a cat, a spoon, and a chair.

If, "Please," and, "You know that," from a mother tell you what an infant or toddler can or cannot do, that's what matters. Don't worry about a parent's deviation from instructions in a test manual.

STUDY OF THE CHILD

Observation

You will learn much about a preschooler from reports of parents and from his performance on test items. You'll discover more by observing him.

With the Parent

In a psychologist's office both parent and child are under stress. The way they act toward one another may not be typical.

Nevertheless, if the older preschooler puts up a tremendous fuss about leaving his mother and going to the testing room with you, you may suspect that the tie between adult and child is knottier than is good for either of them.

If a mother buttons the coat of her five-year-old and helps him with his mittens, it's likely that she always coddles and babies him. If a father placates his rebelling daughter by promising her a banana split when the testing is over, that suggests the little girl queens it over the adults.

Perhaps the child begins to cry. The mother turns her back; the father threatens punishment. Coldness and rejection may be family hallmarks.

Often, when you're talking to the child, he says little or nothing in reply. If his father continually urges him to answer or his mother coaches him with questions and hints, it's probable that neither thinks much of their youngster's competence.

But if the boy or girl leaves his parent without a backward glance and not only answers questions put by the examiner but volunteers exciting information (his father cut himself shaving this morning and said, "Christ!"), it's likely that he's an independent, friendly youngster at ease with himself and the world.

And if the parent talks to his son or daughter in a calm tone, makes requests which help him behave as he needs to in these new surroundings, listens to what he says and answers his questions, and treats him with the courtesy he would show an adult, chances are that the mother or father thinks of his preschooler as an intersting, capable person. The adult has no need to use him as a possession, an enemy, or a helpless dependent.

With the Psychologist

Most infants and toddlers have had little experience with strangers. Wary and anxious, they hold back. The mouth puckers. The tears flow.

Children three and older are more sociable. They're proud they can talk so well; they're eager to try what's new; they want to be friends. An older preschooler who is afraid, resistive, belligerent, or manipulative is advertising his uncertainty, his habit of playing tricks, or his conviction that he's "bad."

Watching him refuse tests, grab materials, or try to run the show, you'll know whether temporary upset or longstanding modes of behavior are responsible for his actions.

Four-year-old Debbie, returning to the testing room after a drink of water, suddenly flung herself into a chair, curled herself into a ball, and screamed: "Don't hit me! Don't hit me!"

The examiner plucked her from the chair and sat her on her lap, facing the desk. Debbie continued to scream, punctuating the racket by slamming the desk drawer open and shut. It was behavior she routinely used to intimidate adults.

Five-year-old Eric revealed his tension by talking non-stop to the examiner. Bragging was frequent.

"I've got one of those," he said when a form board was placed in front of him.

"I can do that," he announced when asked to draw a square.

Obedient, alert, and undemanding, Eric clearly had little confidence in himself.

Three-year-old Jenny happily followed all of the examiner's instructions in the testing room.

With a smile, she confided, "I like you."

The testing over, back in the waiting room the psychologist began talking to Jenny's mother. Suddenly the affectionate, cheerful youngster turned into Miss Hyde. She threw magazines on the floor, bounced on chairs, and grabbed pens and paper from the secretary's desk. Although Jenny managed well when she was the center of attention, she fell apart when she was not.

Physical Evaluation

Height and Weight

A quick glance tells you if the preschooler is in the normal range of height and weight. If he is not, he will be treated differently than others his age. The result can be devastating.

A two-year-old who is as big as a four-year-old will be expected by parents, teacher, sitters, and neighbors to show the conformity and restraint of an older child. He cannot; so he is scolded and told that he is wild and babyish. He grows up knowing he cannot please adults and he stays wild and babyish.

A five-yera-old whose size pegs him as being a year or two younger will be considered unable to do what other five-year-olds do. He will be helped more than he needs to be, excused for failure more than he should be, and given easier tasks that he can master. He grows up thinking of himself as incompetent and he resents work and hardship.

If a preschooler is thin and pale, something is wrong. He may be living on cokes and chips and suffer from nutritional deficit. Or he may be stymied by a years'-long eating problem which his parents have not been able to solve. Tired and weak, he cannot keep up with playmates, think clearly, concentrate, or hold his temper.

Nor can the fat youngster keep up with other boys and girls. Gradually he quits trying, isolates himself, resents other children, and stops maturing. Most overweight children are smothered with parental concern and supervision. Emotional clinging between parent and child is tight.

Attractiveness

Some children are beautiful. They have curly hair, huge soft eyes, and dimples. Most are average: their features are slightly lop-sided; their noses run; their hair is messy; their chins are decorated with scabs. Some are homely: their ears are enormous, their teeth crooked, their body parts disproportionate.

The beautiful child may hear every day from someone that she is *so* pretty. She begins to think of herself as special, and she demands favors from adults and lords it over playmates.

Parents of the average child may wish he was better-looking, but they are used to his appearance and seldom think of it. Nor does he.

The ugly child is taunted by playmates about his big ears and funny teeth. If his parents are embarrassed by his looks, they sigh or perhaps treat him harshly. Studying himself in the mirror, the un-sightly child is ashamed and hides himself under cap and coat worn year-round. Sure that everyone despises him, he either avoids or be-little others.

Abnormalities

Look for physical abnormalities. Take a break half-way through testing and stroll down the hall to the water fountain. Hang behind and watch how the child walks. Is there a limp? Does he trip over his feet? Is he pigeon-toed or knock-kneed? Does he lose his balance or walk on his toes?

If so, he has trouble running when playmates scatter for Hide and Seek. He can't readily obey adult orders to hurry. Annoyed by his difficulty in getting around, his temper and his opinion of him-self deteriorate.

You'll discover from the way he handles toys and test materials whether his small muscles are well coordinated. If he doesn't easily pick up and hold onto objects, it's probable that life at home is a se-ries of errors: he drops his spoon on the floor and knocks over his milk glass at meals; he loses his soap in the bath water; he takes forever to collect and put away his toys. And his mistakes garner him a steady stream of scoldings.

Watch to see whether the youngster can see and hear normally. You may be able to tell from the way he responds to your directions.

During testing, four-year-old Ray sometimes did not hear the examiner's instructions, sometimes replied promptly, and sometimes answered after a few moments' hesitation.

When the child gave no response, the examiner repeated the direction more loudly. It did not help. Yet Ray jumped in alarm at the click of the light switch or stop watch.

A hearing problem or an undependable nervous system? It was important to find out.

Stamina

Judge the child's stamina. Toward the end of the session, or earlier, does he refuse to try test items? Do talking and moving about slacken? Does smiling fade? Does he sag with weariness?

If so, you need to learn if his fatigue is caused by lack of sleep or food, or if it is a chronic condition which does not improve with adequate physical care.

If the child has little stamina, he cannot long tolerate frustration, punishment, stimulation, or direction. Both his daily life and his contacts with others are altered because he is tired.

Speech Evaluation

A thorough, detailed examination by a speech clinic is needed for some preschoolers. But you can discover whether the child's speech is normal for his age.

A one-year-old uses only a few single words; pointing substitutes for talking. A two-year-old can put together two words to make a sentence: "Kick ball." A three-year-old is gabby; talking is the skill he works on all year long. Four- and five-year-olds can and do talk as much and as colorfully as some adults.

If the older preschooler has little to say and his sentences are short and primitive, he may lag in speech development. Or he may be frightened and unable to speak freely in these strange surroundings. Sometimes, when a small child tries to speak, he is always ignored by parents and older siblings. He gives up and stays silent around other people.

Adams and Passman[2] learned that children between the ages of one-and-a-half and five years talk to each other easily and often when they have been successful previously at getting across their meaning with words. But if other children or adults fail to understand them, they clam up and seldom speak.

You will spot the child who stutters, whose words are unclear, or whose voice is hoarse or squeaky. Many such problems are temporary. Some are not; they need attention from speech specialists.

The parents of three-year-old Todd reported that he made no sounds as an infant. Even when he was one and two years old, he never tried to talk. Although he now could remember and repeat what others said, he had trouble speaking his thoughts. After beginning speech therapy, Todd improved steadily.

If you want to learn more about a youngster's speech skills than you can in an hour of listening to him, try the *Zimmerman Preschool Language Scale*. This test takes twenty minutes to give and measures the speech competence of children eighteen months and older. It checks articulation, identifies specific disabilities, and provides a language score related to developmental age.

Testing

The preschooler's behavior during testing tells you much about him. How does he react to failure? To success? Does he know when either has occurred? Fearing failure, does he refuse tasks he believes he cannot do? Or does he swagger through all you offer?

You will learn whether he shines on verbal tests, delights in non-verbal ones, or calmly conquers or collapses with both. He may doggedly stay with a task which is hard for him. Or he may back off at the first sign of difficulty. His actions give you a glimpse at his strengths and weaknesses.

Physical Function

Preschoolers love to show what they can do with their bodies. Instructions to skip, throw, listen, touch, and watch are eagerly obeyed. It's a good way to start the formal part of your study.

NEUROLOGICAL SCREENING. The *Kindergarten Neurological Screening Test for Learning Disabilities,* devised by physicians Ellidee D. Thomas and Gloria A. Rogers, checks the child's preference and knowledge of laterality and his sensory, fine motor, gross motor, and cranial nerve function.

There are twenty-seven tasks, most of which require only a few seconds to do. Some are repeated for scoring accuracy. The youngster is asked to do such things as kick a soft ball, track a moving pencil, hold his arms extended, walk a 108-inch tape, open and close a safety pin, and identify which finger or cheek is being touched when his eyes are closed.

Although scoring is based on the expected performance of kindergarteners, the test also can be given to four-year-olds as a measure of general neurological development. In judging performance, remember that tracking errors in preschoolers may indicate, not neurological malfunction, but immaturity of eye muscles.

An infant in his first year normally changes his dominant hand once or twice and inconsistency in handedness preference can last until the child is seven years old. But over 90 percent of boys and girls establish handedness by the age of two years.

Ideally, a child who is right-handed will also be right-eyed and right-footed, indicating that his brain's left hemisphere coordinates nerves and muscles well. More often, function is mixed: *e.g.,* a right-handed child sights with his left eye, but uses his right foot for kicking.

Some youngsters are ambidextrous. They use the right hand and foot for some activites, the left hand and foot for others, and either eye for sighting.

In general, left-handed children and those with mixed laterality find speaking, writing, and reading more difficult than do boys and girls who are right-handed or whose laterality is consistent.

Other indicators of neurological difficulties are problems with reproducing drawings and wide differences between verbal and nonverbal scores on intelligence tests.

AUDITORY SCREENING. The *Wepman Auditory Discrimination Test* is a series of paired similar-sounding words and paired identical words. The child must judge whether the words the examiner reads are the same or are different. Typical pairings of non-identical words are: *rub-rug, pool-tool, wreath-reef, vie-thy.*

An attentive older preschool child should be able to detect many of the words which are different. If he cannot, although he is trying hard, he should be examined by a physician for hearing acuity.

The youngster who has trouble with sounds misses or misinterprets directions from parents and teachers. This earns him frequent scoldings and he may even be considered retarded.

He also has problems with speech. Hearing incorrectly or imperfectly, he has no model of sounds on which to base his own talking. He makes mistakes often and gradually speaks less and less.

Unable to get across his ideas and wishes to parents and playmates, he is constantly frustrated and angry. He may show his distress by becoming aggressive and destructive or by harming himself.

Intelligence

Intelligence, a word which scares parents, is merely the term used to describe a child's learning capacity. Intelligence is measured by tests which sample the child's ability with a variety of tasks, both verbal and non-verbal. His successes and failures are compared with those of other children his age.

MANAGING THE CHILD. Tell the youngster you have some games to play with him. Then be prepared for much to go wrong. A preschooler is an unpredictable bundle of moods and behaviors. The child may be tired; he may be frightened; he may be angry. If so, he will not do his best and the score will not describe him accurately.

Sattler[11] suggests ways to manage an emotion-blocked child. If the youngster is frightened, avoid introductory explanations and start testing at once. Action chases away worry.

Offer the negativistic child a choice: "Would you like to draw a picture or build with blocks?"

If the preschooler cannot sit still or focus on instructions, give the test as quickly as you can. To help him pay attention and respond, hold his hands or arms or head.

For the non-talking boy or girl, begin with a non-verbal test item. Try speaking to him in whispers, or use a doll as your puppet translator.

Arrange materials ahead of time so that you can move rapidly from one test item to the next. Keep everything out of your rubber-armed young guest's reach. Small dolls, chairs, and animals are fascinating and the youngster will want to play with them. Promise that he may, once he has answered all your questions. You don't let him play with test materials before or during the examination.

be intrigued by the stopwatch and want to work it. You'll
you show him how it stops and starts. Let him try it once
or twice. Then assert yourself as adult-in-charge, retrieve the watch,
and carry on with the test.

Carrying on is what you do despite all distractions. If the preschooler's questions and stories cascade into lengthy interruptions and if you've politely acknowledged them two or three times, you must then ignore his extraneous comments. Proceed with your requests and questions. With luck, he'll tag along.

When the child asks how much longer this foolishness will last, tell him. Say, "Ten more minutes," or, "Just a few more questions," (if it's only four or five.) He won't understand how long ten minutes takes, but he'll know that there's an end ahead. Also, you can tell him that as soon as you're finished, he can play just as he pleases with some special toys.

Keep a supply of small candies nearby and, every so often, give him one. The reward is for following your instructions and trying, not for success. Candy brightens the demanding atmosphere and keeps the young child working cheerfully.

If you anticipate trouble testing a shy, withdrawn non-talker, try the *Peabody Picture Vocabulary Test* as a starter. It consists of a series of cards on each of which are four pictures. You say to the child, "Point to the spoon."

Because he need not speak or handle materials, pointing seems easy to him. Having managed that, he may relax and work with you, answering questions and manipulating objects as you direct.

The Peabody test provides an I.Q. and a mental age for preschoolers two-and-one-half years and older. Jack and Diane Naglieri[9] found that the revised version gives both a lower I.Q. and a lower M.A. than does the older form. In any case, the Peabody is a screening device, no substitute for checking the child's ability with a variety of tasks.

Infant Tests. An infant test, strictly speaking, does not measure intelligence. It checks only the child's development prior to his use of language. It cannot predict his future creativity, memory, or reasoning skills. But an infant test can rule out gross mental retardation or developmental lag.

One widely-used test is the *Cattell Infant Intelligence Scale* for children from two months to five years of age. It consists of five or six test items, with alternates, for each month from two through twelve, for every two months from one to two years, and for every three months thereafter. Items for older preschoolers are taken from the Stanford-Binet Intelligence Scale, Form L-M.

Alternate test items substitute for ones which have been spoiled because someone has walked into the testing room or materials accidentally have been scattered or mismanaged. For infants and toddlers, an alternate also may be used to replace a refused test, in the hope that a different task may prove more attractive. Alternate tests are not a second chance for failed tests. If they are given in addition to regular items to provide extra information, they are not scored.

On the Cattell Scale, test items for the first year include the infant's ability to babble or coo, inspect his fingers, follow a rolling ball, pick up a spoon, lift a cup, pat and smile at his mirrored reflection, play with a string, ring a bell, finger holes in a peg board, find a block hidden under a cup, and mark with a pencil. Many tasks require him to imitate the examiner.

The *Gesell Developmental Schedules* give a D.Q. (developmental quotient) instead of an I.Q. The developmental age earned on the test is divided by chronological age to obtain the D.Q.

Testing begins at one month and continues through five years. Items measure motor, language, adaptive, and personal-social behavior of the infant or toddler. They can rule out gross deficiency.

PRESCHOOL TESTS. The most-used test for children between the ages of two and six years is the *Stanford-biunet Intelligence Scale, Form L-M*. It consists of a variety of tasks, none of which takes long to do. Because of the rapid change in types of questions, tasks, and materials, young boys and girls stay interested and alert.

The test items check the youngster's ability to copy drawings, follow directions, listen, discriminate sizes, reason, and identify likenesses and differences in pictures. They also measure his memory, fine motor coordination, general knowledge, and vocabulary.

There are six tests and an alternate at each age level. These are set at half-year intervals between two and five years, then at one-year intervals. The test starts with the age level at which the child passes every task. It ends with the age level at which he fails every task.

Each test item is given in order, with specific instructions, no word of which may be altered, embellished, or omitted by the examiner. Because the test was carefully standardized using these exact instructions, failure to follow them invalidates the score.

But a question or its pertinent part may be repeated if the child does not understand what is meant or if he was inattentive or did not hear clearly. That the youngster did not hear accurately is obvious when you ask, "What is a ball?" and he answers, "It has eyes and cries."

When you do not understand what the child means by his answer, you may say, "Tell me more about it." Don't do this often, however, lest the youngster believe you are dissatisfied with his replies.

Scoring the preschooler's responses can be tricky. If you are uncertain, refer to examples of pass or fail answers in the manual. Avoid crediting the youngster with more successes than he has earned (the "halo effect") because he is charming, compliant, and compliments you on your shirt. And avoid failing him on every questionable item because he whines, squirms, and steadily announces that he wants to go home.

The testing room should be relatively free from distractions such as outside noise and a too-busy scene which can be spotted from the window. A child's table and chairs should be used for smaller children; a card table or a desk with a kneehole is all right for four- and five-year-olds of normal size.

Don't spend more than thirty or forty minutes on an intelligence test. After that length of time, the child will tire. He'll refuse or fail items he could pass if he were rested. If there is wide scatter (successes and failures on many age levels) which causes testing to go on and on, have the child return another day to finish.

The *Wechsler Preschool and Primary Scale of Intelligence* is standardized for children between the ages of four and six-and-one-half years. Modeled on the Wechsler Intelligence Scale for Children, it is divided into two parts, verbal and performance (non-verbal), and provides an I.Q. for each part, as well as a combined I.Q. Sub-tests measure general information, sequencing ability, observation of details, vocabulary, skill with puzzles, understanding, and memory.

This is a more burdensome test for the child to take than the Stanford-Binet. It requires an hour or more to complete, too long for a preschooler to sustain attention. Furthermore, there is no switching from one type of item to another: the youngster is given questions ranging from easy to difficult in one area (vocabulary, for example) until he fails. Thus he is aware of having failed many times during the examination.

Sattler,[11] after pointing out that the *Wechsler Preschool and Primary Scale of Intelligence* is reliable, valid, carefully standardized, and provides separate verbal and performance I.Q.'s, lists its faults. Besides the lengthy administration time, its floor and ceiling are inadequate and scoring is more subjective than is desirable. On some sub-tests, the examiner is required to ask for additional information after the child has answered, which implies that the answer was poor. Some questions in the Comprehension test are ambiguous and/or emotionally disturbing.

Zimmerman and Woo-Sam[16] compared I.Q.'s earned by kindergarteners and first graders on the Stanford-Binet with those earned on the Wechsler Scale and found that results were similar except for children who scored at the superior level. Bright boys and girls did better on the Stanford-Binet: their mean I.Q. of 129 on the Stanford-Binet corresponded to a Full Scale I.Q. of 117 on the Wechsler.

DRAWING TESTS. Most boys and girls like to draw. Information about the older preschooler's intelligence and perception can be gained from drawings, both free-style and copied.

The *Goodenough Draw-a-Person Test,* standardized for children between the ages of four and ten years, is a quick way to estimate general intelligence.

The child is asked to draw a person; each feature or correct detail earns three months' credit on a point system of scoring. Results correspond well with I.Q.'s earned on the Stanford-Binet unless the boy or girl suffers from nervous system damage or is clumsy with his hands. Then scores are lower on the Goodenough than on the Stanford-Binet.

Abraham,[1] who tested 90 two- to six-year-olds, pointed out that the young child's drawings often lack consistency. He recommends having the boy or girl make several drawings, not just one, so that a broader sample can be scored.

Fadely and Hosler[4] describe inferences which can be made from a youngster's drawing. They note that usually a preschooler places his drawing on 60 percent of an 8½" x 11" sheet of paper. But if he completely fills the page or, in contrast, crowds a tiny figure into a bottom corner, his need to feel more important is clear.

Sometimes the child starts his drawing with the feet and ends up with the head, a reversal which may indicate neurological problems. And if the preschooler puts either light or heavy pressure on his pencil, his fine motor coordination may be faulty.

If he is meticulous and takes a long time to complete his drawing, he may be perfectionistic. Or, if he dashes it off, this may be a clue that he is careless about work.

A handicapped child often either omits or emphasizes in his drawing that part of his body which functions poorly.

Another widely-used drawing test for four- and five-year-olds is the *Bender Visual-Motor Gestalt Test*.[15] It consists of nine geometric figures, one to a card. Each card in turn is placed in front of the child and he copies what he sees.

The Bender measures visual-motor ability and developmental progress. Indications about the youngster's personality and self-control appear in the size of the figures, their placement on the page, and the accuracy with which they are drawn.

Omissions, distortions, reversals, angular problems, and repetitions suggest problems with perception. These may be related to central nervous system malfunction and forecast future difficulty in reading and writing.

The *Berry Test of Visual Motor Integration*, which also provides forms to be copied, has age norms beginning at two-and-one-half years.

TESTING THE HANDICAPPED CHILD. Many handicapped boys and girls — cerebral palsied, deaf or hard-of-hearing, blind or visually impaired — receive an inadequate education because their abilities were misjudged and their training delayed. It is essential that a reasonably accurate evaluation of their intelligence be made during the preschool years.[8]

Testing is not easy. Allowances must be made for the predicament of the cerebral palsied child trying to make his muscles respond to his brain's signals. Chances are good that he cannot place pegs, build with blocks, and string beads. Verbal tests work better, given by an examiner who can interpret, perhaps with a parent's help, the garbled, indistinct answers he gives.

But some cerebral palsied youngsters have one good hand and their skill with non-verbal tasks can be measured. If both hands work reasonably well and speech is limited or impossible to understand, then performance tests may be the only kind you can use.

Expect a slow, labored response to every request. Count on two sessions to determine an I.Q.

The deaf or hard-of-hearing child can be examined with parts of standard intelligence tests. With pantomime, you can convey to him what you want him to do. You must take care not to indicate answers as you demonstrate instructions.

The deaf child can draw with the same competence as a hearing preschooler, so the Goodenough and Bender tests are valuable aids in judging his capacities.

The *Leiter International Performance Scale* is a non-verbal test for children between the ages of two and eighteen. The child selects a block with the appropriate symbol or picture to fit into a frame. There is no time limit and instructions are given in pantomime. The test is useful not only for the deaf but also for young children who have motor defects or problems with sensory reception or speech.

Deaf children often score in the retarded range of intelligence. Although many are below normal in learning capacity, others are not. These suffer from the effects of limited experiences, overprotection, and little or no practice in thinking in words.

Keep working with any deaf child who tests below normal. Try combinations of test items and look for new tests which will give you an adequate understanding of his potential.

The blind child also can be tested, most effectively with verbal questions. The *Interim Hayes Binet Intelligence Test for the Blind* is available for four- and five-year-olds, although Hepfinger[6] considers it tiring and boring because of its repetitive questions.

Partially-sighted children can try some performance tests, such as pegboards and form boards. They can be directed in manipulation of test materials. A partially-sighted child, if well-taught, dresses and feeds himself, so he is accustomed to using his hands well.

Hepfinger[6] suggests that the psychologist study the preschooler's ocular report to learn how severe the handicap is and what surgery, pain, or emotional distress the child has experienced.

If the blind or visually-impaired child you test has been isolated at home and waited on, expect a low score. Teach the parents how to help the child become more self-sufficient and re-test later.

Repeated testing is needed for every handicapped child. If home and school training are on target, his scores will rise steadily, encouraging both him and his family.

Personality, Emotion, and Motivation

Studying the child's physical prowess and intellectual capacity, you have learned much about him and his operating equipment. But what is he like? Does he worry? How does he think of himself? Of his family? What are his daydreams?

Tests will tell you: the child cannot. Although an adult can spend hours with a friend or psychiatrist, spilling out his feelings about spouse, job, mother-in-law, offspring, neighbors, family background, and daily life, a child rarely attaches words to emotion. For the preschooler, feelings are fleeting, brief sparks in his action-loaded day.

Only when emotion is constant and overwhelming is he aware of panic or deep sadness. This happens if his parents quarrel every time they are together, his father whips him fiercely for minor disobedience, or his mother regularly disappears without warning, returning home days later with no explanation.

If you gain his confidence, he will tell you about these things. But he does not relate them to his actions, his mood, and his abilities. You must do that.

QUESTIONS. The *Interview for Children* test can be adapted, expanded, or shortened as you choose. It consists of twenty-six questions, too many for most young children.

Some are:

What is the best thing that ever happened to you? The worst?

What makes you angry? What makes you cry? What scares you?

If you had three wishes that could come true, what would you wish for?

If you were going away to live on a desert island and could take only three people with you, which three people would you take?

If you were an animal, what animal would you want to be? Why?

How would your mother like you to be different?

How would your father like you to be different?

FAMILY PICTURE. The way a child draws a picture of a person tells you how he thinks of himself. If the figure is extra large, very tiny, mutilated, or distorted, you know something is wrong. Ask him to draw a picture of his family and you'll learn more.

Four-year-old Justin began his drawing with his father. Next came the father's car. To Justin, his father was important; to his father, the car was important and the child knew it.

Five-year-old Amanda drew her mother holding her little sister's hand. Then she drew her father on the mother's shoulders. The father drank and steadily lost jobs.

Some children's pictures show family splits: the mother with her son is on one side of the paper, the father with his daughter is on the other side.

The preschooler may draw himself bigger than everyone in the family, smaller, or off to one side, alone. Frequently he does not include himself in the family picture and must be asked to do so.

After the boy or girl has finished his drawing, ask him to tell you about it. As he explains what everyone is doing, you'll discover his point of view about what goes on at home.

STORY-TELLING TESTS. These tests require the preschooler to tell a story about a picture. They are sometimes called apperception tests because the child tends to put himself, his experiences, and his feelings into his stories.

Bellak's *Children's Apperception Test,* for three- to ten-year-olds, consists of ten pictures of animals, dressed and acting like humans: *e.g.,* two adult monkeys are sitting on a living room couch, drinking tea and whispering, while another adult points her finger at a juvenile monkey. Such mixed-up ideas may be more confusing than helpful to a preschooler trying to tell a story. A recent revision of the test replaces animal figures with humans.

The *Michigan Picture Test* is designed for children between the ages of eight and fourteen years. It consists of sixteen pictures, including a blank card, which show school-age boys and girls in various scenes. Some of these pictures can be used with preschoolers.

The *Thematic Apperception Test* consists of thirty pictures intended for older children and adults. But some of these pictures have been used with young boys and girls.

You can create your own test. Collect pictures which feature pre-schoolers in scenes with parents, brothers and sisters, playmates, and school. The characters can be busy at various activities or apparently talking. Obvious emotion (sadness, anger, fright) elicits more dramatic tales.

Precise scoring of apperception tests gives a measure of a child's tension, emotional control, and facility with interpersonal relationships. Usually, however, the preschooler's stories are too brief for this kind of scoring. Also, you can expect him to create stories for only a small number of pictures: six to eight is his limit.

You can discover recurring themes: the child always is afraid or punished or vengeful; the father regularly forgives the child's misdeeds; the mother usually is boss; peers routinely are bullies, are bested, or disappear.

Note the dominant emotion in the stories: fear, anger, pride, delight, envy. Sometimes you can pick out specific worries: the child's parents may separate; he may get into trouble at school; his baby brother reaps all the parental attention; he is bad and about to be sent away forever.

Adding up all you have learned about the preschooler's experiences, relationships, and feelings, you know a great deal about what he thinks of himself and how he gets along with others.

Free Play

Either at the beginning or end of the examination, let the child play with toys you keep in the testing room. It's better to leave free play to the end of the hour; he's tired then, less able to do his best on tests, and playing with new toys rewards him for the effort he's made.

If he won't do what you want at first, however, playing as he likes for ten minutes may soften his steely attitude.

Toys should include books, dolls and their equipment, trucks and airplanes, building blocks, balls, toy musical instruments, toy tools and scrap wood, a pounding set, beads to string, and jigsaw puzzles.

Watch what happens. Does he choose sex-linked, opposite sex-linked, or neutral toys? How efficiently and imaginatively does he play? Does he settle down with one toy or dart about, spending a few seconds fingering each? Is he persistent at building, wood-working, bead-stringing, or puzzle-solving, or does he give up? Is he angry when something won't work? Or embarrassed? Does he handle toys roughly or throw them just for kicks? Is he purposeful or haphazard in play?

Does he include you in his play? If so, does he ask for help, take charge, or treat you as an equal? Does he insist that you play, refusing to play by himself?

Hendricksen *et al.*[5] found that of 38 toys in day care centers serving three- to five-year-olds, most were used for solitary play some of the time. Playing alone, the child need not share, compete, or bend to others' ideas.

If you're not invited to play, sit to one side and take notes. Three-year-old Betsy scolded and spanked a doll for five minutes' straight. Five-year-old Dennis carefully constructed a building from blocks, stared at it, muttered, "Dummy!", and with a sweep of his hand, sent the blocks flying. Four-year-old Ricky pounded a few nails into a block of wood, then moved his supplies to the door and began to pound nails in it. Five-year-old Jessica picked up toys at random and banged them on the floor. Tell-tale play.

With questions, observation, and testing, you'll learn more about the child than anyone else has ever discovered. Knowing what you do, you can explain to his parents why he acts as he does and what can be done about it.

REFERENCES

1. Abraham, A.: (Evolution of human person drawings from ages 2 to 6). *Bulletin de Psychologie, 32*: 323, 1978-1979.

222 *Behavior Problems of Preschool Children*

2. Adams, R. E., and Passman, R. H.: Verbal communication among toddlers and preschoolers in a day-care setting. *Journal of Genetic Psychology, 139*: 159, 1981.
3. Bakwin, H., and Bakwin, R. M.: *Clinical Management of Behavior Disorders in Children,* 3rd ed. Philadelphia, Saunders, 1966.
4. Fadely, J. L., and Hosler, V. N.: *Developmental Psychometrics.* Springfield, Thomas, 1980.
5. Hendrickson, J. M., Strain, P. S., Tremblay, A., and Shores, R. E.: Relationship between toy and material use and the occurrence of social interactive behaviors by normally developing preschool children. *Psychology in the Schools, 18*: 500, 1981.
6. Hepfinger, L. M.: Psychological evaluation of young blind children. *The New Outloook for the Blind, 56*: 309, 1962.
7. Johnson, H. W.: *Preschool Test Descriptions.* Springfield, Thomas, 1979.
8. Murray, J. N., ed.: *Developing Assessment Programs for the Multi-handicapped Child.* Springfield, Thomas, 1980.
9. Naglieri, J. A., and Naglieri, D. H.: Comparison of the PPVT and PPVT-R for preschool children: Implications for the practitioner. *Psychology in the Schools, 18*: 434, 1981.
10. Rabin, A. I., ed.: *Assessment with Projective Techniques.* New York, Springer, 1981.
11. Sattler, J. M.: *Assessment of Children's Intelligence.* Philadelphia, Saunders, 1974.
12. Self, P. A., and Horowitz, F. D.: The behavioral assessment of the neonate: An overview. In Osofsky, J. D., ed.: *The Handbook of Infant Development.* New York, Wiley, 1979.
13. Song, A. Y., and Jones, S. E.: Vineland Social Maturity Scale norm examined: The Wisconsin experience with 0- to 3-year-old children. *American Journal of Mental Deficiency, 86*: 428, 1982.
14. Terman, L. M., and Merrill, M. A.: *Stanford-Binet Intelligence Scale: Manual for the Third Revision Form L-M.* Cambridge, HM, 1960.
15. Tolor, A., and Brannigan, G. G.: *Research and Clinical Applications of the Bender-Gestalt Test.* Springfield, Thomas, 1980.
16. Zimmerman, I. L., and Woo-Sam, J.: The utility of the Wechsler Preschool and Primary Scale of Intelligence in the public school. *Journal of Clinical Psychology, 26*: 472, 1970.

Chapter 20

DIAGNOSTIC REPORT

YOU'VE spent hours writing to fellow professionals, interviewing the parents, and examining the child. What do you have? A mass of raw data, a jumble of facts, some strong hunches.

And a job to do. You must put this cornucopia of information in order so that you can understand clearly what's happening. Only then can you get on with the next step: erasing the child's behavior problems by guiding his parents in new directions and coordinating the separate efforts of physician, speech therapist, and teacher.

A diagnostic report puts you on track. To organize your facts, score tests, relate cause to effect, and choose remedial measures takes from two to four hours.

LENGTH

Reports come in two lengths. There should be a complete, detailed account for yourself and a condensed version for other professionals who work with the child.

Complete Report

For yourself, write a complete report of three to four single-spaced pages. See that it contains every item and impression to which you must refer as you work with the parents. Your report is the work sheet on which you base treatment and against which you compare future assessment of the child.

A clear, detailed account saves time during treatment. Never again need you review the pages of raw data you have assembled. Instead, you have a summary of reports from other professionals, information given by parents, and test findings. Add descriptions and quotations which justify conclusions and flavor your writing with the distinctive events and mannerisms which permit your instant recall of this particular child.

Many child guidance centers use a different colored paper for reports from each professional — pink for the psychologist, blue for the social worker, yellow for the psychiatrist. The color code allows you or any other staff member to locate your report instantly in the child's folder.

Condensed Report

A condensed report goes to other professionals. It is one to two single-spaced pages long, written as a letter. A summation much longer than this will neither be read nor digested. Learn to extract what's important and pack what you have to say into few words.

Keep the condensed report lucid and non-technical. Many physicians won't know what you mean by "performance test." Teachers will get the wrong impression of pupils you describe as "hysterical." Social workers are vague about the label, "LD child."

You also may need a condensed report for staff within your own clinic. Tallent[2] states that many psychiatrists object to a psychologist's making diagnoses and recommendations. They reserve that task for themselves.

Find out what is wanted in your own organization. It may be a short, clear, precise report which lists the tests you gave but summarizes findings as an entity, rather than test by test. Tell what the child is like and specify his assets and liabilities.

CONTENT

A detailed report can be organized in several ways, but should include at least seven parts: problem, history, general observations, test results, diagnostic summary, recommendations, and treatment plan.

Problem

List the problems for which the child was referred and name the organization or individual who sent the child to you. If there was no referral, state that the youngster was brought by his parents.

History

Summarize what you know about the family's structure and background, the child's rearing, activities, education, emotional expression, and physical health. This is information obtained from your interview with the parents and from other professionals.

General Observations

Describe the physical, verbal, emotional, and social behavior of the child during the examination.

Test Results

Report what the child did on each test you gave. His intellectual achievements and failures, his attitude toward himself and his family, the specific worries he bears, and his physical and emotional assets and liabilities should be clear.

Diagnostic Summary

Explain the reasons for the preschooler's unwanted behavior.

Recommendations

List what must be done to remove the problems.

Treatment Plan

List treatment goals, methods of achieving them, and the number and spacing of private or group sessions needed. Place your recommendations in this time frame.

With this summary of your study, you have everything you need to begin making changes in the child's life.

Below is a typical report.

DIAGNOSTIC REPORT

Name: Robert (Robbie) Swift   *Date:* December 1, 1984
Born: June 8, 1979.

Problem: Robbie was referred by Dr. Jonas Williams, the family physician, after several episodes of hyperactivity in his office. The child also is inattentive at school, wets and soils himself, is troublesome at the sitter's, and over-interested in sex.

History: Robbie's father, a welder, presently is unemployed. He is bitter about the lack of available work. Robbie's mother has been a supermarket checker for the past four years. The child has been cared for by a series of sitters, the latest of whom took over in mid-October. He has one brother, who is three years old.

Mrs. Swift suffered an infection during the last three months of her pregnancy with Robbie and labor lasted thirty hours.

The parents report that Robbie is a poor eater who must be coaxed and threatened to down a meal. He gets no more than ten hours' rest a night and often less. His physician noted no major physical problems, but said that he is slightly underweight and excessively active.

Before starting kindergarten, Robbie was in a day nursery for six months. His kindergarten teacher states that he appears to like school, but when she is talking to the class, he looks around the room, interrupts, and sometimes leaves his chair. She has spanked him for touching other children on their genitals.

At home, his playmates are neighbor girls, nine to twelve years old. Sometimes, instead of letting him hang around, they chase him away. He also has played with other children at the homes of his various sitters. His parents were vague about what Robbie likes to play, saying only that he enjoys drawing and using a tape recorder. Most of the time when he is home, he watches television.

"Usually" he dresses himself. Occasionally he washes dishes and vacuums, sloppily, and he objects to this "hard work."

Mrs. Swift feels that her husband gives in to Robbie too easily. With her the child is demanding and, in the clinic waiting room, she made no attempt to control him. Robbie has been punished for hitting his brother; now he makes no attempt to defend himself when the smaller boy hits and pushes him.

Several times each day Robbie is spanked by both parents, either with their hands or a belt. When scolded, he fidgets, turns his head away, rolls his eyes, and sometimes drops to his knees and cries.

The only time he becomes angry is when something he tries to do turns out poorly.

He talks about sex, kisses girls, and wants to sleep nude.

The parents could think of no positive traits in their son.

General Description: Robbie was slight and small-boned. He spoke in a loud nasal tone and could not pronounce *r*, *th*, or *l*.

He talked steadily and tensely to the examiner about colors and shapes, trying to make clear that he knew all about them. During the testing hour, he did everything asked of him and was pleased with his successes. He was alert, asked for no help, and made no demands. At times he hinted that he would like candy from the examiner and when he was given some on leaving, he asked for more to take to his brother.

Test Response

Geometric Figure Drawing. Robbie failed both the square and the triangle.

Kindergarten Screening Test: On the tandem walk, Robbie could not heel-and-toe; he is pigeon-toed. He failed tracking tests at first, but later passed them. Fine motor coordination, knowledge of directions, and sensory reception were normal.

Stanford-Binet Examination, Form L-M: C.A., 5-6; M.A., 5-9, I.Q., 105. Because of insufficient time, the complete examination was not given. Robbie was sure of test items dealing with numbers, vocabulary, and analogies. He could not describe differences in pictures. He passed, barely, drawing a square.

Children's Interview: Robbie's three wishes were for bubbles (he saw a bubble blower in the testing room), a car, and a toy truck. If he could live with only three people on an island, they would be his brother and two friends. His worst and best experiences had to do with dinosaurs and if he were an animal, he would like to be a dinosaur: "I could eat everyone up."

He becomes angry when "someone trying to kill me;" he is afraid of a giant bird that "almost killed me"; he cries if someone "kills me or stabs me." He is happy if people "leave me alone or I eat 'em up." When he is grown, he will "live with my friends or be dead."

Aggression, loneliness, dread, hopelessness, and distancing from reality characterize these answers.

Michigan Picture Test: In one of Robbie's stories, a boy at school failed to draw a circle and square correctly. In another, a boy was spanked by his angry father. Other tales were of beatings, killings, and jail. Robbie mentioned twice, as he looked at pictures, that the boy "got his clothes on." In one story, Santa Claus appeared at school. His stories mirrored his panic and confused thought.

Family Drawing: Robbie drew his father first, then his brother, and finally his mother. Only when asked to do so did he draw himself. He put himself at the bottom of the page, beneath his father's feet. His brother and mother were close together and separated from the father figure.

Diagnostic Summary: Robbie is a lonely child who has no sense of belonging to his family. He is closer to his brother than his parents realize. He resents his mother's abandoning him to sitters and tries to bully her into paying attention to him. He fears his father, who may have whipped him for poor school reports, and he wheedles gifts and concessions from him as a sign of approval.

The father, unemployed, presently is moody and angry, alternately belligerent and indulgent with his son. His mother resents the relationship between father and son, feels isolated in the family, and is burdened by work and responsibility. She has no energy or will left to control or comfort Robbie.

Because he has been cared for by many different adults, each with unique standards, Robbie does not know how to please. Tense, anticipating grownups' displeasure, he loses all control and is overactive. His fear of punishment is founded in the reality of daily scoldings and whippings. Formal school attendance began only a few weeks before he was left with yet another sitter, so that his usual anxiety level was heightened by the need to adapt to two new caretakers and settings within a month.

Robbie obviously has been exposed to sexual stimulation. This preoccupies him and gets him into trouble at school. He may have witnessed sexual intercourse at home or been sexually fondled by older girl playmates or at a sitter's home.

Late hours, insufficient food, constant television, inadequate play and playmates, and problems with speech and locomotion keep him tired, frightened, bewildered, and indignant.

Because he is anxious and apprehensive, Robbie has limited control over his behavior. Wetting, soiling, and excessive activity reflect his fear, loneliness, and uncertainty.

But his learning ability is normal, he wants to please, he can and will follow directions, and he tends to feel protective toward his younger brother.

Recommendations

1. *Physical care:* Robbie needs twelve hours in bed every night of the week, with each parent in turn reading or talking with him before lights out. The parents can learn how to improve Robbie's eating habits. No television-watching should be permitted. An orthopedist can examine Robbie to determine if corrective shoes are needed.

2. *Family relationships:* Each parent should praise Robbie once daily. The family should eat the evening meal together. There should be no interference from parents when the brothers argue or fight. The father should help the mother with housework, refrain from verbally abusing her, and take any job he can get.

3. *Discipline:* The parents should keep a tally count of daily scoldings and punishment given Robbie and decrease both. Physical whippings should end. Punishment can be chair-sitting, isolation in his room, a chore, or retribution for harm done. Acceptable behavior should be taught with instruction, approval, and practice. Robbie should not be corrected or ridiculed for inadequacies such as awkward walking, speaking, or drawing.

4. *Playing:* Play with older girls should cease. Robbie needs time to play alone daily. Once or twice weekly he should play with a friend his own age and sex for one to two hours. His brother should not be allowed to play with the older boys at that time.
5. *School:* Parents should avoid stressing the need for top school performance. They should not make Robbie practice drawing squares and circles. Instead, they should read to him every day.
6. *Self-respect:* Robbie should be taught how to do different kinds of chores and required to do them daily. Nothing should be done for him which he can do for himself, such as dressing, bathing, and brushing his teeth.
7. *Wetting and soiling:* Re-training is needed. Robbie should be sent to the bathroom after meals and every two hours in between to try to urinate or evacuate. Each success is to be rewarded with a penny, and Robbie is to be taken to the store once weekly to spend his earnings. If he soils or wets, he washes out his underwear and pays his parents a penny. There is no scolding or physical punishment for failure.
8. *Sex interest:* Privacy for parental intercourse should be ensured. Constant nudity at home is to be avoided. If an occasional spanking is warranted, it should be done with Robbie fully clothed. He should be told that handling the genitals of others is impolite and should be questioned about when and by whom he has been sexually stimulated.
9. *Public behavior:* Robbie should be prepared for every change. He needs to be told what will happen in new situations: school, the doctor's office, a different sitter. He can be directed in practicing how to behave in each strange setting.
10. *Other caretakers:* Conferences with the teacher and sitter should be held. Robbie's problems can be explained to them and consistent, anxiety-reducing management procedures taught.

Treatment Plan

   Goals: (1) To provide better rearing for Robbie: (2) to increase his confidence and self-respect; (3) to protect him from people who confuse and demean him; (4) to enable him to control his behavior.

   Method: (1) Guide the parents in implementing the recommendations with private consultations. The time will be used for them to describe puzzling and irritating actions of their children, to receive instructions for handling these problems, to ask questions, to be assigned a project to work on, and to report their success or difficulty with the previous assignment.

(2) Confer regularly with Robbie's teacher and sitter to gain their assistance and their evaluation of the child's progress.

Duration of treatment

Eight conferences with the parents will be held, the first four at one-week intervals, the next two at two-week intervals, and the last two one month apart. Project assissgnments will be made in the order given under *Recommendations*. There will be contacts by phone with the teacher and sitter at three-week intervals. At the end of this time (four months), Robbie will be re-evaluated.

A condensed report to the physician who referred Robbie is sent as a letter. It reads this way:

Thank you for referring Robert Swift (b. 6-8-79). I talked with Mr. and Mrs. Swift November 23 and examined Robert November 25.

Robert is the older of two sons. His mother has worked for the past four years; his father presently is unemployed. Robert and his brother have been cared for by a series of sitters.

The child is demanding with both parents, who erratically ignore, indulge, or punish him. He is spanked several times daily, sometimes with a belt. High emotional tension exists between the parents.

There was infection during the pregnancy and delivery was prolonged. Robert often is waited on, eats under protest, gets insufficient sleep, watches TV constantly, and plays, in the neighborhood, only with older girls. He talks about sex, kisses girls, wants to sleep in the nude, and has been spanked at school for touching classmates' genitals. His teacher reports that he is inattentive and restless. He wets and soils himeslf.

Robert is a slight child who has problems with walking and balance. Some articulation and voice difficulties were evident. Fine motor coordination, sensory reception, and directional abilities were good.

He was given these tests: Geometric Figure Drawing, Kindergarten Screening Test, Stanford-Binet Examination Form L-M, Children's Interview, Michigan Picture Test, and Family

Drawing. During testing, he was tense and afraid of failing, but he followed directions, stayed alert, and asked for no help.

Intelligence is normal. Vocabulary and knowledge of numbers are sound, but he cannot draw geometric figures as well as other children his age. Emotionally, he is anxious, lonely, and confused. He dreads punishment, fears death, and is preoccupied with nudity.

Wetting, soiling, and hyperactivity are caused by the unpredictable, emotional behavior of his parents toward him, the varying expectations of changing caretakers, poor physical care, infantilization, and exposure to sex, which may have occurred at home, at a sitter's, or with girl playmates.

These findings have been reviewed with the parents. They will come for eight consultations over the next four months, after which Robert will be re-evaluated. They will learn to give Robert more food, rest, praise, personal attention, privacy, and opportunities to play with boys. They also will manage discipline more fairly, refuse demands, require self-care and chores, and use a reward system to re-train Robert to use the toilet. The source of Robert's sexual interest will be investigated and he will be taught to refrain from sexual touching of others.

Conferences will be held with his teacher and sitter to enlist their understanding of the problems and provide consistency of management.

I appreciate your continuing interest in this child.

Sometimes it's best not to send a written report to the school. A child's file is open to every subsequent teacher the child has. His first or fourth grade teacher, reading an account of his behavior when he was five years old, may prejudge him and never assess him accurately.

Also, parents expect details of what they tell a psychologist to remain confidential. Unfortunately, a few teachers discuss psychological reports in the lounge over coffee.

Instead of a written summary of your findings, talk personally with the teacher. You need to get to know her and how she thinks about the child. She will work well with you once she trusts your understanding of the youngster's difficulties and her trials with him. As you talk, she can make her own notes on what is said to guide her in managing the boy or girl in her classroom.

REFERENCES

1. Hollis, J. W., and Donn, P. A.: *Psychological Report Writing,* 2nd ed. Muncie, Accel Devel, 1979.
2. Tallent, N.: *Psychological Report Writing.* Englewood Cliffs, P-H, 1976.

Part IV.
TREATMENT

Chapter 21

PROBLEMS OF PARENTING

MONSTER or martyr? With parenthood, a normal man or woman can mutate into either. Easy-to-get-along-with, content adults detect disturbing changes in themselves after the birth of a child.

For no clear reason, they snap at mates. Rage, unknown for years, is unleashed at offspring. Despair sets in: a mother wipes endless tears from soggy cheeks; a father glumly isolates himself in the garage or seeks oblivion in bars.

Feelings harass the parent. There is the deep sigh of hopelessness from everlasting infant duty, the sweet reasonableness of explaining to the toddler that he may not drive the car or set the house on fire, the barely hid exasperation with the four-year-old's interminable demands for candy, toys, movies, late bedtimes, and chauffeur service across town to visit friends.

Startling change, incessant challenge, and fluttering worry are a parent's lot.

CHANGE

One of the most baffling features of parenthood is that nothing stays the same.

The young baby, after weeks of unreliability, finally settles into a comforting routine of eating and sleeping. His grateful, weary parents now can count on three or four hours straight to do as they choose, not to mention the miracle of a full night's sleep.

But it doesn't last. Before he's a year old and without any prior warning, the once-helpless infant pulls to a stand. Within weeks he's staggering off, primed with energy, eager to explore the entire world. He abandons his schedule. Naps are shorter and fewer, and by the time he is two years old, he fiercely fights every attempt to bed him down.

Now mobile, he courts disaster. No longer can he be deposited in his playpen for quiet toy-fingering. He climbs on a chair, on the kitchen counter, on top of the refrigerator. He scoots out the front door and into the car-jammed street. He can reach pans of boiling water on the stove, doorknobs guarding basement stairs, medicine cabinets loaded with poisonous substances, drawers hiding knives and scissors. When no one is watching, he wanders far away from home or tumbles into the swimming pool. Someone must watch, every minute.

Steadily growing older, the placid, amiable, smiling baby with whom his parents cooed and cuddled disappears. Now the child can talk. He refuses, he demands, he argues, he insults, he pesters, he lies. He's communicating.

Before long, he has friends: little boys and girls who hang around for hours ruining privacy and needing service, consoling, and directing. When at last they depart for home, rooms are cluttered with toys, crumbs, and used glasses. The toilet is loaded with urine and feces. The next day, right after breakfast, here they are again, pounding on the door.

To do their job, a mother and father must recognize the child's need to be respected, to be proud of himself, to get along with others, and to obey society's moral code.[13] They support these needs when they stay consistent in manner and method. But such uniformity in child-rearing isn't easy when the child keeps changing.

AGGRAVATIONS OF THE CHILD

Psychologists and psychiatrists understand all too well what the child endures. Sympathizing, some censure parents for unwise and intemperate treatment. But taking sides reflects unfair assessment of the home scene. The erratic preschooler, testing and trying his mother and father, dumps on the flames of uproar his own huge pile of flammable materials.

Incessant Problems

Any adult who could predict the number and complexity of problems inserted into his life by parenthood would delay it as long as possible.

The difficulties start with colic, dead-of-night feedings, diarrhea, and spitting up. They go on to thumbsucking, the dragging of pans from cupboards and shoes from closets, and the screams for release from the jail of crib and playpen. Next come episodes of thrown food, torn books, terrible tantrums, and endless talking.

Bred by playmates, wounded feelings, hitting, and name-calling emerge and must be dealt with. Next come parent-sassing, swearing, and losing and mutilating clothes and toys. One memorable day, there's a phone call from the kindergarten teacher: Jonathon refuses to put away toys, keep quiet during stories, button his coat, or sing.

A bottomless box of troubles.

Physical Care

The physical care of a preschooler exhausts his mother. It takes six hours every day to feed, dress, and bathe an infant. Soon he's older, heavier. Before long, he weighs fifteen pounds, then twenty, and all of him must be hoisted out of a crib and into a playpen, stroller, high chair, and car seat. He must be lugged around stores and across streets.

Not only does his mother lift and carry him, she also wrestles with him. As she tries to diaper him, he wiggles and twists to get away. While she's shoving his feet into shoes, he curls up his toes. When she tries to stuff his arm into a jacket sleeve, suddenly the bone turns to jelly.

Her back aches from leaning over the crib and heaving up the mattress to fit on a clean sheet. There are heavy pails of wet diapers to haul to the washer or huge sacks of paper ones to drag outside to the trash can.

The house is a mess. Tinker Toys® sticks and wheels, blocks, doll clothes, tiny dishes, records, books, toy cars, and real kitchen utensils litter every room. Feedings end with puddles of milk and gooey mixtures of plums and carrots spread over high chair and floor. One helpful two-year-old fetched a can of drippings from the stove, carried it carefully to the living room where his six-year-old brother lay ill on the couch, and soothingly dumped it over his head.[13]

Care of the preschooler means confinement at hard labor for his mother.

Teaching Chores

Parents not only are problem-solvers and servants, they also are the child's chief teachers. In a short five years, the youngster must learn to manage a cup, handle a spoon, and eat table food. He must dress himself, use the toilet, brush his teeth, and wash off dirt. He must control irresistible impulses to bite and hit playmates, swear, and take what does not belong to him.

He must also leave the contents of closets and drawers intact, stay out of the street, and keep clear of hot stoves, electrical outlets, the Christmas tree, unsteady lamps, and trash cans. He must say, "Please," and "Thank you," at the right times, set the table, and be quiet when adults are talking.

Parental instruction never ends. But the young pupil objects loudly and fails often; the daily lessons discourage both adult and child.

Experiments in Independence

Parents can put up with a lot if their little one admires their perfect knowledge and politely accepts their wise edicts and sensible rules.

But he doesn't. He dismisses his parents as oracles of information and quotes truth as pronounced by peers: "Potatoes grow on trees";

"Jesus and Santa come down the chimney"; "If you sneeze too hard, the stars will fall out of the sky." *That's* gospel: Beth (age four) said so.

Worse yet, rivals shoot down parental standards of behavior. After an hour with a buddy, the previously unsullied youngster swaggers, blinks, and answers every question with, "What's it to ya?"

Nor does the preschooler depend solely on playmates for new ideas. He has his own. Proving to himself that he's important, he doggedly skirts his parents' wishes and commands. He feeds his spinach to the cat; he kicks his dirty socks under his bed; he shows up in the living room ten times after being put to bed; he dawdles over meals, he never hears requests to come to dinner or to put away his wagon.

Independence for him, frustration for his mother and father.

Volatile Emotion

He's not fluent, so the preschooler cannot win what he wants or say how he feels with words. He uses the only weapon he has: emotion. Ferocious kicks broadcast his displeasure. Piteous sobs announce his fear. Wild, ear-splitting screams pierce the quiet.

His mother and father, years removed from putting on such displays themselves, consider his emotional fireworks abnormal. Certainly the intensity of the upset bears scant relationship to the trifling incidents which provoke it. Disturbed, the adults react either with too-tender compassion or by matching the youngster's dramatics with their own.

Total Togetherness

A small child grows up well in the security of home, where his eating, sleeping, and playtimes are dependable and his principal caretaker is his familiar mother.

But this means that the two of them are comrades for ten or twelve hours each day. Such total togetherness would strain the good will of the most devoted couple, but the constant companionship of mother and child is imposed more by necessity than by deep, time-tested affection.

Also, because she is with her youngster during most of his waking hours, a mother witnesses his every fault. Over and over, he whines, yanks the cat's tail, and picks his nose. His mountain of sins convinces her that both she and her child are failures.

Here is one mother's report of a typical day with her young children. "This is only about two-thirds of what really happened," she says.

Kim is ten days past her second birthday; Shelley is eleven months old.

6:50 A.M. — Shelley gets up, bouncing and smiling until I get her out of the crib. I put her on the double bed to change her. She rolls over, crawls to the edge of the bed and I pull her back. She squeals while I dress her. Take her out and sit her on the living room floor.

7:00 A.M. — Kim gets up and comes out into the kitchen, saying, "Hi!" to everyone. She tries to take my pen. "Oooo! Write! Write!" Sees empty pizza carton. "Pizza, Mama? Pizza, Mama?" Rubs her nose, watches me write again, then says, "K--O--." Shelley is now having her morning snuggle with her daddy.

7:10 A.M. — Daddy changes Kim's diaper and reports that she was singing an original song about kitties while he was changing her. Shelley crawls around the kitchen while I fix her bottle and cereal. She starts to get fussy, saying, "Nah-nah!" (That's me.) Daddy tells Shelley no-no for pulling up on and hanging onto the lid of the trash basket and for touching the stove.

7:30 A.M. — I feed Shelley while Kim brings some toys into the living room. Kim's oatmeal is ready and she rushes into the kitchen and sits in a chair on top of an old phone book. Shelley hangs from the high chair tray while her big sister eats. I adjust Kim's bib when she complains about it and she dips her otameal-covered spoon into my coffee when I'm not looking. Shelley has now gone into the living room and is lying across a toy garage.

7:40 A.M. — Kim is done eating. She comes into the living room with oatmeal on her chin and I clean her up. She finds our Siamese under the aquarium and gives her a smooch on the nose, "Kissy, kitty!" Both girls go back in Kim's room to dig in the toy box. Kim comes out with more toys, shouting, "G.I. Joe Koko!" (G.I. Joe from Kokomo, a rhyme her daddy taught her.) Shelley comes out and kisses the top of the coffee table, twice.

Kim tries to get Shelley to "chase" her through the

kitchen, but Shelley pulls up on the TV stand instead and jiggles her rear to music coming from the television. I tell Shelley no-no for pulling off the felt cover on one of the stereo speakers and turn the speaker sideways so she can't reach it.

Daddy comes in and sits on the floor, putting Shelley in his lap. Kim gives him sugar and he gives Shelley sugar. He's now ready for work and puts on his coat. Seeing this, Kim says, "Bye-bye, Daddy," seven times. Shelley claps instead of waving to him when he leaves.

I turn on a favorite children's TV show and both girls dance (or wiggle), look at each other and laugh. Kim watches TV while Shelley roams around the living room pulling up on shelves and furniture. I let the cat outside.

8:30 A.M. I give Shelley the rest of her bottle, change her diaper, give her a few drops of infant's aspirin as she is cutting another tooth (her seventh), and put her down for a nap.

Kim gets in my make-up in the bathroom, smearing blush on her face. She turns the TV off. I turn it on and tell her she knows better. She gets another bite of her oatmeal, now cold, and follows me around the house talking about her daddy. She insists, "Mama sit!", so I do for a minute and hold her in my lap.

She comes willingly when I say it's time to get dressed, then hides behind her curtains and tries to run out the room while I'm getting her clothes. She laughs about this; she's always teasing. Get her dressed.

She goes back to the TV show while I do the dishes. I let the cat inside. It's really cold and windy out, so I decide it's not a good day to let the kids outside to play, as both just got over the sniffles. The cat is eating her food out of her bowl on top of the kitchen cabinet, as Kim will eat it if it's left on the floor.

When I'm finished, Kim says, "All gone dishes" and brings a box of blocks to show me. She keeps me company while I take a quick bath. She moves the shower door back and forth, washes her face, washes my arm, and tries to wash my hair, but I won't let her.

When we come out of the bathroom, she slams into a corner of the stereo speaker and cuts her face. She cries wildly, but only lets me hold her for a moment before throwing herself on the floor to finish her cry. When she gets up she sobs, "Buggers!" and I wipe her nose and eyes. We go wash her cut and she dries her face herself. I get her Kool-Aid and crackers.

The phone rings. It's a friend of mine and Kim gets a coveted chance to talk on the real telephone, but only smiles into it. While I'm on the phone, she tries to get my attention by climbing up on top of the kitchen table, chewing the end of the popcorn popper plug, and repeatedly asking for cookies.

Put Kim on potty with no luck. Put her in training pants. We watch the space shuttle take off and she says, "Bye-bye, spaceship." I turn the TV off. While I'm adding to these notes, Kim smacks me on the leg with a long, plastic tube and laughs about it.

We go downstairs to fold laundry and she swings up on the exercise bicycle. When she decides to help with the laundry, she sits on top of it. I put away the wash while she bounces on the waterbed.

10:25 A.M. — Shelley gets up. Kim climbs into the crib while I change Shelley's diaper. Both of them come out into the living room while I fix Shelley's lunch. Have to scold Kim for playing with the turntable and she gets mad at me. They follow me into the kitchen and Kim wants me to hold her in the middle of fixing the bottle. Kim gets mad — clenches fists, grits teeth — when I won't hold her and I have to stop her from climbing onto the high chair tray from a kitchen chair. I put Shelley in the high chair and feed her lunch. Kim brings toy phone on which we all take turns talking to Grandpa.

11:00 A.M. — Start to fix Kim's lunch when Shelley begins to cry loudly and I find that Kim has wrapped the toy phone cord around the baby's shoulders and is pulling her over. Rescue Shelley and carry her for a couple of minutes, then deposit her on the floor in front of the cat. The cat wants to go downstairs and I latch the doors at the top of the stairs behind her.

While we wait for the soup to warm up, Kim sits in my lap talking about "pretty yellow" blocks in her hand. I mention that it's lunch time and now she is very happy. "Lunch! Soup!" She raves about her fruit cocktail: "Cocktail! Cocktail!"

Get Daddy's lunch ready while Kim eats. She demands more milk, but as she has poured hers into her soup, I tell her no, that she'll have to spoon it in as it is. I get tired of her doing this at mealtimes. Shelley plays around her sister's chair while Kim eats. Shelley squeals constantly and we can hear her grinding her teeth. Kim gets down from the table, leaving a trail of chicken noodles across the kitchen.

I sit her on the potty again and she demands that "et tu, Mama," so I do, but she doesn't, so I put her in a diaper.

11:40 A.M. — Daddy arrives home for lunch and Kim greets him five times with, "Hi, Daddy!" Both girls follow him out to the kitchen and Kim gets a share of his lunch. Shelley plays with an errant ice cube on the kitchen floor. Daddy snuggles with Shelley after he's through eating, while Kim scatters bread and lunch meat on a bottom shelf in the living room.

Stop Kim from pouring her Kool-Aid into that same long, plastic tube and take it away from her. I find her trying to pour Kool-Aid into her milk cup and take that away. She shouts, "Oh, MAMA!" and I say, "Oh, Kim!" and she laughs.

11:55 A.M. — Daddy gives Kim bye-bye sugar and she insists that he give "Mama sugar, Mama sugar!" which he does. As the door slams behind him, Kim shrieks at the top of her lungs, "SHELLEY SUGAR! SHELLEY SUGAR!"

Kim goes to play in her room and comes out crying that a toy moose has pinched her finger. I kiss it and then I get sugar. Shelley takes a sudden tumble. Her eyes get wide and her hands shake, but she decides not to cry, so Kim and I have a laugh about it. Kim stubs her toe and cries, holding it up for my inspection. I kiss it and she jabbers about her foot.

Kim has brought her little chair into the living room and I pull it back from underneath the coffee table so that she can sit down. Shelley stands beside her, cooing at a doll on the table. Kim hits Shelley in the face with a toy camper and the baby starts to cry. I pick her up and tell Kim to come and kiss her and tell her she's sorry. Kim rushes over, delivers the kiss, and says, "I'm sorry, Sissy." Shelley smiles.

Kim gets going with some serious playing and Shelley gets busy standing up and sitting down all over the living room, but both take time out from their activities to watch every commercial that comes on the TV screen.

12:25 P.M. — Give Shelley the rest of her bottle. She sucks her thumb and grunts amiably while I change her diaper and put her to bed. I drag a giggling Kim out from under her own bed and put her down for a nap too.

12:50 P.M. — Kim gets up and I put her back to bed.

2:00 P.M. — Kim wakes up, but is crabby at first. I get her some Kool-Aid and half of a blueberry muffin. We split an apple a little later. "Ummm, apple." She relaxes on the love seat with her thumb in her mouth.

2:30 P.M. Fix Shelley's food and bottle. Get her up and change her wet tights to thick socks. I feed Shelley while Kim plays.

3:00 P.M. — I turn cartoons on the TV and both girls dance to music. I try to put Kim on potty, but she is so sulky that I just change her diaper.

I open the back door and both girls enjoy a breath of icy cold air and looking out at the back yard. I close the door when it gets too cold and they go back into the living room where Shelley starts pulling out albums. Tell her no-no and put albums back in place.

Give Kim Kool-Aid. She takes it to the living room and shows Shelley her new doggie cup. Spills the Kool-Aid on the coffee table and wipes it up with the slacks I haven't yet put on her.

Kim follows me around wanting me to talk in her toy phone. Then she wants crackers, but when I tell her to finish her apple, she yells, "No!" and wants to sit in my lap. I say no because I'm busy and she leaves the kitchen. She comes back immediately and screams at me about something. I tell her, "Be quiet!" I'm the one who's mad now. End up sitting on kitchen floor with her and talking about her toes. Then Shelley crawls up and we talk about Sissy's diaper, socks, shirt, and hair.

3:45 P.M. — Two neighbor children, Jerry (10) and Linda (7), arrive at the door. I babysit them after school on Monday and Tuesday. While Linda is showing me her school pictures, Shelley gets scared of Jerry out in the living room and starts to cry. Bring her into the kitchen with me while Kim hangs out with the big kids. Take Shelley into her room with me while I straighten up and change her crib sheet.

After fighting over one of Kim's toys and who gets to lie on the big pillow, the older kids settle down for cartoons. The cat comes by for a pat and Shelley grabs her, but after I show her how to pet the kitty, she is more gentle.

4:30 P.M. — Give the big kids apples and Kim finishes hers. By invitation, Kim sits on Linda to watch TV.

4:40 P.M. Fix Kim's supper. Daddy comes home. Kim eats after I chase her down and tickle her.

4:50 P.M. — Jerry's and Linda's dad comes by for them and Linda tells him she would like me to have one of her pictures. Kim surprises him by saying, "Bye-bye, Richard." It's the first time she's ever said his name. Kim eats every bite of her supper and I catch her in the living room to take off her bib.

Daddy gets down on the floor with the girls to play and they stick close by him. Kim chatters non-stop to him and when she trips against the door, she goes to him for comforting. Shelley slaps her hand to her face to play peek-a-boo, peering out between her fingers at us. Daddy gets some cheese and Kim gets her share.

5:15 P.M. — Fix Shelley more bottle and get her bedtime snack ready. Daddy takes Kim to potty, but she doesn't want to and he can't make her sit for long. He puts her in training pants while I start Shelley's tub.

5:30 P.M. — Give Shelley her bath and get her ready for bed. Feed her mashed banana and half a bottle. She gets night-night sugar from Daddy and Kim.

5:50 P.M. — Tuck Shelley in crib with her stuffed puppy. Give her more aspirin.

Start more water in the tub for Kim. She is getting nervous about a big moth in the kitchen. "Go, fly!", so when it lands on a chair we go and look at it. I touch it and it takes off and when I try to catch it, she laughs. We talk about how it is not a fly, but it is a bug and has pretty wings.

6:00 P.M. — Daddy gives Kim her bath. She runs out of her room before he can put on her nightgown, a nightly occurrence. He reports that she was singing a song about "Sissy crying" during her bath. He gets her some milk and two cookies. She wants to share the second cookie with me, but I decline. She acts like she's going to have a bowel movement, so we hurry into the bathroom. She sits obediently on her potty for five full minutes, but still doesn't do anything. Put her in another diaper.

6:30 P.M. — Ask her to help pick up toys, but she is too excited about a special cable TV show that is coming on. She dances and shouts out the names of several of the characters. I pick up the toys alone tonight.

6:50 P.M. — Give her one more cookie (they are small) before the show is over. She says, "Thank you, Mama."

7:00 P.M. — Dances to the music at the end of the show, then gives her dad a good night kiss. Tuck her in bed and wind up her singing teddy bear before turning out the light.

8:30 P.M. — Kim gets up, wanting a drink. Give her one and take her back to bed.

11:30 P.M. — Check on the girls. Shelley is hunched up, fist in cheek, blanket at the foot of the crib. I cover her up. Kim is asleep under her bed. Haul her out and put her in bed.

WORRIES OF THE PARENT

All by himself, the preschooler can give his parents a rough time. Their own insistent worries add pain to every day's events.

Lack of Confidence

Most mothers and fathers have slight confidence in their ability to bring up youngsters. Unsure of themselves and not knowing what to do, they misinterpret normal behavior and over-play their role as parents.

They panic when the child produces his first tentative, "No." Afraid that years of defiance are ahead, they yell, criticize, and punish to block his opposition. They neither see or hear the child's point of view.

They fear he'll get hurt or fall ill and cause them grievous anxiety. To save him from fatal harm and themselves from unwanted extra care, they keep him penned up at home and away from other children.

They worry about spoiling, so they shove him into neighborhood crowds of older children, turn down every request he makes, and brusquely order him to stop crying when he is hurt or sad.

They decide he's a "problem child" when he occasionally hides from visitors, stamps his foot, refuses his beets, or takes change from the dresser. Guilt-ridden, they make amends by letting him do as he chooses and say what he likes.

Their insecurity sets management habits which hurt him and complicate family life.

Imperfection in the Child

Some small children are adorable. They are equipped with dimples, sturdy bodies, pearly teeth, and long dark lashes. But some start life with huge ears and lopsided features. They are skinny and funny-looking. Gazing at what they have wrought, parents blush.

Not only may a small child look as though he's near disaster, sometimes he is. Preschoolers have heart problems, ulcers, bone deformities, and blood diseases. Some must wear thick glasses; others cannot hear. Treating these ills costs time and money. Concern about the present and future health of the youngster drains his parents.

If the boy or girl falls behind the norm in walking, talking, feeding hmself, or toilet training, his mother and father worry that he is retarded. They are ashamed and dread the critical comments of relatives and friends.

Before too long, the youngster meets his lifetime associates: one- and two-year-olds who grab his toys and push him down, three- and four-year-olds who jeer at and desert him. A mother and father, dreaming of a popular, friendly, in-charge son or daughter, are dismayed by their youngster's inept social talents.

Imperfections — dozens of them — depress the adults.

Disappointment in Parenthood

Adults idealize parenthood, seeing themselves as the prominent figures in a family portrait of beauty and harmony. Reality strikes hard.

The mother, home alone with her small children, yearns for adult companionship. Worn out from an endless round of work, she has neither energy to look after her hair and figure nor time to do what pleases her. She considers herself a dumpy drudge, forgotten by everyone busy in the exciting world outside her home.[6]

Friendships with other people sour. Childless couples regard the new mother and father as settled and burdened; they seldom call or come to see them. Two sets of new grandparents revert to type and shower their adult children with warnings and criticism.

Life-style changes. Interior decorations now are a crib and scales, a playpen and high chair. Space disappears as stacks of blankets, sleepers, and sweaters stuff drawers, and powder cans, bottles, pacifiers, and plush dogs clutter the house. Wallets empty at each trip to the store for diapers, formula, and strained vegetables. Whimpers and loud bellows disturb the day's plans and the evening's peace.[4]

Parenthood may divide the couple. Perhaps the new father, shoved aside by his busy, tired wife, turns demanding or distant. Or, wary of the tiny infant and, later, of his self-sufficient young son, he will have nothig to do with his child.

250 *Behavior Problems of Preschool Children*

Osborn and Morris[9] asked kindergarten boys if their fathers (1) looked after them when their mothers were busy, (2) put them to bed, (3) took them to school, or (4) read to them. Only half of the fathers helped in one way; a mere 4 percent helped in all four ways.

Many young women have no man around to help at all. Divorced or never married, they rear their preschoolers alone. The children, especially boys, are difficult to handle.[7]

Some dutiful parents try too hard. They spend hours reading to and playing with the child; they let him join them at cooking or car repair whenever he asks; they are angels of patience when he hits or fusses. but the sacrifices churn up resentment. Although they bow to their youngster's will in many ways, they subtly dominate him in others. Parent and preschooler remain annoyed and uneasy with one another. Family life is troubled.

The problems of parenting are enormous and constant. Mothers and fathers seeking help merit respect.

REFERENCES

1. Bandura, A., and Walters, R. H.: *Social Learning and Personality Development.* New York, HR&W, 1963.
2. Bell, R. Q., and Harper, L. V.: *Child Effects on Adults.* Lincoln, U of Nebr Pr, 1980.
3. Church, J.: *Understanding Your Child from Birth to Three.* New York, Random, 1973.
4. Clarke, J. I.: *Self-Esteem: A Family Affair.* Minneapolis. Winston Pr, 1978.
5. Ditzion, J., and Wolf, D.: Beginning parenthood. In The Boston Women's Health Book Collective, Inc.: *Ourselves and Our Children.* New York, Random, 1978.
6. Kitzlinger, S.: *Women as Mothers.* New York, Random, 1978.
7. Levy-Shiff, R.: The effects of father absence on young children in mother-headed families. *Child Development, 53*: 1400, 1982.
8. Murphy, L. B.: Coping devices and defense mechanisms in relation to autonomous ego functions *Bulletin of the Menninger Clinic, 24*: 144, 1960.
9. Osborn, A. F., and Morris, A. C.: Fathers and child care. *Early Child Development and Care, 8*: 279, 1982.
10. Smith, D. B., and Roth, R. M.: Problem-solving behavior of preschool children in a spontaneous setting. *Journal of Genetic Psychology, 97*: 129, 1960.
11. Spock, B.: *Problems of Parents.* New York, Crest, 1962.
12. Stith, M., and Connor, R.: Dependency and helpfulness in young children.

Child Development, 33: 15, 1962.
13. Verville, E.: *Behavior Problems of Children.* Philadelphia, Saunders, 1967.

Chapter 22

ERRORS OF PARENTING

M ISTAKES? Legislators and bus drivers, surgeons and accountants, astronauts and parents: all make mistakes.

No single error in his rearing permanently damages a youngster. Nor do hundreds of scattered errors. A child is both flexible and tough. But steady, skewed mismanagement in one or more aspects of the preschooler's life does harm.

How he thinks of himself and how he behaves with others take a drastic down-turn when any one of nine mistakes persists. They are (1) indadequate physical care, (2) warped social growth, (3) ruined self-respect, (4) overprotection, (5) rejection, (6) severe punishment, (7) permissiveness, (8) failure to teach responsibility, and (9) distortion of parental function.

INADEQUATE PHYSICAL CARE

Everyone knows that a small child needs proper physical care, but many mothers and fathers fail this basic test of concerned parenting. Thousands of youngsters are malnourished, fatigued, overstimulated, and pushed beyond their limits of tolerance.

252

The Errors

Insufficient Food

Welfare workers, relatives, and neighbors find children alone in cold houses barren of food. The family's limited cash is spent on alcohol and entertainment.

Some middle-class and upper-class youngsters live on sandwiches and cereal because no one ever prepares a meal for them. One child reported that his supper, the night before, was popcorn.

Other boys and girls starve in the midst of plenty. They consume quantities of tea, cokes, corn chips, and candy bars, refusing nutritious foods. Their parents look on as the children grow pale and weak.

Lack of Sleep

Many preschoolers don't go to bed until their parents do because life is easier that way. There's no fussing late at night and no need to read a story. The child is grateful for the chance to sleep.

Naps are skipped or inserted at odd hours. When a bored, lonely mother needs to get out of the house, she shops or visits and her little one goes along. At night, the parents haul the child to movies and ball games they want to see, his need for sleep ignored.

Overstimulation

Adults like the distraction of a crowded life. Talking, listening, watching, going, and doing spark dull days. But preschoolers do not have the stamina to cope with constant stimulation. They need to play alone and to run free outdoors.

Too many small children have time for neither. They sit in front of the TV set for hours daily, bombarded with emotion-rousing sights and sounds. Their physical, emotional, and intellectual capacities wither.[47,96]

Parents sign them up for classes intended to make them graceful, athletic, mannerly, or artistic. Once there, they must take orders and criticism from a teacher, compare their performance with that of other boys and girls, and try to do well what they may not wish to do at all.

Community living exhausts them. Infants deposited in day nur-series a few weeks after birth and older preschoolers sent to nursery school face a barrage of directions, challenges, and conflicts. Worn out, they long for a slower, easier, less social life at home.

The Effects

The tired, pressured, overstimulated, or undernourished pre-schooler not only fails to mature steadily, he reverts to earlier days. He cries often and cannot stop his tears. He hides behind his mother, sucks his thumb, and soils himself. He whines that he cannot brush his teeth or button his shirt.

His time at school is wasted. When his kindergarten teacher re-views the days of the week, her words slide past him. He forgets that he was assigned to cut out animal pictures from magazines at home and bring them to class the next day.

If he spends hours daily at television-watching, he has no time to create, explore, reason, and investigate.[96] Unused, intelligence dims.

The physically depleted youngster, irritable and intolerant, will not pick up his coat or take his bath when told to do so. Dragged away too often from play and never able to do what he wants, he balks at every adult request, whether or not it is reasonable.[16]

WARPED SOCIAL GROWTH

From an early age the child is ready to mingle with his peers. Playing, he learns what to expect from others and how to get along with them.[87] He talks more, handles his body better, is emotionally more free, and grows more independent than if he has no playmates. He develops a personal morality based on his experiences with other boys and girls.[84]

Early social seasoning determines for years his attitudes toward and relationships with others. Kagan and Moss[53] report that passiv-ity during the first three years of life is related to timidity in social contacts throughout the early elementary school years. Physical ag-gression toward peers remains stable for the first ten years of life. A child's habits of dominance and competitiveness do not change from the time he is three until he is fourteen.[52]

The youngster who has no playmates, whose friends are predominantly younger, older, or of the opposite sex, or whose playtime is disrupted by sibling or parent interference grows up socially warped.

The Errors

No Playmates

Some children have only rare contacts with peers until they enter public school. By then they lag far behind classmates in social development.

But if they are around other youngsters from an early age, social growth is steady. Like physical development, it follows a set pattern. Normally, the one-year-old plays alongside another child but shows little interest in him. A two-year-old notices the other boy or girl and gets acquainted by snatching his balloon and shoving him. The three-year-old's belligerence reduces to name-calling, and the four-year-old can share, cooperate, and compromise during play.

A kindergartener who has never played with other children starts at the beginning. He pushes or ignores his classmates and they, unused to such treatment, consider him peculiar and keep their distance.

Younger Playmates

Playing with a younger boy or girl tucks a feather in the preschooler's cap. He's boss, and he dispenses information and philosophy with the aplomb of Solomon. The recess from competition with age-mates is a welcome breather.

But if younger children are his *only* friends, he's in trouble. Classmates won't tolerate his dictating to them, nor can he keep up in games and sports they've practiced and he hasn't. They desert him and, at school, he's lonely.

Older Playmates

It's worse if a youngster's sole companions are older than he.

They often mock, humiliate, and rebuff him. He never can be sure they'll let him play; he never makes the decision about what to play; he never can count on having a good time. He learns to give in and take his lumps.

His classmates find him over-eager and fawning. They look down on him and avoid him.

Opposite-Sex Playmates

Preschoolers play with children of both sexes and experiment with each other's toys. Small boys feed dolls; small girls swoosh around toy airplanes.

But soon sex differences clarify. Boys' play activities between three and six years accurately predict their adult sex-role interests. Preschool girls, talking for their dolls and interested in playmates' ideas and lives, demonstrate the involvement with people typical of their sex.[36]

Boys' play is more consistently active than girls'. Boys run, yell, climb, and seldom are still. Girls run, climb, and shriek, but they also play happily for an hour in one spot.

A boy whose only friends are girls spend much of his time playing school or house; a girl whose only friends are boys wrestles, flings snowballs, and plays cops and robbers.

None of these play activities is undesirable for either boys or girls. But the youngster whose play consists only of that more typical of the opposite sex never develops the skills and interests of his own. By the time the child is nine, when the two sexes part company,[89] he is in desperate straits. A hybrid, he fits into neither sex's slot.

Interference With Friendships

SIBLINGS. When a child has a friend visiting, the parent often insists that his younger or older sibling be allowed to play too. This edict ruins the host youngster's chance to learn from peer play: family squabbles swallow up the time. The younger sibling grabs toys, chatters, and makes demands. The older one grabs toys, jeers, and sometimes runs off with the guest.

PARENTS. Some mothers stage manage the child's social life. They choose his friends, tell the youngsters what to play, and plan every detail of parties and excursions.

When every social contact is produced and directed by his mother, the preschooler loses interest in being with other boys and girls.

The Effects

Social withdrawal starts early and can lead to later aggression and lawlessness. It happens when a youngster does not learn how to get along with peers or how to play and think like children of his own sex. Afraid, he refuses to play when someone invites him to do so. Other children consider him snobbish, leave him alone,[84] and soon his only companions are adults.

The girl or boy who spends no time with peers is unaware that they, too, have problems and self-doubts. Watching from a distance, he is sure that everyone is totally confident and capable. In sad contrast, he is all too aware of his own uncertainties and feeble skills. Discouraged, sure he is a failure, he gives up trying to improve himself.

The friendless youngster, certain neither of his competence or likeability, regresses to crying or thumbsucking, or, as he grows up, becomes fearful, rigid, or compulsive.

With no playmates to distract or comfort him, the young child notices every fleeting ache and each tiny cut. Soon he hurts all over, all the time, and must stay home from school.

A boy or girl unacceptable to like-sexed peers rejects them and adopts traits of the opposite sex. Atypical and lonely, he later may turn resentful, suspicious, and irrational.

RUINED SELF-RESPECT

A child sees himself as his parents do.[4,43] If they believe he is a joy to be with and a credit to the family, he is proud. But if they deceive, ridicule, and humiliate him, he is sure he is worthless. Although parents may not intend to send that message, their degradation of him ruins his self-respect.[80]

The Errors

Lying

To a small child, trust is vital. He knows little about the world; he cannot control what happens to him. He trusts his parents to tell him the truth.

Some mothers and fathers don't. Smiling, they tell him they're taking him to the park. Thirty minutes later, he's in the doctor's office waiting for shots. He turns around, after talking to the sitter, and his parents are gone; they have sneaked out the back door. They say his friend can't stay for lunch today but tomorrow he can; the next day they promise the same thing.

Somehow they never get around to telling him that he's adopted or that his mother really is his stepmother or that the family is going to move because his father got a new job. He learns these momentous facts from his grandmother or a playmate and concludes that his parents think so little of him that lies are what he deserves.

Ridicule

Ridicule, blatant or subtle, broadcasts a parent's belief that the child is inadequate.

Neither listening or judging, the adult automatically and always refuses the youngster permission to try a grand, original scheme or to do what he's planned for the next hour. To him, the child's ideas are foolish, sure to fail, and he tells him so.

Or, the youngster never does anything right. After he's made his bed, his mother smooths the spread. Following behind while he sets the table, she straightens the silverware he puts out. When he appears for breakfast, shirt buttons awry, she unfastens them and does them up correctly.

Many parents do for the child what he needs to do for himself. If his son momentarily is tongue-tied at a visitor's question, the father answers for him. When a playmate snatches a daughter's sand bucket, her mother retrieves it and gives it back to her. The preschooler concludes that he can manage nothing by himself.

Humiliation

A child is humiliated when he is treated rudely, his rights are not respected, and his limitations are reviewed in public.

Rarely are boys and girls granted the courtesy they are expected to show others. A youngster is taught to answer when spoken to, to keep quiet when someone else is talking, to ask rather than demand, to give in to others' wishes, and to thank those who do something for him.

But his parents don't reply to his comments or questions. They interrupt his lively story of the movie he saw. They crossly dispense orders, insist on what they want, and never offer a "Thank you," when he watches a small brother or picks up magazines in the living room. The vast difference in courtesy between the way his parents treat him and the way they treat everyone else heralds his insignificance.

He also is humiliated when his rights are not respected. Small brothers and sisters are allowed to use his toys; he must share with them candy given him by an adult for whom he's done a favor. He cannot ban anyone from his room; he cannot play in private with a friend; his ancient, favorite sweater is thrown out with no by-your-leave.

And while he listens in shamed silence, his mother talks to a neighbor about how he stutters and wets his bed. In the presence of dinner guests, his father scolds him for reaching for the bread and commands him to stop talking.

The Effects

The degraded child distrusts everyone and, told that he is peculiar, withdraws completely. He talks only to himself, his monologue blotting awareness of his sorry state.[21,49]

The deceived child is terrified by his parents' lies. He can neither predict what will happen next nor count on his mother and father to protect him. When he hears about a murder, a flood, or a tornado, he is sure that similar disasters will strike him and his family. He suffers from nightmares and, whenever his parents try to leave him, he screams in fear.[64]

A preschooler whose trust has been violated turns aggressive. Although he rarely pays back his deceptive parents for mistreatment, he attacks younger children. When he is older, he speads false rumors about classmates and cons them out of toys and money.

The child whose self-respect is gone has few original ideas and little interest in trying them. He is convinced that he is worthless, inferior to everyone.

OVERPROTECTION

A newborn infant would die if his parents did not feed and protect him. But before he is a year old, he is busy evading his mother, feeding himself, and exploring. At three or four years, he deserts his parents for peers, now the important companions and models in his life.[86] By that time, if food and water were available, he could survive without adult help.

If unneeded care is prolonged, parent aid is instantly available, and the child's actions and contacts are restricted, he is overprotected.

The Errors

Prolonged Care

The older preschooler stays immature if his mother dresses him, wipes him after a bowel movement, bathes him, brushes his teeth, makes his bed, picks up his clothes, and serves on order whatever food he wishes. He never gets the chance to learn the skills nor gain the confidence he needs to look after himself.

One woman, loaded spoon in hand, chased her husky five-year-old around the yard. She was sure he wouldn't make it through the day if he skipped one bite of his breakfast.

Unnecessary service can continue without change for years. Some adolescents are coddled and served in the same ways they were as toddlers.

Instant Aid

If the child cries or complains and his mother quickly comforts him, if he gives up and his father immediately takes over, he learns that he is never expected to endure unpleasantness. He knows that adults will do his schoolwork, fight his battles, give him what he wants, supply presents and sympathy when he is disappointed, and rescue him if gets in trouble.

Restricting Action and Contacts

The overprotective parent is her child's constant companion. She drives him to school, watches his dancing lesson, sits with him while he colors, and rarely allows him to play with another child. When she does, the other youngster's selfishness and poor manners are pointed out. If there's quarreling, the visitor is sent home for good.

To keep her child close, the mother warns again and again that other boys and girls will hurt him. Nor does she allow him to become attached to his teachers; she preaches that they are mean and unfair.

Alone with his mother, dependent on her in every way, the growing preschooler stays as helpless as an infant.

The Effects

At kindergarten, for the first time in his life the child is expected to work, to stay seated, to obey orders, and to manage alone. The overprotected youngster cannot. Mooning and fiddling, he resents being asked to do such unpleasant and difficult tasks.

And, because he has his parent for a friend, he dodges age-mates.[42] Other preschoolers dislike the girl who hangs on adults and the boy who runs to them for help.[61]

Both aggressive and negativistic behavior are common in the overprotected boy or girl. He refuses orders, evades work, and, despite his easy life, feels disgruntled and exploited.[26]

He retains for years erratic, immature behavior, sleeping with parents, wetting the bed, and eating dessert first at meals.

He fails to develop normally. Alertness, communication, and learning stall and his innate capacities lie dormant.

REJECTION

In a devastating reversal of the overprotective adults's hovering, the rejecting parent offers his child no affection, attention, care, or interest. He abandons him to look after himself or turns him over to someone else to rear.

Some rejecting adults are totally irresponsible. But many intelligent, usually dutiful men and women never have understood that their child needs them in his life. They are unaware that they are the reason he tries to do his best.

Happy, self-reliant, courageous preschoolers have mothers and fathers who explain, listen, give emotional support, exercise control, and require responsible, independent behavior from them.[62] It is the attitudes of parents which determine how small children behave.[57]

Rejecting parents avoid their boys and girls and give them insufficient protection and care.

The Errors

Avoidance

It's easy to avoid a child. A mother stashes her infant in his crib in a distant room and busies herself with chores, TV, or visitors. She never checks on him; she ignores his crying. A father shrugs off his preschooler when he wants to snuggle and talk, ordering him to go away and stop bothering him.

Sharing none of his own life, the parent tells the youngster nothing about his work or what he thinks. He considers the child an unpleasant appendage of marriage, something expected by society and his own parents, but of no concern or interest to himself.

Some rejecting parents regard their preschooler as property. When guests come, the youngster is displayed briefly, like a new car. For others, grandly slighting or dismissing the child, he serves as an ego-booster. For most, the son or daughter is considered a nuisance.

Insufficient Protection and Care

Rejection spills over into danger.

Small children are turned out of their homes to roam alleys and wander off to shopping centers. They are left by themselves in the house while parents visit neighbors or go to bars.

A five-year-old, alone in a dark room watching TV while his mother worked, was killed by a policeman who glimpsed the toy gun the child kept for protection.

Preschoolers die in fires they start while parents are gone.

Sometimes rejecting parents hire caretakers, with mixed results. Schachter[78] reports that two-year-olds at home with their mothers earned higher intelligence scores on tests than two-year-olds of employed mothers. Youngsters sent to day nurseries grow self-sufficient, but Rubenstein *et al.*[75] found that they also are more fearful and throw more tantrums than children kept at home. Some preschoolers are victimized by sitters: they are denied needed food and freedom to play, cruelly punished, or sexually abused.

The Effects

The rejected child, of no importance to his mother and father, has no energy or enthusiasm for learning. He lags behind his age-mates in speech, intelligence, and manual skills.[79] Because they surpass him in every way, he avoids them.

He tends to fear people. One small boy was given a radio as a substitute for his mother's companionship and kept in his crib long after he could walk. On the rare times he was let out, he huddled in a corner and covered his eyes when anyone came near.

Sometimes the abandoned boy or girl is wary of adults but will approach children. But because he is over-eager to please, they consider him odd and avoid him.[19]

The rejected child may comfort himself with a doll or special toy as replacement for the absent parent. If he attaches himself permanently to objects, instead of people, he accumulates dozens by stealing.

He also worries about what may happen to him. No one looks after him, controls him, or cares what he does. He is free to hurt or kill himself and certain that he will. Prasad and Prasad[73] found increased anxiety among older preschoolers whose mothers were employed. Shunted among several caretakers, the youngster stays tense, never knowing when he will offend and be punished.

To gain attention, spurned preschoolers bestow endless kisses, cry, and disobey, behavior which causes parents to dislike them even more.

If the child is branded by his parents, he quickly acts the part assigned him. Three-year-old Matt brought home a playmate's ball and his father labelled him a thief. From that time on, Matt took everything he spotted. Five-year-old Claudine left her doll out in the rain and denied it. Her mother called her a liar and she became one, making up a dozen fanciful tales a day.

SEVERE PUNISHMENT

All children are punished. Adults show disapproval in ways ranging from a disappointed glance to a life-threatening beating. To learn self-control, a youngster must be corrected when his behavior is unacceptable. But authoritarian mothers hinder intellectual growth in their sons and daughters[20] and hostile, punitive parents create disturbed children.[6,41,54,56]

Punishment which is too severe includes harsh deprivation, constant criticism, or physical abuse of the child.

The Errors

Harsh Deprivation

Taking away privileges is a time-honored punishment for children's misbehavior. But the sentence may be more severe than the crime warrants.

Because she lied about eating some cake, four-year-old Ashley was not allowed to play with her friends for two weeks.

Because he left his yard after being told to stay there, two-year-old Chad was kept indoors for three weeks.

Because he hit his father, five-year-old Paul was not allowed to watch TV for six weeks.

Sometimes penalties pile up to such mountainous heights that the child never works his way free of them. Harsh deprivation occurs when the parent punishes not only the current misdeed but tries to prevent its repetition[69] by "teaching him a lesson he'll never forget."

Constant Criticism

Parent standards can be incredibly high. A strict father expects instant obedience and perfect self-discipline from his three-year-old. A mother, noting that a young visitor is polite, thoughtful, generous, and flattering, unhappily compares him with her own rude, selfish, disobedient preschooler. Unaware that the visitor is putting on a brief, impressive show of manners, quite different from his everyday behavior at home, she condemns her own youngster's shabby actions.

Over-correcting, parents pounce on every failure: their small sinner didn't finish his cereal, put his clothes in the hamper, speak clearly, share his teddy bear, or come when called. He did pull the dog's tail, spill his milk, track in mud, lose his shoe, and jump on the bed.

Criticized hundreds of times daily, the miserable preschooler knows he can do nothing right.

Physical Abuse

A million cases of child abuse are reported annually and another million are suspected. Labelled the "battered-child syndrome" by Dr. C. Henry Kempe,[11] attacks on youngsters are increasing.

Physicians treat children with broken arms, legs, ribs, and skulls, as well as burns and bruises. Boys and girls are beaten with belt buckles, fists, and hammers. Their hands are held over gas flames; they are chained to furniture, smothered with plastic bags, kicked, drowned, and burned with cigarettes.

Two-thirds of the battered children are under three years of age, and a premature infant or one with a difficult neonatal period is at high risk.[40] Many abused preschoolers die.

Parents are responsible for the injuries, as well as boy friends of single mothers, sitters, and relatives. The abusing adults were themselves physically hurt or emotionally abandoned as children. They are impulsive, indifferent to the child's needs, embroiled in conflict with their children and spouses, and convinced that severe punishment benefits the youngster by teaching him how to behave.[30,55,81]

Some help is available. Laws now require anyone witnessing or suspecting child abuse to report it to the authorities. Parents Anonymous is a self-help group whose members meet regularly and phone each other when rage overwhelms them. Instruction about children, home visits, counseling, and help with child care for young, single mothers and high-risk families is denting the incidence of abuse.[29,74]

The Effects

The severely punished youngster is beset with physical problems. Brooding about his unworthiness, convinced that he deserves the beatings, he eats poorly, sleeps fitfully, and stumbles when he tries to run or skip.

At school, he mulls over the criticism, penalties, and pain he suffers daily at home. Afraid, distracted, and angry, he is too disturbed to learn and remember.[5,12]

The severely punished child rarely gets along with other boys and girls.[88] Either he attacks them or he is deferential and meek. They leave him alone; he hates them. Sometimes, copying his parents' rigid standards, he disapproves of his classmates' rowdy ways and disdainfully isolates himself from them.[68]

When he is with his parents, he cowers, miserably accepting orders, blame, and condemnation. Never knowing when he will be scolded or whipped, he lives in constant fear. Blocked from behaving or even thinking as he chooses, he turns servile.[2] Dreading senseless punishment, he behaves aimlessly and impulsively.[91]

Beaten boys grow up to become adult rapists and child molesters.[39]

PERMISSIVENESS

Severe punishment damages the child; permissiveness destroys him and imperils others.

Every boy and girl learns self-control by first obeying the edicts of adults responsible for him.[14] A disciplined youngster feels secure, is satisfied with himself, and can set and work toward goals. He fits into and contributes to society.[23,28,35,41]

Normally, the preschooler concentrates on what he wants, hitting and screaming to get it. if he is not taught sounder ways of acting, he stays self-centered and demanding all his life.[69]

Parents who ignore, reward, defend, or encourage misbehavior fix it firmly as their youngster's method of managing others and getting through his days.

The Errors

Ignoring Misbehavior

Every small girl, at times, protests she did not hear her mother's command to put away her toys. Every small boy, at times, earnestly pledges never again to hit his sister. If a mother always believes her child, forgets what happened, and turns to other matters, the youngster gleefully behaves as he chooses, sure that his actions will be ignored.

Some children try hard to change a bland parental attitude. Four-year-old Lucas repeatedly cursed and kicked his father but got in return no more than a gentle admonition. The child's attacks became more frequent and vicious.

Rewarding Misbehavior

Misbehavior not only may be tolerated, it may be rewarded. If the child yells angrily when his parents decide to go to Arby's and, to appease him, they go instead to McDonald's, he finds that selfishness and temper pay. If he demands that his mother fix him a sandwich and she does, he learns that rudeness brings quick service.

Some children, told they'll be paid for chores, wiggle out of work every day. Even so, the money is handed over. Disobedience gets these boys and girls everything.

Defending Misbehavior

Defense of misbehavior is a giant step over the ethical border.

Four-year-old Jimmy refuses to set the table as his mother asks, but she does not press him. Instead, she excuses his behavior by telling herself that it's her job to get meals ready. Or she recalls that he fought with his best friend earlier and reasons that he's had enough bad things happen for one day.

A crying playmate tells Jimmy's father that Jimmy punched him.

"What did you do to deserve it?" asks the father.

When the preschooler is in trouble with other adults, his parents defiantly stand in his corner. Three-year-old Melanie picked the neighbor's prize tulips. Her father says it's the neighbor's fault: she should have fenced her yard. The kindergarten teacher reports that Jeff won't take his turn passing out crayons and paste. His mother retorts that children shouldn't wait on one another.

Encouraging Misbehavior

Some parents, with conspicuous or secret wishes to rebel, not only defend but encourage misbehavior.

A father instructs his small son to smash the face of the playmate who called him a baby. A mother grins when her young daughter displays the doll dress she sneaked out of the store.

Five-year-old Rena regularly calls her mother names; her father laughs. Four-year-old Gary always disobeys his father; his mother eggs him on.

Brutality, law-breaking, scorn: actions promoted in the preschooler by an admiring parent.

The Effects

The permissively-reared boy or girl, with no internal or external controls, is desperate. He knows that he cannot judge accurately which of his actions endanger him socially or physically. Worried about the total responsibility he bears for what happens to him, he is impulsive and aggressive.

He hits, yells, bites, kicks, and scratches everyone within reach.[8,12,58] As he grows older, he rarely attacks adults, knowing their power to retaliate,[9] but he continues to hurt small children. He also sets fires and brutalizes animals, classmates, and strangers. He wrecks possessions, disobeys, refuses to do schoolwork, and retaliates instantly for real or fantasied abuse.[53] Trying to be important, considering himself to be above rules, he steals, lies, and cheats.[68]

The aggressive preschooler, permitted to behave as he chooses, becomes the adolescent who experiments with sex and drugs, runs away, and abuses — sometimes murders — parents.[3]

The child who is never taught moral behavior does not know it exists. He acts impetuously and selfishly with both family and friends, believing whatever he does is right.[62]

LAX TRAINING IN RESPONSIBILITY

A child is born eager for action; he must be taught to be lazy. The youngster who learns early to work and to manage money is fortunate. He grows up to be dependable. He can cope with stress.

The irresponsible child works neither at home or at school. He believes that money, gained in any way possible, is solely for his pleasure.

The Errors

Omitted Home Chores

A two-year-old's favorite toys are a tiny broom and a play lawnmower. The work his mother and father do is great fun, he thinks, and he wants to do it too.

But his enthusiasm fades. Once he gets busy with friends and creates projects of his own, he dislikes being interrupted to help his parents.

Also, any task which bogs down into daily routine strikes him as boring and unnecessary. As often as he can, he escapes making his bed, taking his dishes to the sink, and cleaning the bathtub.

A secret reason he avoids chores is that he is unsure how to do them. If his work doesn't measure up, he is sure to be scolded, so he decides it's better not to try.

Giving up, as the child steadily refuses their requests that he work, a mother and father fail to train him to do regular chores. Without daily practice, his skills stagnate. And, used to service, he protests fiercely that his parents have no right to ask him to work.

Evasion of School Requirements

A five-year-old has few demands made of him at school. But if he does not learn in kindergarten to obey the teacher's directions and to complete his work, he is doomed to sad days in first grade.

Sometimes the adults excuse his non-conformity because he's younger than the others or his home life is chaotic. Or they decide to let him find out for himself the consequences of idleness.

Parents and teacher who allow the kindergartener to dally and who neglect to teach him work habits are setting him up for enduring trouble at school. Sontag and Kagan[83] found that achievement during the first five years in school is related to adult success.

Faulty Use of Money

Too often, money is bestowed, not earned. The child gets a handout regularly or on demand, with no connection to work, and thinks that cash is his by right. He learns to con, beg, and argue for money.

Most youngsters are allowed to spend money just as they choose. The preschooler buys candy, ice cream, and toys, and believes that money is for treating himself. He becomes the teenager who squanders cash on expensive tickets, snacks, jeans, and haircuts. He will be the adult who buys himself a sports car with money needed for groceries and utility bills.

The Effects

The irresponsible child, neither studying at school nor working at home, knows that his age-mates are steadily gaining in ability and achievement and that they think little of him.[7] He dislikes them, keeps his distance, and is uninterested in them.[38]

As a preschooler, he spends his time with adults, entertaining and flattering them. Older, he plays up to members of the opposite sex. In a parody of adulthood, he experiments with sex in his early teens; girls run off with older men.

He is ashamed of himself. His father, working in the yard, tells him he's in the way; his mother, fixing dinner, shoos him out of the kitchen. He sadly concludes that he is useless. He becomes a mimic, unable to think his own thoughts or try his own ideas.

He scorns adults for not insisting that he finish tasks they set. Walsh[93] found that school underachievers were negativistic, evasive, and complained when criticized.

The irresponsible adolescent, embarrassed by his daily school failures, quits when he legally can. Sure that a pay-check will prove his worth, he seeks work. But soon he is back home; the job was too hard, the pay too small, and his co-workers did not like him.

DISTORTING PARENTAL FUNCTION

A child learns how to act by copying the behavior and attitudes of his like-sexed parent.

Unisex is a myth. Preschoolers know their parents differ: mothers are more generous, protective, and helpful than fathers; fathers are more punitive and knowledgeable than mothers.[22,51]

When the like-sexed parent is atypical, the small child is bewildered. Instead of imitating the distortion, he may copy the opposite-sexed parent or any other person he knows.[46]

Five variations of normal parent function disturb boys and girls: (1) parental absence, (2) reversal of mother-father roles, (3) reversal of parent-child roles, (4) identification of the child with the spouse, and (5) assumption of peer status by the parent.

The Errors

Parental Absence

No FATHER. Divorces are legion; thousands of mothers rear their youngsters alone. Preschoolers are upset by the family split and often blame themselves. But as long as one parent looks after them, they worry less than older children about a father's absence.

The young boy or girl who sees his father only on alternate weekends, or not at all, is confused about what men really are like. True, his mother tells him: to keep from upsetting the child, she proclaims his father to be a wondrous person or, still bitter, she denounces him as a blackguard. The preschooler believes her and is baffled by the contrast between her words and his own perception of the man who is his father.

No MOTHER. Sometimes a boy or girl is reared by his father because his mother is ill, has died, or has deserted the family. More fathers now are granted custody of children when there is a divorce.

When the father takes charge, children may not suffer severe emotional pain; his strength becomes theirs.[32] But if he considers his youngster a nuisance, a burden, or a chain on his freedom, he may treat him harshly and leave him alone too often. The child grows independent but, also, insecure.

A boy or girl with no mother usually is cared for by a series of housekeepers, women relatives, and sitters, each of whom expects different behavior. Rarely is he in the good graces of any of the women who look after him, so he feels rootless and unwanted. If his mother has deserted, he dreams of her return and rebels against the orders of those who take her place.

THE BANISHED PARENT. Sometimes a mother or father is physically present in the home but so ostracized by the spouse that, in effect, he does not exist.

The mother erases the father by degrading his abilities and earnings, contradicting and ridiculing his ideas, ignoring his wishes, and keeping the child close to her all the time.

Or the father gets rid of the mother. He criticizes and abuses her, countermands her orders, and takes the child's side against her in arguments. The mother disappears as a force in the youngster's life.

Reversal of Mother-Father Roles

Magazine articles regularly report the duties and thoughts of house-husbands, men who have taken over the care of house and child while their wives earn the living. Although a few insist that they enjoy their home-bound days, most abhor them. The women resent footing all the family bills and regret their lost closeness with offspring.

In half of families with children both parents hold outside jobs, which causes the youngster to wonder how important his father is. Not only does his mother run him and the house, she also works outside so there'll be enough money. Obviously, his father is not too competent.

A mother normally assumes major responsibility for child care. Sometimes her habit of reigning over the youngster drifts into elbowing aside her husband. She is the one who handles the money, paints the house, mows the lawn, and by wheedling, scheming, or demanding always gets her way.

To balance matters, a man may take on duties his wife rejects as boring and traits she considers soft. He dons an apron to cook and wash dishes; he puts the children to bed; he hangs out the laundry. The father becomes the considerate, helpful, patient parent; the mother, the feared dictator.[91]

Reversal of Parent-Child Roles

The child may transmute into a parent. If his mother stays in bed and does no work, if she is shattered by every problem, the pre-schooler learns to fetch her medicine, cold cloths, and food. She basks in his concern and rewards him with effusive gratitude and praise.

With no responsible adult to take charge, the youngster also acts as parent to younger siblings, feeding, commanding, and punishing them.[91]

Identifying the Child with the Spouse

Sometimes an adult attacks and demeans his child because that's how he'd like to treat his spouse.

An alcoholic father, ashamed of his failure to support his family and act as head of the household, resents his wife's steady efficiency. But he dares not disparage her, so the child substitutes.

A mother, upset with an officious, debasing husband, but dependent on him for money, scolds and rules her son.

"You're just like your father!" she shouts at her hapless boy.

Sometimes a woman, unhappy with her husband, longs for a girl child to serve as best friend. If her youngster is male, she tells him daily that she wanted a girl. One little boy, devastated by his mother's refusal even to look at his new baby brother, began to dress up in her clothes. Years later, a confused adult, he underwent a sex-change operation.

The Parent As Peer

Insecure parents want their children to be pals. To win them, they abandon adulthood and behave as though they are peers.

They constantly kid a son or daughter, smilingly address him as "Goofy" or "Ugly," wisecrack when he comes with a complaint or is hurt, and rarely take him seriously if he asks for advice or information. When he has a friend over, the adult joins the children, playing and talking as they do.

Or, the parent takes the youngster everywhere he goes. He convinces himself that the child is so fond of him that he'd hate being left behind.

Mother-daughter dresses and father-son T-shirts further advertise the adult's need to share his child's identity.

The ultimate attempt of the parent to become his child's peer is sexual molestation. Fathers woo or coerce daughters into sexual play; mothers handle the penises of their small sons and laugh at erections.

The Effects

When his mother and father do not act as normal, responsible parents, the child's days are clouded with emotion. Often, he is depressed.[67] If he must take on an adult's duties, looking after himself, younger siblings, and a parent, he stays tense with worry.

The child of divorce assumes that the break-up was his fault. And surely, if the marriage was a mistake, so was his birth. He feels as lonely as the illegitimate child[33] and grows passive and indifferent.

The youngster's competency and emotional stability rest on his being able to adopt a clear, traditional, and appropriate sexual identity.[37,66] A boy feels little respect for a deserting father or one who does not support the family. Identifying with him, he is ashamed of himself and his sex.[63] His mother is the admirable adult, so he tends to adopt feminine traits.

Bender and Grugett[15] report that homosexual men have never thought of themselves as males. They were reared by domineering, belittling mothers, abusive fathers, or in homes missing one parent.

A girl brought up without a father or with one demeaned by the mother may be belligerent and coarse. She apes men in dress and haircut, competes fiercely with them at work and play, and may turn lesbian. She is proving to the world that she doesn't need men.

The child unable to identify with his like-sexed parent, for whatever reason, is a misfit who hates himself and everyone else. Boys reared alone by working mothers rebel.[15,45] Youngsters taught by fathers to despise their mothers become selfish and aggressive.

Anger and fear overwhelm the molested boy or girl. Adams-

Tucker[1] states that moderate to extreme emotional disturbance occurred in girls molested by their fathers at an early age and over a long period of time. Coerced into sexual acts, the young child fears the adult's anger and suffers silently and alone.[31,40] Later, there is deep resentment of the parent's betrayal.

A parent who plays the part of peer and encourages his son or daughter to defy rules and authority paralyzes him with anxiety. Rarely does he find courage to act or think on his own.[91]

Parenting errors cause psychophysiological complaints, stunted development, social withdrawal, emotional problems, sexual confusion, imitative behavior, and, in time, moral and intellectual deterioration.

REASONS FOR PARENTING ERRORS

There are six reasons why, unintentionally or deliberately, mothers and father harm their children: (1) ignorance, (2) fatigue, (3) a need to be important, (4) a wish to avoid trouble, (5) identification with the child, and (6) immaturity.

Ignorance

Nothing prepares adults for the never-ending problems and mysteries of child-rearing. To do the job well, every parent needs instruction. Physicians, books, a mother-in-law, friends, and experience all help. But knowledge may not be sought; information given may not be remembered or used.

Also, everyone tends to treat his children as he was treated. It's an imprint that won't go away. If the adults' rearing strengthened them, their sons and daughters will benefit. If it crippled them, subsequent generations will suffer.

A mother and father reared by lackadaisical parents don't know what good physical care is. They look after their own child on whim or if his screams command attention.

Few parents realize that a youngster's earliest companions determine whether he grows or lags socially.

Lax training in responsibility is an error of omission. Time slides by as adults fail to teach working, earning, and sensible spending.

A small child is rejected because parents don't realize their unique importance to him. Involved in adult activities and friendships, they seldom touch base with him and he grows up without parental guidance, interest, or love.

Fatigue

A parent's too-busy life ensures that there will be gaps in child-rearing. Fatigue and limits imposed by the clock smother adults' good intentions.

Too often, a boy's or girl's physical welfare is bypassed in the everyday turmoil. If both parents work and the preschooler is cared for by someone else, his parents don't know what he's eaten nor how much rest he's had. When the family finally assembles at six o'clock, everyone is exhausted. Dinner is a quick pizza and the child gets to bed when his parents do.

Weary mothers and fathers cave in quickly when there's opposition, teaching a youngster that he always can get his way. Every preschooler stocks an assortment of ways to test and pester his parents; tired mothers and fathers settle for half-hearted corrections. A youngest child or a brace of children born ten years after the first set seldom get the consistent, reasonable discipline given older sons and daughters.

Boys and girls are rejected because parents are too busy and worn out to give them the attention they crave. Some young couples have a baby a year, and the mother is so tired from her endless 18-hour days that postpartum depression, infanticide, and suicide sometimes occur.

Some fathers are workaholics. Paid and voluntary jobs crowd their days and leave no time for sons and daughters. News stories report the vandalism, drug-dealing, and suicide of adolescents whose fathers are prominent workers in the church, Scouts, Little League, and civic committees. Chances are good that the fathers were never home when their children were preschoolers who needed their interest and affection.

Mothers schedule hours of volunteer duties which benefit others and neglect their own boys and girls. Half of all mothers work for pay. Drained of energy and patience, they snap at the child who wants advice, sympathy, cuddling, or help.

The Need To Be Important

Everyone needs to feel important, but child-rearing practices should not be based on ego-building.

Parents who must "look good" hurt their youngster by copying the unwise methods of other mothers and fathers. If neighbor boys and girls are allowed to watch eight hours of TV daily, stay up till ten o'clock, and eat what and when they choose, unsure parents don't buck the trend. When adult friends enroll their preschoolers in dancing and gymnastics classes, parents trying to march in step do the same.

Reflected glory is sought by mothers and fathers who dedicate themselves to bringing up a child who stars, socially or athletically. They arrange for him to play with boys and girls from the "best" families; they plan elaborate parties for him; they send him to the top-rated private nursery school. Or they diligently take him to swimming or ice-skating lessons, hire a private coach, and supervise hours of daily practice.

To avoid embarrassment, some parents dominate every facet of the child's life, making sure he never fails in public.[17] They control him from morning till night and do for him what they fear he cannot do well. Overpunishment stems at times from an adult's need to mold his youngster's behavior into error-free performance.

The shaky mother or father delights in feeling superior to his child. Deliberately, the parent fails to keep promises, invents stories about the preschooler's past, gives him wrong answers to questions, or brutalizes him.

An overprotecting parent, manipulating the child's actions with strong censure or doting approval, glows with a feeling of his own power. Or, the adult may be doing what comes naturally. Levy[59] notes that many overprotective mothers are competent, responsible women who, from an early age, cared for younger siblings or an incapacitated parent.

Sometimes a woman working at a prestigious job never shifts, when home, from her public, in-charge ways. She is brusque with or indifferent to her preschooler, maintaining her proud sense of being somebody to whom others defer.

Men and women who consider themselves economic, social, or personal failures try for importance by humiliating their offspring and spouses. As children, they themselves were dominated by lordly parents.[60]

Avoidance of Trouble

Parents can be cowards. Dreading conflict, they set no rules: their children do what they like and the peace is kept.

To avoid emotional scenes, weak parents lie. Knowing a youngster will cry when they leave without him, they sneak off. When he must visit the dentist, they bundle him into the car, announcing a trip to his grandmother's. If the mother must have surgery, they say nothing to the child. If the father is leaving for good, he exits the preschooler's life without a farewell.

For some parents, backing away from trouble isn't enough: they run away from offspring. Many a mother of preschoolers admits that their problems make her feel helpless and stupid. She takes a full-time job and turns them over to someone else to rear.

Identifying With the Child

Some mothers and fathers squeeze into the youngster's shoes. Most women empathize with their children; if the father scolds his son or daughter, his wife scolds *him*.

It may be the father who is overly protective. If he remembers endless tongue-lashings from his own parents or if his wife is hard on the preschooler, he is gentle and sympathetic with him. Seldom does he correct the child. Never does he urge him to do his best.

Tender-minded adults know that foul weather, playmates' abuse, school failure, and disappointment distress their youngster, so they do their best to shield him from such hardships. But difficulty strengthens, not weakens. Adults should discover what a son or daughter can do for himself and let him do it.[65] As he copes with stress, the preschooler struggles, achieves, and feels good about himself.

Identification with the child can cause harsh rearing. Mothers want perfect daughters; fathers want outstanding sons. Youngsters name their same-sex parent as the more dominant and punitive of the two.[50]

Adults severely punished as children treat their boys and girls the same way. Justifying their actions, they declare, "A whipping never hurt me!"

Immaturity

Maturity demands selflessness, but some adults focus on nothing but their own feelings, wishes, and troubles. Although such mothers and fathers can learn to be adequate parents, the lessons will not come easily.

Immature adults need to be liked, are concerned only with themselves, and base their behavior on jealousy or hostility.

Need To Be Liked

Some friendless, insecure adults turn a child into a best buddy. While the parent watches TV at night, the youngster must keep him company until finally he sags into sleep on the floor. The tired son or daughter is hauled along on every shopping trip and visit, to every movie, concert, and ball game. The parent need go nowhere alone, but the worn-out child is cross from fatigue, tardy in development, and cheated out of leading his own life.

Sometimes a mother or father is lonely because the spouse is busy elsewhere and uninterested in the family. Or the marriage partner is lost because of divorce, desertion, or death. The child must replace the absent spouse.

When the adult's need to be liked comes first, overprotection and permissiveness are his automatic ways of dealing with his child.

Self-concern

Some parents think only of themselves and what they want. To them, the child is a bother whose conversation is boring and whose activities are dull.

Told to play with her troubled son thirty minutes daily, one mother asked, "Why should I lower myself to his level?"

A self-centered father neglects his child and spends all his free time with his own friends.

Or, pitying herself, a mother complains to her son or daughter about her severe headaches and painful back. She tells stories of mistreatment by neighbors, relatives, and her husband. Winning the youngster's service and sympathy, he becomes parent to her.

Jealousy

Adult jealousy can deny a preschooler friends. Resenting intruders on their turf, parents chase away youngsters who taunt, influence, or attract their child. They forbid him to play and teach him to distrust others.[9,91]

After the birth of their first child, a young father often feels isolated from his wife, displaced by the infant who now claims her total attention. Jealous, he retaliates either by criticizing or ignoring both his spouse and his child. As the son or daughter grows older, he refuses to intercede when his wife cannot handle the youngster.[70]

Sometimes a father appropriates the child for himself and excludes his wife from outings, conversations, and visits to his family. Jealous and resentful, the shut-out mother treats the youngster harshly.

Hostility

An adult who considers himself a failure is hostile toward everyone.

Guilt-ridden, he is alert to the misbehavior of his son or daughter. If the preschooler lies about taking a cooky, helps himself to an apple at the grocery store, or throws a rock at a playmate, the parent heaps scorn and punishment on him. He justifies his strong reaction by insisting that he is trying to save his child from repeating mistakes he has made.[91]

If the parent cheats or steals, he attacks his child in token punishment for his own actions.[64,71]

A hostile, weak partner in a troubled marriage persecutes not the mate, but the child. He cannot risk losing his spouse.

A hostile adult may even convince himself that his child deliberately fails in school or fights with neighbor boys and girls to put him in a bad light as an inadequate parent. Furious, he slanders, degrades, and punishes.

An angry parent, frustrated by difficult living and working conditions, may use his child as a scapegoat. He yells at and beats him instead of solving the problems which plague him.

Sometimes a mother or father never outgrows a childish wish to outwit and defy authority. He brags that he runs red lights and cheats on taxes. Or he resents his capable spouse and treats the child badly to distress his mate.

Ferret out the reasons for parenting errors and you can guide mothers and father into new and better habits.

REFERENCES

1. Adams-Tucker, C.: Proximate effects of sexual abuse in childhood: A report on 28 children. *American Journal of Psychiatry, 139*: 1252, 1982.
2. Anderson, G. L., and Anderson, H. H.: Behavior problems of children. In Pennington, L. A., and Berg, I. A., eds.: *An Introduction to Clinical Psychology*. New York, Ronald, 1948.
3. Aubry, J.: (Serious manifestations due to absence of maternal care.) *Evolution Psychiatrie, 1*: 1, 1955.
4. Ausubel, D. P., Balthazar, E. E., Rosenthal, I., Blackman, L. S., Schpoont, S. H., and Wellkowitz, J.: Perceived parent attitudes as determinants of children's ego structure. *Child Development, 33*: 173, 1954.
5. Ayer, M. E., and Bernreuter, R. G.: A study of the relationship between discipline and personality traits in little children. *Journal of Genetic Psychology, 50*: 165, 1937.
6. Bakwin, R., and Bakwin, H.: Discipline in children. *Journal of Pediatrics, 39*: 632, 1951.
7. Baldwin, A. L.: Pride and shame in children. *Newsletter, Division of Developmental Psychology, American Psychological Association*: 1959, Fall.
9. Bandura, A., and Walters, R. H.: *Social Learning and Personality Development*. New York, HR&W, 1963.
10. Bankart, C. P., and Anderson, C. C.: Short-term effects of prosocial television viewing on play of preschool boys and girls. *Psychological Reports, 44*: 935, 1979.
11. Battered-child syndrome. *Time, 80*: 60, 1962.
12. Becker, W. C., Peterson, D. R., Luria, Z., Shoemaker, D. J., and Hellmer, L. A.: Relations of factors derived from parent-interview ratings to behavior problems of five-year-olds. *Child Development, 33*: 509, 1962.

282   *Behavior Problems of Preschool Children*

13. Bee, H. L.: Prediction of IQ and language skill from perinatal status, child performance, family characteristics, and mother-infant inter action. *Child Development, 53*: 1134, 1982.
14. Bernhardt, K. S.: How permissive are you? *Bulletin of the Institute of Child Studies, 18*: 1, 1956.
15. Bender, L., and Grugett, A. E., Jr.: A follow-up report on children who had atypical sexual experience. *American Journal of Orthopsychiatry, 22*: 825, 1952.
16. Bleckmann, K. H.: (Children who are under too much pressure.) *Praxis der Kinderpsychologie und Kinderpsychiatrie, 6*: 273, 1957.
17. Block, J.: Personality characteristics associated with fathers' attitudes toward child-rearing. *Child Development, 26*: 41, 1955.
18. Block, J. H., Block, J., and Morrison, A.: Parental agreement-disagreement on child-rearing orientations and gender-related personality correlates in children. *Child Development, 52*: 965, 1981.
19. Bowlby, J.: Some pathological processes set in train by early mother-child separation. *Journal of Mental Science, 99*: 265, 1954.
20. Camp, B. W., Swift, W. J., and Swift, E. W.: Authoritarian parental attitudes and cognitive functioning in preschool children. *Psychological Reports, 50*: 1023, 1982.
21. Despert, J. L.: Some considerations relating to the genesis of autistic behavior in children. *American Journal of Orthopsychiatry, 21*: 335, 1951.
22. Droppleman, L. F., and Schaefer, E. S.: Boys' and girls' reports of maternal and paternal behavior. *Journal of Abnormal and Social Psychology, 67*: 648, 1963.
23. DuBois, F. S.: The security of discipline. *Mental Hygiene (N. Y.), 36*: 353, 1952.
24. Ellerstein, N. S.: *Child Abuse and Neglect.* New York, Wiley, 1981.
25. Elrod, M. M., and Crase, S. J.: Sex differences in self-esteem and parental behavior. *Psychological Reports, 46*: 719, 1980.
26. Erikson, E. H.: Growth and crises of the "healthy personality". In Kluckhohn, C., Murray, H. A., and Schneider, D. M., eds.: *Personality in Nature, Society, and Culture.* New York, Knopf, 1956.
27. Farina, A.: Patterns of role dominance and conflict in parents of schizophrenic patients. *Journal of Abnormal and Social Psychology, 61*: 31, 1960.
28. Flynn, T. M.: Parental attitudes and the preschool child's self-concept. *Child Study Journal, 9*: 69, 1979.
29. Fontana, V. J., and Besharov, D. J.: *The Maltreated Child: The Maltreatment Syndrome in Children — A Medical, Legal, and Social Guide,* 4th ed. Springfield, Thomas, 1979.
30. Friedrich, W. N., and Wheeler, K. K.: The abusing parent re-visited: A decade of psychological research. *Journal of Nervous and Mental Disease, 170*: 577, 1982.
31. Fritz, G. S., Stoll, K., and Wagner, N. N.: A comparison of males and females who were sexually molested as children. *Journal of Sex & Marital Therapy, 7*: 54, 1981.
32. Frumkin, R. M.: Childhood supervision and mental disorders. *Alpha Kappa*

Deltan, 24: 8, 1953.

33. Gardner, G. E.: Separation of the parents and the emotional life of the child. *Mental Hygiene (N Y.), 40*: 53, 1956.

34. Garmezy, N., Farina, A., and Rodnick, E.,: Direct study of child-parent interactions: I. The structured situational test. A method for studying family interaction in schizophrenia. *American Journal of Orthopsychiatry, 30*: 445, 1960.

35. Geisel, J. B.: Discipline viewed as a developmental need of the child. *Nervous Child, 9*: 115, 1951.

36. Goodenough, E. W.: Interest in persons as an aspect of sex difference in early years. *Genetic Psychology Monographs, 55*: 287, 1957.

37. Gray, S. W.: Perceived similarity to parents and adjustment. *Child Development, 30*: 91, 1959.

38. Harris, D. B., Rose, A. M., Clark, K. E., and Valasek, F.: Personality differences between responsible and less responsible children. *Journal of Genetic Psychology, 87*: 103, 1955.

39. Hartogs, R.: Discipline in the early life of sex-delinquents and sex criminals *Nervous Child, 9*: 167, 1951.

40. Haughton, P. B. T.: Child abuse: Early diagnosis and management. In Rodriguez, A., ed.: *Handbook of Child Abuse and Neglect*. Flushing, Med Exam, 1977.

41. Havighurst, R. J.: The functions of successful disciplne. *Understanding the Child, 21*: 35, 1952.

42. Heathers, G.: Emotional dependence and independence in nursery school play. *Journal of Genetic Psychology, 87*: 37, 1955.

43. Helper, M. M.: Parental evaluations of children and children's self-evaluations. *Journal of Abnormal and Social Psychology, 56*: 190, 1958.

44. Hess, R. D., and Goldman, H.: Parents' views of the effect of television on their children. *Child Development, 33*: 411, 1962.

45. Hoffman, L. W.: Effects of maternal employment on the child. *Child Development, 32*: 187, 1961.

46. Holmes, M. H.: The child's need for identification. *Mental Health (London), 10*: 64, 1951.

47. Huston-Stein, A.: The effects of TV action and violence on children's social behavior. *Journal of Genetic Psychology, 138*: 183, 1981.

48. Jensen, L., Peery, C., Adams, G., and Gaynard, L.: Maternal behavior and the development of empathy in preschool children. *Psychological Reports, 48*: 879, 1981.

49. Jersild, A. T.: *Child Psychology*, 7th ed. Englewood Cliffs, P-H, 1975.

50. Kagan, J.: The child's perception of the parent. *Journal of Abnormal and Social Psychology, 53*: 257, 1956.

51. Kagan, J., and Lemkin, J.: The child's differential perception of parental attributes. *Journal of Abnormal and Social Psychology, 61*: 440, 1960.

52. Kagan, J., and Moss, H. A.: *Birth to Maturity*. New York, Wiley, 1962.

53. Kagan, J., and Moss, H. A.: The stability of passive and dependent behavior from childhood through adulthood. *Child Development, 31*: 577, 1960.

54. Kearsley, R., Snider, M., Richie, R., Crawford, J. D., and Talbot, N. B.: Study of relations between psychologic environment and child behavior. *American Journal of the Disturbed Child, 104*: 12, 1962.

55. Kempe, R. S., and Kempe, C. H.: *Child Abuse.* Boston, Harvard U Pr, 1978.

56. Kinard, E. M.: Experiencing child abuse: Effects on emotional adjustment. *American Journal of Orthopsychiatry, 52*: 82, 1982.

57. Kotaskova, J.: (Changing influence and importance of some stimuli for the child during socialization.) *Psychológia a Patopsychológia Dielala, 11*: 405, 1977.

58. Lafore, G. G.: *Practices of Parents in Dealing with Preschool Children.* New York, Columbia U Pr, 1945.

59. Levy, D.: *Maternal Overprotection.* New York, Norton, 1966.

60. Lu, Y.: Parent-child relationship and marital roles. *American Sociological Review, 17*: 357, 1952.

61. McCandless, B. R., Bilous, C. B., and Bennett, H. L.: Peer popularity and dependence on adults in pre-school age socialization. *Child Development, 32*: 511, 1961.

62. Maccoby, E.: *Social Development.* New York, HarBraceJ, 1980.

63. McCord, W., McCord, J., and Verden, P.: Familial and behavioral correlates of dependency in male children. *Child Development, 33*: 313, 1962.

64. McDonald, R. L.: Intrafamilial conflict and emotional disturbance. *Journal of Genetic Psychology, 101*: 201, 1962.

65. Murphy, L.: Preventive implications of development in the pre-school years. In Caplan, G., ed.: *Prevention of Mental Disorders in Children.* New York, Basic, 1961.

66. Mussen, P. H.: Some antecedents and consequents of masculine sex-typing in adolescent boys. *Psychological Monographs, 75*: 506, 1961.

67. Mussen, P. H., Young, H. B., Gaddini, R., and Morante, L.: The influence of father-son relationships on adolescent personality and attitudes. *Journal of Child Psychology and Psychiatry, 4*: 3, 1963.

68. Peck, R. F., and Havighurst, R. J.: *The Psychology of Character Development.* New York, Wiley, 1960.

69. Phillips, E. L., Wiener, D. N., and Haring, N. G.: *Discipline, Achievement, and Mental Health.* Englewood Cliffs, P-H, 1960.

70. Plotsky, H., and Shereshefsky, P. An isolation pattern in fathers of emotionally disturbed children. *American Journal of Orthopsychiatry, 30*: 780, 1960.

71. Porter, B. M.: The relationship between marital adjustment and parental acceptance of children. *Journal of Home Economics, 47*: 157, 1955.

72. Powell, K. S.: Maternal employment in relation to family life. *Marriage and Family Living, 23*: 350, 1961.

73. Prasad, M. B., and Prasad, A.: Social and emotional development of pre-school children of employed mothers. *Journal of Social and Economic Studies, 3*: 73, 1975.

74. Rodriguez, A.: The abusive parents. In Rodriguez, A., ed.: *Handbook of Child Abuse and Neglect.* Flushing, Med Exam, 1977.

75. Rubenstein, J. L., Howes, C., and Boyle, P.: A two-year follow-up of infants

in community-based day care. *Journal of Child Psychology and Psychiatry, 22*: 209, 1981.

76. Rubin, K. H.: Social interaction and communicative egocentrism in preschoolers. *Journal of Genetic Psychology, 129*: 121, 1976.
77. Savage, A.: Child abuse thrives on ignorance, disbelief. *Rocky Mountain News,* Denver, April 5, 1983.
78. Schachter, F. F.: Toddlers with employed mothers. *Child Development, 52*: 958, 1981.
79. Schenk-Danzinger, C.: (Social difficulties of children who were deprived of maternal care in early childhood.) *Vita Humana, 4*: 229, 1961.
80. Serot, N., and Teevan, R. C.: Perception of the parent-child relationship and its relation to child adjustment. *Child Development, 32*: 373, 1961.
81. Serrano, A. C., Zuelzer, M. B., Howe, D. D., and Reposa, R. E.: Ecology of abusive and non-abusive families. *Journal of the American Academy of Child Psychiatry, 18*: 67, 1979.
82. Slater, P. E.: Parental behavior and the personality of the child. *Journal of Genetic Psychology, 101*: 53, 1962.
83. Sontag, L. W., and Kagan, J.: The emergence of intellectual achievement motives. *American Journal of Orthopsychiatry, 33*: 532, 1963.
84. Sorokin, P. A., and Grove, D. S.: Notes on the friendly and antagonistic behavior of nursery school children. In Sorokin, P. A., ed.: *Explorations in Altruistic Love and Behavior.* Boston, Beacon, 1950.
85. Spock, B.: *Baby and Child Care.* New York, Dutton, 1976.
86. Stendler, C. B.: Critical periods in socialization and overdependency. *Child Development, 23*: 3, 1952.
87. Stott, L. H., and Ball, R. S.: Consistency and change in ascendance-submission in the social interaction of children. *Child Develoment, 28*: 259, 1957.
88. Straker, G., and Jacobson, R. S.: Aggression, emotional maladjustment, and empathy in the abused child. *Develop mental Psychology, 17*: 762, 1981.
89. Sutton, R. S.: An appraisal of certain aspects of children's social behavior. *Journal of Teacher Education, 13*: 30, 1962.
90. Ucko, L. E., and Moore, T.: (Parental roles as seen by young children in doll play.) *Vita Humana, 6*: 213, 1964.
91. Verville, E.: *Behavior Problems of Children.* Philadelphia, Saunders, 1967.
92. Vogel, E. F.: The marital relationship of parents of emotionally disturbed children: Polarization and isolation. *Psychiatry, 23*: 1, 1960.
93. Walsh, A. M.: *Self Concepts of Bright Boys with Learning Difficulties.* New York, Columbia U Pr, 1956.
94. Wang, J. D.: The relationship between children's play interests and their mental ability. *Journal of Genetic Psychology, 93*: 119, 1958.
95. Wilkins, W. L.: Social peers and parents. *Education, 73*: 234, 1952.
96. Winn, M.: *The Plug-In Drug.* New York, Viking, 1977.
97. Witty, P., and Kinsella, P.: Children and the electronic Pied Piper. *Education, 80*: 48, 1959.

98. Zahn-Waxler, C., and Chapman, M.: Immediate antecedents of caretakers' methods of discipline. *Child Psychiatry and Human Development, 12*: 179, 1982.

Chapter 23

TEACHING PARENTS: PRIVATE CONSULTATIONS

YOU understand the pressures, irritations, fears, and disappointments of these parents. You have identified the traps in which they are caught, the bad habits which chain them. You know their preschooler, both his strengths and his weaknesses, better than they do. You have decided what must be done to quash the emotion-based behavior which has antagonized adults and earned punishment for him.

How will you get his mother and father to change, to do what is best?

PARENT FEELINGS

Put yourself in their places. When they appear to listen to your report on their child, they walk through the door dreading the next hour. They still feel guilty because their son or daughter is not behaving or learning as he should. They still think it must be their fault and that you will say so and scold.

They fear the worst. Will you announce that their child is severely disturbed, that the outlook is bleak, that he must come to see you weekly *ad infinitum* at a high fee, or even that he must be sent away to a special residential school or hospital?

287

You're the authority, but they're not sure about you. Bristling inside, they come prepared to argue. They believe they won't like what you say, so they don't like you.

To avoid sinking in this muddy mess, they plan to distance themselves from the whole unsavory business. They tell themselves that making things better is your job, not theirs. They'll stand aside while you remodel their youngster.

Dread, antagonism, rejection of responsibility: these are their feelings as they wait for your pronouncements about their child.

PRESENTING DIAGNOSTIC FINDINGS

Introduction

Stay relaxed. Start by thanking the parents for their help. Without all the information they gave, you could not have figured out what was happening. Tell them you enjoyed getting to know their son or daughter, that they have much to be proud of. This is always true.

Remind yourself that you are no oracle and they are no dunces. Treat them as equals who are temporarily flustered by the importance of this meeting.

Tell them that you will review each test. You will be talking steadily and they are to interrupt, ask questions, and make you explain anything which is unclear. Say that you want them to know everything you know about their preschooler.

Reviewing Tests

Describe the child's behavior during testing, balancing the negative with the positive.

If you must state that Vicki was reluctant to try what you asked of her (she hid under your desk), add that sometimes she overcame her hesitancy and then tried hard to do her best.

If you must report that David isn't skilled at taking care of property (he threw everything he got his hands on), tell them also that once he gets interested, he concentrates well. (Fascinated with the operation of your stopwatch, he refused to give it back.)

Name every pleasing trait you observed during testing. Leave the impression with the parents that you approve of their youngster. They need to approve of him too.

Review the physical tests first, then the intelligence tests, and finally the emotion and motivation tests.

Give the name of each test and state how it is administered and what it measures. This puts the mother and father in the testing room with you and their child; their displeasure at being excluded from your private encounter vanishes. Reporting on each test also convinces them that you were thorough; you got lots done in the hour or two you spent with their youngster.

What their son or daughter did on tests is totally new information to parents. More often than not, they are astonished by their child's abilities, thoughts, and feelings. They are equally surprised by his failure to do something they consider simple, but the failure explains for the first time why he has difficulty at school or can't keep up with playmates.

What you say must be clear. Avoid terms they do not understand. If you do use a technical term, such as *performance I.Q.*, explain it.

Choose your words with care. "Brain damage" is scary. "A poorly functioning central nervous system" sounds less drastic and irreversible.

Conclusions

Finally, tell them why the child behaves as he does, pointing out the cause-and-effect relationships revealed by the examination. Stories and similes illustrate what you are talking about.

Liken the constant activity of their anxious youngster to the behavior of the hapless victim of rowdy cowboys shooting at his feet. In terror, he hops this way and that, trying to avoid the pain he knows will surely come. Only when the shots cease does his erratic, mindless jumping-about end.

Contrast the effects of violence and calm on a child's actions by re-telling the fable of the wind and the sun. Each wagered that he would be first to remove the coat of the man walking beneath them. The wind blew and blew, as hard as he could, but the man wrapped his coat more tightly around himself. Then the sun beamed steadily, gently. Soon the man loosened his coat, then took it off.

After you have finished presenting your diagnosis, ask the parents, "Does all this make sense to you?"

Nearly always they agree that it does. They are relieved to have explanations for actions which have puzzled and alarmed them for so long. Ask them if they have questions or disagree with anything you have said. If so, explain again as simply and completely as you can.

Diagnosis of Retardation

Take extra care when you must tell parents that their preschooler is retarded. Even though they may expect this, your verdict will stun and wound.

Begin by asking them at what age level they believe their child functions.

They'll hedge, "He does some things as well as any child his age."

Then they'll peg accurately their four-year-old's abilities as nearer those of a two-year old.

Agree that they are right. Your tests confirm their observations.

They will ask a torrent of practical questions. They'll want to know about schooling, how to deal with skeptical relatives, how much to expect of the child, what to say to friends and neighbors, and whether the retardation will upset the family 's other children.

Hidden behind every question is the unspoken one: must they care for this youngster all of their lives?[6]

Reassure them. Describe training, recreational, and vocational facilities available to their child. Let them know that many young adult retardates live together in homes with supervisors and work to support themselves. Even more manage alone, holding jobs and even marrying. Whether their child will achieve this level of independence depends on his capacity (and you will re-test regularly) and his training.

A mother and father feel both helpless and useless in their strange, unwanted role as parents of a retarded son or daughter. Emphasize that their child needs them to bring him up well. They must teach him to work, to be kind, to care for himself, and to control his behavior, just as they do their other boys and girls. When they know they have a job to do, but it's not a lifetime sentence, they feel better.

PRESENTING THE TREATMENT PLAN

Trying to absorb the deluge of facts and conclusions you have given them, parents still have misgivings over what you will say about treatment.

Set them straight at once. Ask if getting rid of the problems is what they want to do. It will be. Then give them hope. Tell them that a preschool child is not set in his ways. He quickly changes his behavior when he is handled differently.

He also responds promptly to his parents' wishes. His mother and father are the most important people in the world to him. Despite appearances, he desperately wants to please them and he is miserable when he believes he does not.

But he is only a small child. His good intentions, like those of his elders, seldom are enough to curb actions which get him into trouble. He needs to be taught, gradually and continually, how to behave. And the method of instruction must not confuse and frighten him.

Explain that teaching him will be their task, both because they live with the child and because they are the ones he values most. You will steer them in the right direction and keep them on course.

Add that you have a long list of steps they can take. Because there's no way they can do everything at once, you would like them to come in eight times, once each week for the first month, every two weeks the second month, and once during each of the third and fourth months. Then you will re-examine the youngster and everything should be much better.

Describe what will happen in your one-hour consultations. First, they will tell you how their son or daughter reacted to the changes they made and together you can judge progress. Then they can talk about any problems which developed during the week and, with you, figure out why they happened and what to do next time. Finally, you will explain what they need to do before you see them again. Let them know that they can call between appointments if they hit snags.

Tell them you will talk with the teacher, doctor, speech therapist or any other professional working with their child, so that everyone handles him in the same ways. You'll fill them in on these conferences and you'll keep in touch regularly with the other professionals.[2]

List the goals you hope to reach during the next four months; ask if these are what they want. Perhaps they'll add more, but it's unlikely they'll delete those you name.

Find out if they have questions about these plans and answer them.

Then set a regular appointment time, one which is best for them. Offer to see them first thing in the morning, during the noon hour, even at night or on Saturday if necessary. Make it easy for the father to come. If both parents work on the new ideas, they'll back each other up. If one is left out, he may sabotage the efforts of the other.

They may ask for a copy of your report. Legally, they are entitled to it. But, to make sure your frank observations do not harm your rapport with them, ask for a week to prepare a summary, explaining that the detailed report is a working paper for yourself. In the summary, include the essential results of the study and the plans for remediation which you have discussed with them.

Finally, give them one task to begin with. This should be a simple one: *e.g.*, cut TV-watching to thirty minutes daily. Explain why this is important.

Warn them not to tell their preschooler that the reason he can't keep on the television is because "the doctor said so." If their child is to retain his trust in them as competent to care for him, they must not appear to be slavishly taking orders from an outsider. They must take credit (or blame) for the changes.

They should tell the youngster they've talked it over and decided he's watching too much TV. From now on the limit is thirty minutes a day.

Remind them that they can ask you, when they next come, about any behavior which has frustrated or perplexed them. Suggest that they make a note when it happens so they won't forget to bring it up and thus be caught with the same problem again.

THE CONSULTATIONS

You have only eight hours to achieve miracles. You must motivate the parents, your on-the-scene agents, to do what is needed; you must answer accurately the questions they raise; you must underscore progress and deal with stalemate; and you must be satisfied wih less than perfect compliance with your plans.

Not only do you want life to improve for the child, you also want the parents to gain in confidence, self-respect, and knowledge.

The hour will go faster than you and they like.

Parent Stalling

Don't waste time on the weather or the latest election. Plunge right in. Ask how cutting TV-watching to thirty minutes a day is going.

Perhaps they'll say, "He surprised us. He didn't complain as much as we thought he would."

But probably they'll say, "He really doesn't watch all that much. We don't like to set rules about it."

Or, "We didn't start that. It was a different kind of week. We were gone a lot and the sitter lets him watch all he likes."

In other words: strike-out, first time up. Expect this, and you won't feel betrayed or discouraged. It will remind you again that parents are human. Humans tend to stick with old, comfortable ways. There's no risk of an unpleasant, emotional blow-up from the child, one they're sure they won't manage well.

Also, you gave them a lot to digest in your session last week. They're still chewing on bits and pieces of what you said: "He's good with words . . . he can't draw a square . . . he's afraid all the time . . . he likes his brother . . . those older girls may have fooled around with him . . . he's punished too much . . . ."

Trying to remember, dwelling on one remark you made, living with mingled feelings of guilt, relief, anger, and sympathy, they don't get around to following orders. In fact, they can't see that reducing television-watching matters at all.

Tell them again why it matters. Their uptight son needs time in his day, hours of it, to play with other boys, to do chores, to be with them, to create. He doesn't need to re-live vivid scenes of anger and cruelty at night when he's in bed. He doesn't need to sit for hours staring at a small, bright screen. He doesn't need to be certain that the world is a frightening place. Turning off the television is the initial, giant step toward restoring his health, stimulating his intelligence, calming his sleep, and rousing dormant social skills.

Sometimes parents are slow to follow instructions because they resent being told what to do. They're paying you good money to cure their child, but you're not doing the work. They are and that's unfair.

When you suspect self-pity and firm reluctance to exert themselves, repeat what you said before: they live with the child — you don't. They are important to the child — you're not.

Tell them that if they can get the hang of what it takes to bring up a child well, they'll be able to manage future problems (and they will surely come) with confidence and success. Rearing a child who grows up to be an adult they are proud of is the greatest satisfaction any parent can have. But bringing up a son or daughter takes thought and effort. This is their chance to become experts at it.

Sometimes mothers and fathers drag their heels because they want to talk with you forever, not just eight times. They like the idea of spilling out all the worries they've either bottled up or unloaded on relatives. If they don't solve the problems, they can keep coming.

This is flattering, but it puts you in the same category as relatives and friends who listen patiently, sympathize, sigh, and wait unwillingly for the next woeful tale.

You're supposed to be more useful than that. Put an end to delaying tactics by saying you know it's difficult to get started on a new program, but that the three of you have only eight sessions in which to accomplish a great many changes. Review the goals. Ask again if this is what they want.

Solving Problems

Then go to the events of the week which disturbed them. Perhaps the child, in a fit of temper, knocked all the glasses off the dinner table. Or he disappeared for three hours. Or, suddenly, he's smothering them with hugs and kisses and telling them over and over that he loves them.

Ask what they did about the problem. They'll expect the question, though they may blush at their own behavior. Whatever they say, just nod. Make no comment. Knowing they must tell you what they did serves as a brake to future impulsive reactions.

Find out their theories on why their preschooler acted as he did. Sometimes they'll say they have no idea. Usually, however, after thinking a few seconds, they'll answer vaguely, "He was angry . . . tired . . . jealous."

Sometimes they'll pin it down. "His brother grabbed his dessert and that was the last straw. Danny had pestered him all afternoon."

Or, "I'd scolded him a dozen times that day. I guess he'd had more than he could take."

Or, "Maybe he's trying to apologize for his bad behavior."

Right or wrong, their thinking about why the child behaves as he does signals a leap into objectivity. Before, they responded with reflex displeasure and punishment. Now they try to make sense of the youngster's actions.

Accept their ideas as possibilities, probing further if they're off-the-cuff generalities. Then add any they've missed: *e.g.,* a child who continually shows affection for his parent is asking the parent to show some for him. He needs proof that he is loved because he's sure that he is not.

Next, ask the mother and father what they believe is the best way to handle knocking glasses off the table, running away, or exaggerated affection. If their ideas are sound, say so. If not, suggest another solution, explaining why it will work.

Reviewing distressing events this way, a mother and father gradually learn to think before they act, to see matters from the child's point of view, and to do what is needed to keep the youngster on an even keel. By the end of your eight consultations, they are well able to understand what happens and to choose fair, workable solutions by themselves.

Closing the Hour

After you have talked over the problem behavior of the child, give the parents the new task they are to do next week: *e.g.,* praise the youngster once each day. Be sure they understand that they also must cut television-watching to thirty minutes daily. Duties don't fade away if they're skipped; they stack up. Write exactly what they are to do and hand them the list.

Then have them tell you why the new assignment is important. They should be able to come up with at least one reason: "He'll be encouraged to do better." Ask for any other reasons, let them think, and hope they'll find more.

When they figure out the point of certain changes, there's a solid push to make them. They see their connection with the problems, they find that what they do affects the way the child acts, and they discover that they can get the kind of behavior they want if they know what they're about.

Next, summarize in two or three sentences what you have talked about during the hour and what they are to do next and why. Say a few kind words about their reasoning and, if they followed your instructions, what they did the previous week.

Close by asking if they have any other questions or comments. Then get ready for a blockbuster.

Most parents, especially during early consultations, save their most devastating experience to relate in the final few minutes. The grim memory of it has lurked for an hour; courage to report the startling or embarrassing incident has not surfaced. Now, urgently, it does. Do your best to listen, review the parent's ideas, and add your own in the time you have left.

Because critical developments bubble up so often when time has lapsed, you need to watch the clock carefully toward the end of the hour. It's not that you don't want to give as much time as is really needed, but rather that part of your job is to teach the parents to plan ahead. Just as you know before they come what you want to accomplish, so should they. If they decide ahead of time what they want to talk about, they won't drag in difficult topics at the last minute.

And if you begin and end every session on time, that tells them you are dependable and responsible. You want them to copy you in those ways.

Ending Consultations

Each time you change the consultation interval (from weekly to every other week, and from that to monthly), ask the parents if the stretch-out is all right with them. Nearly always, it is. They've gained confidence and are ready to shorten the crutch. Say again that they can phone you about problems which trouble them in between your meetings.

Before the last session, remind them that this will be the final one scheduled, that you will then re-examine their child and tell them what changes the tests show.

After you have done so, ask if they would like to come in once or twice more or if they believe everything is going well now.

Some parents will choose to return; most will not. Those who do come in after an encouraging re-evaluation often have little to say. No major problems have developed. They have handled day-to-day conflicts without undue emotion. Usually they agree that more consultations are not needed.

Tell them that they may phone or return to talk any time. If they want you to re-evaluate the child in a year, they can set up an appointment for this.

Your suggesting various ways they can keep in touch tends to dissipate the clouds of concern they feel at carrying on alone.

If you've done your job (and been lucky), the parents now know a great deal about their preschooler, they have abandoned destructive habits in dealing with him, they understand why he does what he does, and they are able to teach him how to act as they want him to.

Everyone in the family is calmer. Everyone feels more kindly toward one another. Probably they feel kindly toward you too.

REFERENCES

1. Brody, S., and Axelrad, S.: *Mothers, Fathers, and Children.* New York, Intl Univs Pr, 1978.
2. Brusiloff, P., and Schulman, R.: Parental intervention: A growing alliance. *Family & Child Mental Health Journal, 7:* 30, 1981.
3. Curtis, J. M.: Effect of therapist's disclosure on patients' impressions of empathy, competence, and trust in an analogue of a psychotherapeutic interac-

tion. *Psychological Reports, 48*: 127, 1981.
4. Fleischman, M. J.: A replication of Patterson's "Intervention for boys with conduct problems." *Journal of Consulting & Clinical Psychology, 49*: 342, 1981.
5. Nielsen, G.E.: *Helping Children Behave.* Chicago, Nelson-Hall, 1974.
6. Noland, R. L., ed.: *Counseling Parents of the Mentally Retarded.* Springfield, Thomas, 1970.
7. Rogers, F. K.: *Parenting the Difficult Child.* Radnor, Chilton, 1979.
8. Wilkes, J. R.: Involving parents in children's treatment. In Noland, R. L., ed.: *Counseling Parents of the Emotionally Disturbed Child.* Springfield, Thomas, 1972.

Chapter 24

TEACHING PARENTS: REMEDIAL CLASSES

I T'S fun to teach classes in child management.
Parents act differently in a group: they're more thoughtful, less dependent.

When several people work together, change is more certain than when you must coax one set of reluctant parents to try new ways.[5]

You'll learn from the members of your class. They'll be fast, accurate thinkers; they'll come up with reasonable answers to every question you ask, answers it has taken you years to tease from cases and books. They'll use methods you've never thought of, methods which make sense and work. What they know and do teaches you respect for their parenting ingenuity.

CLASSES VERSUS PRIVATE CONSULTATIONS

Remedial classes are preferable to private consultations in every way but one: only mothers attend. Sometimes a lone father, working night shift, will come, but that's rare.

Still, fathers often ease out of private consultations. They find excuses to stay away, sometimes because they don't want to do what you say and sometimes because they're embarrassed at talking child-rearing with a psychologist.

Mothers welcome help. A mother shares thousands of experiences with her son or daugher; a father, not nearly so many. A mother is sad when her youngster is sad, delighted when he's delighted; a father finds his child interesting and expects to be proud of him. A mother, conscientious and worrying, is burdened 24 hours a day by parenthood; a father assumes all is well and relegates parenting to odd moments.

And many young women, divorced, are bringing up their children alone. They are after all the knowledge and skills they can get.

Not only do women want help, they also like to get it in groups. Although they stall over tasks you set them privately, they'll undertake them when others do. Class assignments are a shared experiment, not a reminder of their own mistakes.

And every mother who listens to the disasters other women endure instantly cheers up. Her youngster doesn't set fires, soil himself, beat up the neighbor child, or refuse to eat anything but peanut butter and jelly sandwiches.

Guilt drifts away. In this class are intelligent, lively, reasonable, *normal* women, each of whom has trouble understanding and dealing with her little one. Problems with children must be natural, nothing to be ashamed about.

LEADING THE CLASS

So here you are with your eager, curious mothers. How do you make your course worth their while?

This is how: (1) teach them what you know; (2) provide a setting for them to share experiences and insights, to think, and to act. If you are to succeed you must plan well and stay vigilant.[1]

Although a woman enjoys talking herself, she doesn't like to hear only the rambling thoughts and strong opinions of strangers no wiser than she is. She comes to learn from you and she counts on you to direct the class so that time is used well.

As expert-in-charge, you needn't be pompous. Quite the opposite: avoid lengthy, murky lectures; don't insist that only one idea (yours) is correct; and never ridicule what a class member says or side with one against another. Stay honest, cheerful, and supportive. And keep your class busy.

ORGANIZATION

Number and Length of Sessions

Twelve sessions is a good number. If you explore a different topic at each meeting, you'll have time to review the basics of child-rearing. With three months of weekly thought and action, stressful parenting cools into calm know-how. And there's time to set new habits firmly enough so that the old ones don't ooze out again.

Ninety-minute meetings work well. An hour isn't long enough for all you must do. Two hours drags and wearies.[2]

It's best to meet every week, so classes can be shoe-horned into a mother's seven-day schedule. Avoid summer; vacations interfere and crucial sessions are missed.

Participants

You don't want a crowd when your class is for troubled mothers. Six to eight are enough. Everyone gets to know each other; everyone gets a chance to talk. Yet with half-a-dozen families represented, there'll be a rainbow of opinions, ideas, and experiences.

It's possible to hold classes for as few as three mothers or as many as ten, but these are the outside limits. You can't sustain a workmanlike atmosphere with only two women: time slips away in casual talk and irrelevant anecdotes. With more than ten, you'll remain strangers and never get the feeling of cameraderie which keeps everyone coming.

How do you get a mother to join the group? Include class attendance in your treatment plan and tell her about it when you present your diagnosis.

Say the class deals with principles and techniques for managing preschoolers. You'll be discussing such topics as discipline, responsibility, playmates, and getting along in the family. You'll meet twelve times, once a week for a one-and-one-half hours, and the group will consist of six to eight parents.

You would like her to come. You are sure she'll have much to contribute. Let her know that everyone has a good time, but also that you get the job done. Add that class members may phone or come in for a private consultation any time.

The father will be in your office as you describe the class, so you invite both parents to come. If he says he can't take off work every week for three months, probably he can't. Tell him you'll miss him, but that his wife can fill him in on what goes on.

Even if she also holds a job, it's likely she can arrange to come. Some employers, sympathetic to mothers with upsetting children, let them go for help without penalty. Others allow them to make up lost time. Some will excuse employees but dock their pay. A working mother usually gets to most sessions, skipping those she thinkswill be less useful in her situation.

If the mother agrees to join the class, find out if there is any day or hour she cannot come. When you have recruited enough mothers, write each a letter, giving the location, time, day of the week, and date of the first meeting. Ask them to bring a small notebook and a pen or pencil. A day or two before the first session, call to remind them.

It's unnecessary to limit the class to parents whose youngsters have identical problems or like personalities. A mix teaches more. The only similarity should be the children's age: all participants should be seeking help for preschoolers.

Agenda

Every week except the first, the class begins with your summation of the discussion and conclusions of the previous week. This prods memories and puts everyone in the mood for work.

Then ask each mother to report what happened as she carried out the week's assignment. Youngsters' comments and reactions to the new methods or rules are funny and soon everyone is laughing. These real-life tales prepare each mother to smile, not panic, when her own child tries his clever dodges. Tell the mothers they did well and that they are to continue the assignment for the duration of the course.

Then announce the topic for the day. Set the stage with a brief introduction, stressing the subject's importance and touching on controversy or misconceptions it arouses.

Next, divide the class into small groups of two, three, or four people and send them to different areas of the room. If the class's total attendance is three, split up just the same. You join one of the mothers.

Hand one member of each group a typed question. This designates her as chairman. She reads the question aloud and sees that everyone gets to talk about it. Appoint another mother in each group secretary. She writes what each person says and reports to the full class. Rotate the jobs of chairman and secretary so everyone serves.

Every group gets a different question and five minutes to answer it. Then the class reassembles and each secretary reports her group's answers. Solicit other ideas from the full class, compliment them on their conclusions, and summarize.

The technique of small group discussion has been used for years to entice idea-sharing. But it can founder. It does so when too many persons form a group, when there is no designated leader or recorder, and when the allotted time is too long. A thirty-minute discussion can deteriorate into rambling vagaries which annoy rather than inform.

With a five-minute time limit, the mothers think quickly and incisively. With a chairman and a secretary, the meeting is businesslike. And with no more than three or four participants, everyone speaks up.

Once accustomed to talking with two or three women and soon acquainted with everyone in the class (because you designate group members and vary them each time), no one hesitates to express opinions when the full class comes together.

Divide into small groups once or twice during each session. Well handled, this procedure serves as a break, sharpens thinking, and routs strangeness.

After the small group questions and answers have been reviewed, continue discussion by asking other questions which deal with various aspects of the day's topic. Get in as many as you can; each mother will pick up on facts and ideas pertinent to her own problems.

Then have the class members write next week's assignment in their notebooks. Usually it will be not one task, but two or three. Sometimes there will be five or six suggestions, so tell them to choose any two. More often than not, they'll try all of them. Ask what the purpose of this assignment is. They'll know. What they are to do is the direct outcome of conclusions they've reached during class.

Finally, summarize the session. Then, if there are left-over moments, ask if there are questions — on any child-rearing problem. Get the other mothers' ideas if there's time; if not, give your own.

Topics

The topics chosen alert mothers to common errors in child-rearing.

Watch the order of events. If emotionally-charged subjects are introduced too soon, there can be a breakdown in objective thinking and the carrying out of assignments. Other disastrous sessions may follow the pattern and class members begin to drop out. Start with innocuous topics and postpone painful ones until the group is cohesive and everyone is well acquainted.

This sequence works well:

1. The Preschool Child: Motivation and Traits
2. Fatigue and Behavior
3. Independence and Competence
4. Discipline (1): Why Children Disobey
5. Discipline (2): How To Teach Obedience
6. Responsibility
7. Self-respect
8. Play and Playmates
9. The Family: Brothers and Sisters; Grandparents
10. The Family: Father *vs.* Mother
11. Problem-solving
12. Summary and Evaluation

THE CLASSES

The First Meeting

What happens at the first meeting can decide whether everyone or anyone comes to the second. The mothers are curious about what the class will do for them. They're also lonely; you're the only person they know and you must be shared. And they're uneasy at being in this group assembled to learn how to bring up their own children. They hope they won't say something stupid.

Keep things sensible. Don't try for "oneness" by having everyone sit in a circle. You've asked them to bring notebooks and they'll be writing, so put the chairs around a conference table. You sit at one end. There'll be room for your papers and you can see everyone. This is a class.

Business Matters

Tell them you're glad to see them. Say that after today the class always will start and end on time.

INTRODUCTIONS. Then ask each mother to introduce herself, tell where she's from (if different suburbs or parts of a county are represented), and give the sex and age of the preschooler about whom she's concerned.

Don't ask for other details about themselves, their families, or the problems of the child. This is only a nod at getting acquainted, a reminder that they're all swimming in the same cold water.

The age and sex of their youngsters-in-trouble characterize the group. Perhaps they're evenly divided between five-year-olds and two-year-olds, or most are boys. These are interesting facts which unite these strangers right away.

THE COURSE. Next, describe the course again: there will be twelve meetings and you will review major aspects of child-rearing. Say that they'll find they already know much of what you'll talk about. But it's easy to forget what you know in the heat of a momentary problem. The class will jog memories. Add that if each of them takes home one new idea a week, her time will be well spent.

ASSIGNMENTS. Tell the mothers they'll be given an assignment every week, not something to read, but something to do. No task will be difficult, but each will require time and energy. Say that if they fail to do the assignments, they'll enjoy themselves during the next three months, but when the class ends, there will have been no change in the child. Each week you'll talk over what happened when they tried the assignment and they can look forward to fascinating stories.

Hand out class schedules which list topics and dates. Then say you hope they'll make it to every session, but that illness or other crises do occur over a three months' period. Anyone who must miss a meeting but wants the assignment should call another member of the group, not you, to get it.

Make this procedure clear from the start. Otherwise, you'll be caught in lengthy phone conversations in which you review the entire ninety-minute session for one or more absentee mothers. You don't have time for that.

It's not unusual for some members of your class to go out for coffee after the meeting is over. They get to know one another well and don't hesitate to get in touch when they've had to miss a session.

So that no one feels you've slammed the door on out-of-class contacts with you, add that usually there'll be time for questions at the end of each session, and that any of them may phone with a problem or come in for a private conference.

TIME LIMITS. Remind them that you have only a one-and-one-half hours to deal with each topic, there are eight of you, and women love to talk; therefore, everyone should remember to speak briefly so that time is fairly shared.

Setting the Tone

FEELINGS. If you bypass recognition of the mothers' unhappy feelings, they'll never lose them. Brooding about their hard life interferes with clear thinking and the will to change. So begin by letting them know you understand what they've gone through.

Re-create for them the delight and pride they knew when their children were born. Then talk about what happened next: as an infant, the child cried and cried and could not be consoled; a year later he regularly wet on the living room rug and emptied drawers, closets, and wastebaskets; two years after that he sassed and refused to take his nap. Their child, of such hope and promise, turned into a sad disappointment and they became depressed, anxious, and guilty.

How do parents deal with such a letdown? It's natural to look for someone or something to blame: the child's other parent, cousin, nursery teacher, grandmother, or HIM — a thoroughly miserable specimen of humanity.

Joy, despair, blaming: these are the usual feelings of mothers whose hopes and standards are too high.

Problems with children are the rule, not the exception. Every youngster parades four or five each year. As time goes on, the problems differ, but they're always in plain sight. Parents who brag, "We've never had a minute's trouble with our Desmond," have never spent a minute with Desmond.

CHALLENGE. Tell the mothers that theirs is the most important job in the world. If everyone brought up children well, emotional disturbances, crime, even war, would shrink to manageable levels. Remind them that their task is unique. No one can replace them as mothers of their own children.

Now that you have alternately consoled and inspired them, say that if they faithfully attend this ladies' aid society and complete their assignments, they will become the world's best mothers.

Baseline

Now it's time to mark their starting point. Ask each mother to write in her notebook everything which is wrong with her child, everything she'd change if she could wave a magic wand and make it happen. This catalogue of her child's sins is private, not read to the class.

The list is a beginning, a baseline. When the twelve sessions are over, each mother can review today's inventory to see what faults have disappeared. Many will be gone.

When everyone is finished, introduce the day's topic.

1. The Preschool Child: Motivation and Traits

Purpose

To alert parents to the admirable qualities in their children.

To help them accept their youngster's limitations as normal and temporary.

To teach them to monitor what they say and do, so that the preschooler is encouraged, not discouraged.

Introduction

Many difficulties with small children develop because adults know too little about youngsters at different ages. Parents either expect the child to show the same control and wisdom they do, or they fail to change as the child grows: they treat him, year after year, as though he still were a helpless infant.

Also, it's easy to forget that children, even little ones, feel the same way everyone else does about how others act toward them. They respond just as their mother and father do to approval and disapproval.

Today's task is to figure out (1) what the preschooler wants and needs from his parents to do his best and (2) what he is like.

Discussion Questions

1. What is the difference between loving and liking? (To the child, loving is food, clothing, protection, hugs. Liking is respect for what he is and can do. The child takes love for granted as a right; he knows that liking must be earned.)
2. Which does your child want from you? (Liking.)
3. In what ways are children like adults? (How they feel about the way they're treated; need for praise, approval, achievement, independence, comforting.)
4. In what ways are they different from adults? (Limited self-control, knowledge, and experience; short memory; no build-up of fear and anger — they forgive quickly and forget emotional scenes and punishment; reflex, strong emotion resulting in physical and verbal attacks.)
5. What discourages the child? (Constant scolding, correction, name-calling, punishment, rebuffing affection, abandonment.)
6. What makes him want to do better? (Praise, teaching him what to do, letting him do all he can by himself, certainty that parents care what happens to him.)
7. What makes him want to do worse? (Severe punishment, lying

to him, unfair treatment, obvious preference for someone else.)

8. How does a child learn what his parents think of him? (By what they say and do.)

9. Do parents ever give the child false ideas of what they think of him? (Often. They overdo discipline and he believes he can't please them. They try for his affection by waiting on him and excusing poor behavior and he believes they think he is incompetent.)

10. Describe the preschool child, considering his temper, neatness, courage, daring, pressure, competitiveness, confidence with peers of both sexes, confidence with adults, self-control, self-evaluation, talents, interests, and skills.

11. Which of his negative qualities are normal for his age? (Poor memory, limited self-control, ready emotion, negativism, sloppiness, carelessness with belongings.)

12. Which will disappear without attention from adults? (Most either disappear or weaken as child grows older.)

13. Which will not? (Training helps a child remember, gain self-control, inhibit strong emotion.)

14. Write down two experiences in your own child-rearing which were helpful and why.

15. Write down two experiences in your own child-rearing which were destructive and why.

Assignment

1. Spend 30 minutes each day alone with your child, doing what he wants to do. Let him take the lead and do most of the talking. You go along with him, listen, and learn what he is like. Write down what you do each day and what you find out about him.

2. Praise the child once each day. Record what you praise him for. Don't gush. Just mention what he did that you liked. It needn't be anything grand.

Closing

Ask why this assignment is made. Summarize the discussion. Invite questions.

2. Fatigue and Behavior

Purpose

To make the parent aware of the child's physical needs.

To accustom the parent to provide adequate rest, food, and exercise for the child.

Introduction

Prevention of fatigue is one of the easiest ways a parent has of making sure that the child behaves well; yet it is one of the most neglected. The preschooler's day of work, play, and every kind of stimulation exhausts him. He needs a child's schedule, not an adult's.

Typical Schedules

Ask each mother to re-think the previous day for herself and her child. She is to add the hours each spent in routine activities (dressing, bathing, eating), in work or school, in play or recreation, and in sleep. Time for routine activities will be about the same for adult and child; the mother will spend more time on work, less on recreation; the preschooler should have twelve to fourteen hours' rest, the mother, eight.

Discussion Questions

1. Compare adult and child schedules; discuss the implications of each and the changes needed.
2. What are the characteristics of a tired child? (Temper, balking, headaches and stomach aches, anxiety, imitative rather than original behavior, regression.)
3. What happens in a child's daily life to make him tired? (Too little sleep, too many people around, too much TV, too little food, too little exercise.)
4. What are the effects of television? (Long stretches of sitting, over-stimulation internalized, sleep disturbance because of long-lasting effect of emotion-arousing programs, lack of time to develop imagination or to exercise.)
5. What does food have to do with fatigue? (Protein deprivation

causes lag in intellectual growth — research confirms this; breakfast and snacks at school helped both pupils and teachers. The body requires vitamins and minerals found in fruits and vegetables, milk, cereals.)

6. What happens in nursery school or kindergarten to tire the child? (Following orders, sitting still, competing with classmates, trying new activities, thinking, performing.)
7. How does having time to himself help a child develop well? (A reprieve from outside stimulation; uses his imagination and intelligence to entertain himself; pleases himself by choosing his own activities.)

Assignment

1. Restrict television-viewing to 30 minutes daily. The program should not be an exciting one nor watched within two hours of bedtime. No TV at all is better.
2. See that your child plays outside every day for at least one hour and preferably for two to four hours.
3. Begin an early, regular bedtime. He needs twelve hours at night and a one- to two-hour rest or nap, depending on his age, after lunch.
4. Record everything he eats during one day this week.
5. Visit his school and stay as long as you can; if possible, for the entire time he is there.

Closing

Ask why this assignment is made. Summarize the discussion. Invite questions.

3. Independence and Competence

Purpose

To encourage parents to permit children to learn self-care.
To teach parents to deal with children's complaints and demands.

Introduction

Every child arrives in the world wanting to grow and to learn, to be independent and competent. These built-in desires conflict with a human pleasure in being waited on and having one's own way.

The immature child is not as competent as other boys and girls his age. He stays that way if he is waited on, pitied, over-managed, protected, or allowed to dictate to his parents.

Discussion Questions

1. What do you do for your child which he could do for himself? (Review what happens with dressing, eating, sleeping, washing, using the bathroom, driving him to playmates' homes, cleaning up after him.)
2. Why does he not do these things himself? (Parent takes over because its' easier, quicker, less messy; parent underestimates competence; child believes he can't manage alone.)
3. What demands does your child make? (Review common requests for money, food and treats, service, attention.)
4. How does giving in to a child's demands keep him infantile? (Retains the need for instant gratification typical of babies; cannot tolerate refusal; never learns to meet his own needs.)
5. What refusals are common with your child? (Going to bed, eating, picking up toys and clothes, coming to meals, doing chores, sharing.)
6. How does giving in to a child's refusals keep him babyish? (Always gets his way; never learns to do what's difficult or disagreeable; does not obey and thus develops no self-control.)
7. What happens when parents sympathize with the child about his unpleasant teacher or his hard or boring schoolwork? (He gets a go-ahead signal to disobey the teacher, shirk work, and criticize anything he dislikes about school.)
8. How do selecting friends, managing play, defending the child from playmates keep him infantile? (Doesn't learn to get along with a variety of playmates or initiate own play; believes he can't handle peers without parents; fears playmates and testing himself.)
9. How does constant association with adults keep a child babyish? (Cannot live up to adults' high standards, so he doesn't try and may regress; he's treated as a toy or is over-directed or overprotected; he gets no practice in give-and-take with peers.)

10. What is the value of stress, independence, and hardship? (They strengthen courage, promote confidence, teach coping skills, and lessen fear of failure, loneliness, or abandonment.)
11. What is the child like who remains babyish? (Loses interest in trying what's new, becomes hesitant and withdrawn, cries often, cannot get along with playmates, lets parents feed, dress, and entertain him.)

Assignment

1. Record during the next two days: (1) everything you do for your child which he could do for himself; (2) every demand he makes of you, every excuse he makes for himself, every refusal of a reasonable request.
2. On the third day, and from then on, end one service.
3. On the fourth day, refuse one demand.
4. On the fifth day, work out a schedule for gradually turning over self-direction to your child.

Closing

Ask why this assignment is made. Summarize discussion. Invite questions.

4. Discipline (1): Why Children Disobey

Purpose

To make parents aware of the many reasons why children disobey and thus to moderate adult emotional reaction to disobedience.

To alert parents to erroneous teaching practices which increase disobedience.

Introduction

The word *discipline* means "punishment" to nearly everyone. It's better to think of discipline as training a child to obey reasonable orders. In this way, he develops self-control and then can behave according to accepted standards.

Discussion Questions

1. Why do children disobey? (Too many orders; he forgets; the request is unimportant to the child; parents are inconsistent; he wants to be independent; he doesn't want to do what is asked,; he's learned he can disobey without penalty; he doesn't know how to do what is asked; parents forget their own orders and don't follow through on them; he's too young to control his actions; he's tired and cross.)
2. List everything for which you correct your child and everything you tell him to do. (Compare lengths of lists and discuss how much a preschooler can learn at one time.)
3. What practices of parents contribute to disobedience? (Uncertainty about the importance of their orders or demands; using various kinds and degrees of punishment; expecting perfect behavior; permitting child to refuse an order; doing for the child what they have told him to do; parental disagreement on what to require.)
4. How does too much punishment cause disobedience? (Child can't please parents, so he quits trying; he's so frightened of anticipated punishment he can't remember what he's supposed to do; anxiety causes him to lose what self-control he has.)
5. How does too little punishment cause disobedience? (He never knows when adults mean what they say; he concludes that nothing the parent says is important; there is no deterrent to disobedience.)

Assignment

1. Keep a tally count of every correction, criticism, or direction you give your child each day of this week.
2. Record each time he obeys a direction.

Closing

Ask why this assignment is made. Summarize discussion. Invite questions.

5. Discipline (2): How To Teach Obedience

Purpose

To review with parents a variety of successful teaching techniques.

To teach them to distinguish between morals and manners.

To encourage them to pace training so the child can absorb it.

Introduction

Understanding why a child disobeys and why teaching efforts often are unproductive is a first step toward training him in self-control. There are sound methods of teaching the child to obey. Parents need to keep their expectations realistic if they are to succeed.

Discussion Questions

1. What happens if the child is constantly ordered about or criticized for bad behavior? (He gets worse; he's convinced he's bad, so he acts that way.)
2. What happens if obedience is never acknowledged? (He stops trying. He gets no credit for remembering or for self-control, so it must not be important.)
3. How can obedience be taught? (Always follow through on every request; have the child repeat what you want him to do: *e.g.*, return and close a door quietly after slamming it — every time; instruct him in the correct way to do a task; supervise him while he's learning; praise and thank him for compliance; use mild punishment to help him remember; give him a choice — either he may do what you ask or give up something he wants; limit the number of correct behaviors you try to teach at any one time.)
4. What are some kinds of punishment which work well? (Isolation in room; an extra chore; logical consequences of misbehavior — coming indoors if he leaves the yard without permission; retribution — repair a sibling's smashed toy or mop up spilled milk; spanking — one swat for a dangerous act such as running into the street, fire-setting, turning on stove, poking knife into electrical socket.)

5. How do you reward obedience? (Mention good behavior; use a star chart for success; reward with small toys or treats or time alone with parent.)

6. What do you do when the child refuses to obey? (If he's two years or younger, pick him up and carry him where you want him to be; if he's older, give him a choice: he sets the table or he doesn't eat dinner; repeat your direction — "Pick up your toys" — over and over until he complies.)

7. If you should not correct a child for everything he does wrong, what should you correct and what should you ignore? (Don't get after him for poor table manners, sloppy appearance, accidental loss or damage of clothing or toys. Set habits of courtesy and carefulness by example and gradual, non-emotional instruction. Failing to share or be a good sport when he loses and crying when he's hurt are normal emotional responses to trouble for which he should not be scolded. As he grows older, he'll do better. You must correct (1) behavior which is physically harmful to him or to anyone else (eating candy before supper, staying up till midnight, climbing on roofs, throwing rocks, kicking) and (2) behavior which interferes with the rights of others (deliberately destroying others' property, intruding on privacy, jeering, rule-breaking.)

8. What if the child obeys, but protests and sulks? (Pay no attention to his show; thank him for obeying.)

Assignment

1. Choose one kind of behavior you wish your child to learn.
2. Ignore all other misbehavior this week, unless someone is endangered or harmed.
3. Decide what teaching method you will use and stay with your plan all week.
4. Record sucess and failure during the week.

Closing

Ask why this assignment is made. Summarize discussion. Invite questions.

6. Responsibility

Purpose

To encourage parents to use the twin teaching tools of work and money to train the child in responsibility.

Introduction

A child does not suddenly become a responsible person when he reaches the age of eighteen. He learns responsibility from the time he is young by working and earning money which he uses to meet his needs. Chores and money are teaching tools, widely neglected, often from carelessness but sometimes for emotional reasons.

Discussion Questions

1. Describe an adult you know who is irresponsible. How did he get that way?
2. What kinds of work can preschool children do? (Make beds, wash and dry dishes, dust, sweep, set and clear table, empty wastebaskets, clean yard, cook — salads, puddings, toast, sandwiches — carry laundry, feed pets.)
3. What if the child does the work poorly? (Train him to do it right: work with him, watch him do it, re-train when necessary, but don't expect him to do it as well as you do.)
4. What if the child refuses to work? (Insist that the work; chores must be finished before he plays; let him know his help is needed; offer to work with him; say you'll help him.)
5. Should boys and girls do different kinds of work? (Every kind of house and yard work should be learned by both boys and girls. It's knowledge they'll use for a lifetime.)
6. What are the benefits to the child of doing daily chores? (Learns how to do many tasks; becomes proud and confident; feels useful and grown-up; earns praise.)
7. What is wrong with giving a child an allowance? (He thinks of unearned money as rightfully his; he spends it solely for pleasure and believes that's what money is for.)
8. What is wrong with giving a child money whenever he asks for it? (He thinks it's instantly available; he doesn't understand that

someone had to work for it; he puts no damper on his own
wishes.)

9. What is wrong with placing a child in the position of having to
ask for money when he wants or needs it? (It's humiliating to be
dependent on someone else's whims; it teaches the child to beg,
to con, or to demand money.)

10. What does a child learn if he is paid for chores? (Work produces
money; his work is important because it's worth cash; he learns
that he can provide for his own needs.)

11. How should a child spend the money he earns? (Preschoolers:
toys, treats, gifts, charity, savings; older children add hobbies,
clothes, dues, school supplies.)

12. Should a child be paid for everything he does? (Not for care of
his clothes and room; not when his help is needed in an emergency.)

13. Some parents insist that children should work because they are
members of the family and should not be paid for chores. What
happens in such a family when children are asked to work?
(They wiggle out of it.)

14. What is the value of a planned schedule of work and pay? (Child
knows what's expected; there's no nagging or arguing over
chores; child can count on a definite income and budget accord-
ingly.)

Assignment

1. Set up a system of earning money by doing daily chores, preferably both indoors and outdoors.

2. Money is to be used for (1) giving (presents to others, church
school), (2) saving, and (3) fun. No additional money is given
the child for any of these purposes. The child must do the work;
he should be taught how to do it well. Chores can be varied each
day or remain the same for a week or a month. Making his bed
and cleaning his room are unpaid chores. The child should be
paid daily or weekly and taken weekly to the store where he can
spend some of his money.

Closing

Ask why this assignment is made. Summarize discussion. Invite questions.

7. Self-respect

Purpose

To alert parents to the damage caused a child's self-respect by disparagement, deception, or degradation.

To remind them that self-respect is lost when a child is overprotected or allowed to behave selfishly.

Introduction

Sound mental health, obedience to laws, self-discipline, the persistence to achieve, and respect for others all are based on respect for oneself. A child is born with a huge amount of self-respect. The way he is treated determines whether he keeps or loses it. If he grows up despising himself, he will resent and attack others and may destroy himself.

Discussion Questions

1. How does a child lose his self-respect? (He fails to use his abilities; others downgrade him; he's treated as though he is worthless.)
2. What does parental opinion of the child have to do with what the child thinks of himself? (Everything; the child believes the parents' evaluation is correct.)
3. How do adults teach the child that his ideas and his achievements are worthless? (Criticize them; improve on them; refuse to let him experiment with ideas.)
4. How does lying to the child damage self-respect? (It tells him he's so unimportant there's no need to be honest with him.)
5. What acts of courtesy is the child taught? (To say, "please" and "thank you"; to share his belongings; not to argue with adults.)
6. How do adults treat him in these respects? (Rarely thank him; seldom say, "please"; don't let him use their possessions; dispute what he says.)

7. What does he learn about himself from this treatment? (He's unworthy to be treated as courteously as his parents treat strangers.)
8. How does invasion of privacy contribute to a child's lack of self-respect? (Parental insistence on brothers and sisters playing whenever he has a friend over or failure to protect his privacy when he wants to play alone convinces him he's not important enough to have rights.)
9. How does discussing the child in his presence humiliate him? (He's treated as though he does not exist or has no feelings.)
10. How does laughing at him, calling him names, swearing at him, or using sarcasm humiliate him? (It tells him he is inferior to everyone else.)
11. How does anticipating his needs damage his self-respect? (If his parents answer for him when an adult asks a question, wait on him when he doesn't need it, fetch his teddy bear to forestall crying when he's taken away from home, he learns that he is helpless and, thus, worthless.)
12. How does permitting him to get away with aggressive, selfish, or babyish behavior damage his self-respect? (It's implied he's too young to do better; therefore, he thinks of himself as infantile.)

Assignment

1. Say "please" when requesting your child to do something and "thank you" when he has complied.
2. Do not improve on his work.
3. Let him try every idea he has unless it might be dangerous.
4. Keep every promise you make, whether or not he remembers. Write down what you promise; when you keep your word remind him that you made the promise.
5. Never laugh at him or call him names.

Closing

Ask why this assignment is made. Summarize discussion. Invite questions.

8. Play and Playmates

Purposes

To teach parents how play and playmates help or harm the child.

To suggest techniques for handling problems which develop from play.

Introduction

A preschooler's playmates usually are accidentally acquired; yet inappropriate playmates, or none, can affect the way a child thinks of himself and the kind of person he becomes. Also, if the child has no time for play, either alone or with others, he is harmed.

Discussion Questions

1. What is the value of playmates to a preschooler? (They challenge and comfort him; they expose him to new ideas and ways of doing things; he learns to compromise and share; he grows up with his own generation.)
2. What problems do playmates present to the mother? (They make a mess; they complain about her child; they need supervision so they won't get hurt; they invade family privacy; they damage property; they disturb her child when they insult, control, or desert him.)
3. When a child associates only with adults, how does he develop socially? (He acquires adult values, vocabulary, and mannerisms and doesn't fit in with peers.)
4. How does the child develop socially if he plays with no one but his own brothers and sisters? (He always holds the position of boss or slave, depending on his age; there are more fights and emotional scenes than with peers; he turns to parents to settle disputes; there is no variety of personality in companions; he fails to develop play skills appropriate to his age group.)
5. What happens to social development if the child plays with only one other friend? (Misses the variety of sex and personality; adjusting to one child, he considers others atypical: he fears them or isolates himself from them.)
6. What happens to social adjustment if the child plays only with

youngsters of the opposite sex? (He learns the wrong play skills
and preferences for his own sex; he feels awkward around children his own sex.)

7. What happens if the child plays only at his own home? (He
    never learns that other families live differently from his; he gets
    no practice in leaving home and looking after himself in a new
    setting.)

8. What happens if the child plays only with older children? (He's
    abused or petted; he must follow orders; the play is inappro-
    priate for his age.)

9. What happens if he plays only with younger children? (He
    dominates them and gets in trouble when he tries the same thing
    with age-mates; he plays at a less skilled level than he's capable
    of and then cannot keep up with age-mates.)

10. What kind of play is typical of preschool children? (Active; us-
    ing toys common to both sexes; imitative of adults; outdoor
    play. Girls like dolls, tea parties, drawing; boys like building,
    climbing. Both like trikes, wagons, sandboxes, swings, slides,
    teeter-totters.)

11. How often and how long should preschool children play to-
    gether? (Three times weekly; one to one-and-one-half hours
    each time.)

12. What should parents do if the child hits and kicks playmates?
    (Isolate him briefly; have him apologize; then let him try again;
    discuss others' rights.)

13. What should parents do if their child is submissive? (Talk about
    what he would like to do and let him know he can tell playmates
    what he prefers; let him play temporarily with younger chil-
    dren; let him win some disputes with them — the parents.)

14. What should parents do if their child has an imaginary play-
    mate? (This doesn't harm the child, but it means he's lonely; see
    that he has real playmates regularly.)

15. How do you manage toy-grabbing? (Set a rule that no child
    may take a toy from another. He may have it only when it is put
    down. Watch, remind, and enforce the rule.)

16. How do you manage picking up when play is finished? (Allow
    time for this; promise a story or cooky after toys are put away.)

17. In what ways should the parent be involved with playing pre-

schoolers? (Separate for ten minutes if there's constant quarreling; limit the number of toys youngsters play with; keep some toys to be played with only when the child has company; limit the length of playtime; limit the number of children playing together; limit the location of play — not in parents' bedroom, the kitchen, the bathroom, siblings' rooms; interrupt exhausting play with a story, a snack, or listening to records.)

Assignment

1. See that your child plays alone with a child his own age and sex at least twice next week, alternating homes.
2. Set up any rules or practices which will make playing go more smoothly.

Closing

Ask why this assignment is made. Summarize discussion. Invite questions.

9. The Family: Brothers and Sisters; Grandparents

Purpose

To remind parents that brothers and sisters are an asset to the child.

To teach them how to handle quarrels and jealousy.

To help mothers and fathers understand why grandparents act as they do.

To aid them in overlooking grandparents' nuisance behavior and in ending harmful behavior.

Introduction

Besides a mother and father, there are others in the family who influence the mood and actions of the preschooler. Brothers and sisters both challenge and protect him. Learning to deal with them strengthens him and makes him more resilient.

Grandparents may spoil, ignore, or humiliate the child and/or his parents. They should be valued for their help; they should not be allowed to cause trouble for the family.

Discussion Questions

1. What are the advantages to the child of having brothers and sisters? (On the spot playmates; practice in meeting rebuffs; sharing of parents — he's not over-dependent on them; behavior models near his own age — adults aren't his sole models; learns compassion as he comforts beleaguered siblings; learns to handle jealousy; stretches his abilities trying to catch up with older siblings; knows he's not the only family member reaping praise or punishment from parents; gains colleagues who endure what he does.)

2. What are the disadvantages to the child of having brothers and sisters? (Loss of sole parental attention; little privacy; rare success in getting his way; suffering abuse and ridicule; unfair treatment by parents — he's blamed for a sibling's misbehavior or parents allow a brother or sister to use or ruin his belongings.)

3. What are the advantages for parents if they have more than one child? (Variety in offspring; easier and better rearing because attention is divided; realistic attitudes about youngsters' abilities and thus lower standards and a more relaxed home life; assistance with child-rearing — siblings serve as playmates, teachers, and combination challenger and champion.)

4. What are the advantages for parents if they have only one child? (Less cost; less noise; no children's arguments to monitor.)

5. What are common complaints of brothers and sisters about one another? (Interfering with play; using, sometimes ruining, toys and clothing; being left out; pestering; hitting or name-calling; an easier life for one than the other; parent favoritism; differing privileges; work assignments not equitable.)

6. How can you best handle physical fighting? (Ignore; send outside; separate for an hour; assign each battler thirty minutes of chores.)

7. How can you best handle complaints of parental unfairness? (Keep records of decisions concerning disputes, requests, chore assignments.)

8. How can you best handle arguing? (Ignore; time the fight — most children settle quarrels in ten minutes; send them away to yell out of earshot.)

9. How can you best handle complaints of pestering, toy-wrecking, interfering with play? (Put locks on doors; require each to get permission of the other to use possessions or to play; protect privacy and play with friends.)
10. How do grandparents help the family? (Babysitting; affection for and pride in the child; counsel for child and parents when requested; teaching the child skills and passing on knowledge.)
11. How do grandparents hurt the family (Unasked-for advice or criticism; playing favorites; comparing cousins; giving excessively expensive gifts; protecting children from parental discipline; dropping in uninvited.)
12. What can you do to help grandparents become a plus, not a minus, in your family's life? (Use them as sitters only if they volunteer; invite them to dinner and visit them regularly, but not frequently — agree on the intervals; don't permit favoritism; train yourself to ignore unasked-for advice, child-shielding, and inappropriate gifts.)

Assignment

1. For three days, record every dispute between brothers and sisters: what it's about, how long it lasts, and how it's resolved.
2. For three days, record every complaint brothers and sisters make to you about one another and how each is resolved.
3. Choose one method of handling arguments and follow it the rest of the week.
4. Choose one method of handling complaints and follow it for the rest of the week.
5. Put hooks on doors and toy chests.
6. Require each child to have the other's permission before playing with him or with his toys.
7. For three days, record everything grandparents do which bothers you.
8. Choose one problem and solve it.

Closing

Ask why this assignment is made. Summarize discussion. Invite questions.

10. The Family: Father *vs.* Mother

Purpose

To help women understand and support their husbands.

To teach mothers how to strengthen the bond between a child and his father.

Introduction

Many mothers come to child guidance clinics blaming the youngster's problems on his father. He is too harsh; he is too lax; he spends no time with the child. A protective mother constantly tries to ease the strain between father and child or to defend the youngster. This causes the bond between father and child and also between husband and wife to weaken.

Women who understand how men differ from them — and why it's important that they do — avoid much conflict over child management.

Discussion Questions

1. What burdens do men have that women do not have? (Financial support of the family; thirty to forty years of work; must be on their best behavior all day; face competition with other men; can't show feelings; either take orders from superiors or are responsible for work errors of subordinates.)

2. What does a man want from his home? (Peace and quiet; respect.)

3. In what ways are men different from women? (Less interested in details and insignificant events; more indifferent to feelings; concentrate on one matter at a time; strongly involved with job success; concerned with own image; maintain a casual, not a close, relationship with others.)

4. What are a mother's and father's differing roles in the family? (Father represents achievement and is the provider and protector; mother gives care and comfort; she is the child's confidante. These roles hold even if both parents work.)

5. In what ways do fathers treat their children differently than mothers do? (Spend less time with them; urge them to do their

best, to achieve, to control their feelings, to take adversity stoically; mothers devote themselves to entertaining, teaching, or serving their children; they yell at them for minor misbehavior and for causing them extra work or trouble; they sympathize, protect, give in, and buy them presents.)

6. Why is it desirable that fathers and mothers treat the child differently? (If both treated him the same, he would either be challenged to show extraordinary courage and self-control — and he would fail, or he would live with over-attention and constant emotional reaction to everything he did — and be bound too closely to his parents. He needs balanced treatment.)

7. What can a mother do to help father and child get along better? (Praise each to the other; support the father; pass on to each the compliments child and father make in private about the other; see that they have time alone; don't intervene in disputes; don't take child's side against the father.)

8. What can you do to cause your husband to feel more important in the family? (Serve him first at meals; get his breakfast; clean the house; meet his needs; accept his presents; avoid correcting and criticizing him; go out with him.)

Assignment

1. Praise father and child to each other once this week.
2. Select one day to say "yes" to everything your husband suggests — not arguing, refusing, or revising.
3. See that father and child have time alone once this week.
4. Keep out of arguments between father and child. Leave the room if necessary.
5. Go out with your husband once this week.

Closing

Ask why this assignment is made. Summarize discussion. Invite questions.

11. Problem-solving

Purpose

To teach parents to examine problems before acting.

To demonstrate that every problem can be solved.

Introduction

Mishandling problems or allowing them to fester annoys and shames parents. They dislike the child who disappoints them; he grows lonely and afraid.

Solving problems helps both child and parent. The adult's confidence steadies as he discovers he can handle trouble. The child, pleasing his mother and father, is reassured and comforted.

Problems can be solved by observation, study, and a teaching plan.

Discussion Questions

1. Parents often describe problems this way: "She has a temper," or, "He won't mind." Change these broad statements into ones which identify specific action which you can correct. ("She throws a fit when you ask her to pick up her toys." Or, "He leaves the yard when I've told him he can't.")
2. Why should the problem be re-stated this way? (An action can be altered or eliminated; when several similar actions are changed, the unwanted trait also disappears.)
3. How can you learn more about the problem you want to solve? (Record how often and when it happens and whether other events usually precede it; read; talk to friends and relatives.)
4. Where can you find reading material about problems with pre-schoolers? (Libraries, bookstores, child guidance clinics, university nursery schools.)
5. What difficulties can reading about problems cause you? (Authors contradict one another; some solutions and theories are farfetched and confusing.)
6. What can you do about this? (Take notes on what makes sense to you; forget the rest.)
7. What difficulties can talking with friends or relatives about

problems cause you? (Differing ideas; emotional reactions; you feel obligated to try what they suggest and report results.)

8. How will you handle this? (Try ideas which you like and are reasonable; if there are none, use none.)
9. List all the teaching methods you know. Choose those you prefer. (Reward — praise, toys, treats, trips to zoo or lake, time with parent; punishment — an extra chore, isolation, revoking privileges; retribution; repetition of command; practice of correct behavior; use of logical consequences; giving a choice.)
10. How long should you use a teaching method to solve a problem? (At least one month.)
11. How can you tell if there is progress? (Keep records.)

Practice

Divide the class into small groups; give each a problem to solve. Pass out child care books as reading resources.

PROBLEMS. (1) Doug, age four, often pushes his little sister and grabs her toys. (2) Whenever her mother is on the phone, Pam, age three, climbs into her lap, pulls her hair, talks to her, and demands drinks of water. (3) Nicky, age five, frequently brings home toys which belong to his friend and candy he has taken from the grocery store.

Assignment

1. Select one problem your child has. Identify it as a single act of misbehavior.
2. Learn about it by keeping records, reading, and talking with others.
3. Choose the teaching techniques you will use.
4. Begin re-training, keeping records of progress.

Closing

Ask why this assignment is made. Summarize discussion. Invite questions.

12. Summary and Evaluation

Purpose

To consolidate knowledge gained in the class.

To demonstrate the effectiveness of methods taught by comparing the behavior of the child three months ago with his present behavior.

Introduction

Remind the mothers that during the past three months they have accumulated a sizable collection of child-rearing techniques. Everyone has tried most of these. If they have continued to use them, they should now be solid and automatic habits.

But if someone has started a new method only to drop it in a few days, she need only remember that the entire list is in her notebook. When her child next gets far off track and she doesn't know what to do, she should begin again, doing every assignment in turn.

Discussion

Read each assignment. Ask the mothers again to give the reasons why it was made.

Closing

Ask each class member to look at her original list of what was wrong with her child and report if there has been improvement. There will be.

Point out that each mother is responsible for the changes in her son or daughter. Thank all of them for conscientious work and clear thinking, announce that they are now experts at mothering, and tell them they may phone or come in any time they have questions.

MANAGEMENT PROBLEMS

It's always possible that someone's remark, mannerism, or emotion will sidetrack group goals, even cause members to desert the class. When the group is tilting off balance, take charge. Just as pupils in a noisy classroom expect their teacher to quell the racket and get on with teaching, your students count on you to do the same.

Here are common problems which detour the group.

Monopolizing Time

A certain anxious or domineering mother always is first to speak up. On and on she rambles, detailing her experiences and expounding her opinions. Listen as long as time allows (two minutes, at most); then interrupt. Compliment her ideas. Ask others for theirs, or state the next question and call on someone to answer.

At the end of the session, repeat your first-day caution: time must be shared and comments abbreviated.

Ridiculing Others' Ideas

Occasionally a mother proposes an idea or backs a theory discredited by current knowledge. Someone hoots at the suggestion and embarrasses the mother who mentioned it.

Rescue her. Never let anyone remain an outsider or feel unequal to others in the class. Say that the theory is well-known and has been debated a long time. It has its supporters and detractors. Thank the flustered lady for bringing it to the group's attention.

You needn't take sides. You're merely establishing that everyone is entitled to a courteous hearing.

Dictating To Others

Often, one mother will describe a problem with her youngster and another will tell her what she should do. The helpful one may be correct, but her dictatorial manner offends.

Try a two-pronged approach. First, ask the others if they've been in that situation and what worked for them. This soothes the sting: the problem is common and there are various ways to handle it.

Second, ask if anyone else would like ideas from the group about trouble they're having. Someone will speak up, solutions will be offered, and the first mother no longer feels she's the dummy of the bunch. With luck, she'll regain her self-esteem with a useful thought to pass on to someone else.

Diverting Remarks and Questions

The mothers in your group have a lot on their minds.

Mr. Wilson is thinking about how Ray clipped Lori a good one yesterday. Before long, in the midst of a sensible discussion about TV-watching, she'll ask, "What should you do about a boy who hits his little sister?"

Answer if you like, but you'll be sorry if you do. Once the mothers discover that you'll handle anything, any time, the class's 90 minutes will be shredded with their immediate worries. Your course will never be taught.

Instead of replying, tell Mrs. Wilson she can ask the question again at the end of the class period. Be sure to save time for it. You can also say that she should just keep coming; a session on brothers and sisters is scheduled.

Non-participation

In many groups there is one person who nods and smiles but never talks. This won't happen if you divide the class into small groups each week. Getting to know everyone and practicing thinking aloud, even the shyest person will speak out in the full group.

But the competition is unnerving. Glib, eager women are first on stage. Quieter ones won't fight for the chance to speak and their sage comments are lost.

If two or three in the class are not heard often, call on them. And if everyone but your modest mothers has offered answers to your question, ask if they have anything else to suggest. They will have. Soon they'll talk without your invitation.

Failure To Perform Assignments

Usually, everyone in the group will try at least part of the weekly assignment. But there can be one person who ducks her duty. And for certain assignments, perhaps two or three will arrive with excuses.

Make little of their lapses. If you scold, they'll leave forever. But remind them that unless they do the assignments, there will be no change in their children. Then review what happened with the preschoolers of mothers who tried the new tasks.

When you give next week's assignment at the end of the hour, tell the delinquents to work on the chore they skipped, as well as the new one.

Faulty Conclusions

Every question you ask should have several possible answers so that most of the mothers' ideas are acceptable. Sometimes, though, after a bad week, their thinking is muddy. Answering your question, they come up with old wives' tales or the latest peculiar psychological scam.

Bring them back to reality. Explore the validity of what they've said and refute it with facts, from their own experience, if possible. Then ask for more ideas.

They have none. Silence descends. Someone hazards a guess and you shake your head. They panic and try again, uncertain for what you're fishing. Finally they give up and you produce the answer. They laugh in relief. So do you.

You don't want to play many scenes like that. Study your question and, before you form another class, re-phrase it. It should guide them into producing sensible answers.

Disagreeing with You

You trot out a firmly-held belief and an unkind mother says, "Oh, I don't agree with that at all. You're wrong."

Although that's possible, if you know as much as you should, it's more likely that the disagreeing mother is wrong.

Don't humiliate yourself with a lame defense such as pointing out that you've seen hundreds of cases and what you say is correct. Instead, ask the other mothers what they think. Some will agree with you; some will admit they're with your challenger.

Then, with questions which elicit answers to back you up and with facts based on research studies, justify your stand. If you can't, chalk up the debacle to experience and figure out, that day, how you'll handle the opposition next time.

Finally, support your adversary. Tell her you're glad she brought up the point, that it's a commonly-held view and important to discuss.

To learn from your remedial classes, the mothers must trust your competence. If you not only know what you're talking about, but you also circle roadblocks smoothly, they will.

REFERENCES

1. Allen, E. E.: Multiple attending in therapy groups. *Personnel & Guidance Journal, 60*: 318, 1982.
2. Auerbach, A. B.: *Parents Learn Through Discussion: Principles and Practices of Parent Group Education*. New York, Wiley, 1968.
3. Glass, S. D.: *The Practical Handbook of Group Counseling*. Baltimore, BCS Publishing Co., 1969.
4. Kozloff, M. A.: *A Program for Families of Children with Learning and Behavior Problems*. New York, Wiley, 1979.
5. Pevsner, R.: Group parent training versus individual family therapy: An outcome study. *Journal of Behavior Therapy & Experimental Psychiatry, 13*: 119, 1982.
6. Pollak, G. K.: *Leadership of Discussion Groups*. New York, Spectrum Pub, 1975.

Chapter 25

TEACHING PARENTS: PREVENTIVE CLASSES

DON'T limit yourself to rescue work in your office. Try to keep parents away from your door. If mothers and fathers know enough, their children escape serious trouble. Some psychologists spend half their time in preventive work.

Preventive classes help an isolated mother worry less about her puzzling, irritating, demanding small children. As she meets with other mothers, she discovers that children of the same age act the same. Her youngster is normal; his problems are ordinary.

Most clients of child guidance clinics are elementary school children spotted by teachers as deviates from the norm. Parents of pre-schoolers, unfamiliar with what to expect and what to do, often are unaware that their youngsters are warped. They don't get help when they should. Preventive classes teach facts and techniques which break up problems before they cement into habits. It's easy to get rid of fussy eating, tantrums, babyishness, and jealousy when the child is young and pliable. But if nothing is done then, a much greater effort is required later to uproot settled moods and behavior.

SPONSORS OF PREVENTIVE CLASSES

Child Guidance Centers

Surprisingly, few child guidance centers sponsor preventive

335

classes. Staff members busily plug jagged holes in dikes and waiting lists for help are long.

Even so, time should be set aside for preventive work. None is more valuable than classes for parents of preschoolers.

Schools and Nurseries

Public school psychologists sometimes conduct preventive classes for parents.[3] Meetings led jointly by the psychologist and kindergarten teacher answer many questions.

Private nursery schools usually are directed by graduates in developmental psychology. Because most parents who send their children to nursery school are keenly interested in doing their best by their youngsters, preventive classes taught by the school's staff are well attended.

Day nurseries often do not have college-educated teachers interested in the child's home life. But Head Start nurseries are charged with involving parents in their programs. Mothers work alongside teachers, learning both from example and instruction. Evening classes provide more guidance under less hectic conditions.

Health Departments

City and county health departments schedule regular child health conferences. A pediatrician or a pediatric nurse associate examines preschool children and administers required immunizations.

On the staff at some child health conferences is a part-time psychologist who works with the health center's nurse in answering mothers' questions. A preventive class, taught jointly, grows naturally from the practical assistance both give.

One nurse recruited more than twenty mothers to attend a four-session class. Another arranged a series of meetings for mothers of twins, several of whom came regularly to the center.

Mental Health Associations

Mental health associations, run by concerned laymen, sponsor at least one all-day educational session annually. The topic varies each year and anges from alcoholism to worry. Every few years a program on preschoolers emerges, with speakers, films, and discussion groups.

Sometimes a spin-off class, meeting four to six times, is offered mothers and fathers who attend the one-day meeting. If it's held at night, both parents can come.

ORGANIZATION

Number and Length of Sessions

You can't schedule as many sessions for a preventive class as you do for a remedial class. People come for a variety of reasons, but seldom is there a compelling problem which guarantees faithful attendance. Plan for three to six meetings. More mothers will come to all the sessions if there are only three or four.

Ninety minutes is the best length of time for each meeting. That's long enough to get something done and short enough not to bore or tire.[1]

Participants

The more, the better for preventive classes. You're trying to reach everyone responsible for a preschooler. Rather than limiting the group's size, plan to adapt your program each time to the many or the few who show up.

Mothers attending classes sponsored by health departments and Head Start day nurseries often are poorer and less educated than those in groups organized by schools or mental health agencies. Keep this in mind so that you don't use middle class words (such as *sibling* or *peers*) in discussions. And when you talk about toys, stress the fact that no costly ones are needed.

Many of these women have heard of psychologists but never known one. They're wary of you, sure you're on the child's side and unsympathetic to their burdens. This is your chance to clear up their misconceptions. Once the mothers discover you know your business and also understand what they go through, they acquire a resource for help they hadn't considered before.

Set up a nursery in a nearby room, complete with toys and attendants. If mothers must arrange care for their preschoolers, many won't come. Or they'll bring them to the meetings and then miss much of what goes on.

Topics

Anything related to preschoolers' rearing will be welcomed by your mothers. Most are new at the game. But the following topics have proved successful in preventive classes:

1. *Discipline.* Every mother wants to know how to get her child to obey — on one request. Refusals dent the parents's ego and scare her into believing that the youngster is getting out of hand. Mothers need to know that there are logical reasons why children disobey. They need to use teaching methods which don't breed enmity.

2. *Eating, Sleeping, and Toilet Training.* Most of the dozens of daily contacts between mother and child center around life's essentials: eating, sleeping, and going to the bathroom. If there is little conflict during these frequent encounters, mother and child like each other. But if there is unending friction, both are discouraged. Mothers need to learn how to manage these trouble spots.

3. *Emotion: Crying, Fear, and Anger.* The tears, fears, and fury of a small child frighten and confuse his parents. If they know why he acts as he does and what to do about it, both they and the youngster lead more peaceful lives.

4. *Independence.* Some parents find it hard to permit independence. Too often it translates, for them, into defiance or risk-taking. Or they fail to let their preschooler take care of his own needs because they don't realize that he can. If you teach parents of a preschooler to encourage independence, they take a giant step toward making sure he grows up happily and, one day, starts adult life with confidence.

5. *Learning and Learning To Get Along.* Surveys show that parents of preschoolers worry about how smart their child is. The intelligent youngster is a jewel in his parent's crown; the slow one, an embarrassment. What a mother does to help her child learn determines whether he looks forward to or dreads school.

The child also must learn to get along with people. He's not very old before he either likes and adjusts to other boys and girls or fights and distrusts them. Early attention to harmful social contacts prevents later distress.

Programming

In preventive classes, you can experiment with several teaching devices. Because the mother's motivation to change is slight, you need to get across many ideas in a short time, knowing that what catches the interest of one mother slides by another. Variety in programming intrigues and keeps class members returning.

At the first session, outline what you intend to cover during the course. Hand out this schedule in printed form, so there's no confusion about what will be discussed when. Include dates, leaders' names, information about the nursery, and a phone number to call.

Sometimes you can start the class with a short, factual background on the day's topic, given by the psychologist, nurse, or teacher. Assume that your audience is uninformed but intelligent. Don't talk longer than ten minutes; five is better. Women grow restless when they must stay quiet. Besides, no one absorbs quantities of facts at one hearing.

Try films. There's a visual impact which lingers. Have pertinent questions ready for discussion when the picture is over.[7]

You can use part of your class time to answer mothers' written questions. You'll get queries on what's bothersome at the moment and chances are that the same problem worries several other mothers too. You or the nurse or teacher may reply, or you may invite the other mothers to help out with ideas. But when you've invited questions, make sure that you end up with clear and accurate answers.

At one meeting, bring in a new pilot: a child psychiatrist, perhaps, who can talk on such subjects as differences between boys and girls (many parents don't realize they exist and unfavorably compare their sons and daughters); the unique stance of the first child with his parents; contrasts between mothers and fathers in rearing policies and practices; and dealing with family jealousies. A guest can lecture, lead discussion, answer questions, or all three. He should be a lively, knowledgeable person.

One psychiatrist charmed a class by asking, "What does your four-year-old say when you tell him he can't have a candy bar?"

"I hate you!" chorused the mothers.

Instantly, each knew that her child didn't hate her and she need no longer dread turning down requests. And here was a *psychiatrist* who knew what went on behind a home's closed doors!

At every session it's wise to include small group discussion. Divide the parents into four sub-groups, hand out various questions, appoint a leader and recorder, and allow five minutes for answers.

Remember that these women are strangers. Their thinking may be stymied by loneliness and they won't talk freely in the large group. Also, some mothers are used to action, not reflection; revving up brain cells to ponder a question takes getting used to. There may be women in your class whose skill with words (and spelling and writing) is minimal; their ideas will be expressed vaguely. Getting together in a small group helps. Everyone may talk; everyone must think; everyone takes responsibility for solutions.

It's nearly useless to give action assisgnments at the end of the session. Still, that may be exactly what some mothers are looking for. Suggest something new for everyone to try, but don't count yourself a failure if you get only blank stares the following week when you ask what happened. Rather than habit-changing, look for gains in attitude toward the child and competence in handling conflict.

Summarize each meeting so the mothers leave reminded of a few essentials about the subject you've discussed.

Also, you or the teacher or nurse can prepare a one-page condensation of information covered in the session. You'll know ahead of time what points you want to get across, so the abstract can be ready to hand out that day.

THE CLASSES

1. Discipline

Introduction

Parents are upset when their child disobeys. So is the child; he wants to behave so that others approve of him. A mother and father usually believe their youngster is disobeying deliberately. He's not. He's acting his age. Small children learn only slowly, after hundreds of practice trials, what they're expected to do.

Discipline is a gradually-diminishing job for parents. It's most needed when the child is a preschooler, required less for the six-to-twelve-year-old, and dwindles during adolescence. It works this way only if the child steadily develops the self-control which replaces adult commands and rules.

Discussion Questions

1. What is the purpose of discipline? (To teach acceptable behavior.)
2. When does discipline begin in the child's life? (At birth: he must wait for food, changing, and cuddling.)
3. List everything for which you correct your child. (This was one group's list: "fighting; acting smart; bad manners; picking her nose; leaving house without permission; calling names; crying when he doesn't get what he wants; temper tantrums; writing with lipstick on the mirror; messing things up; putting fingerprints on the mirror."
4. Why does a child disobey? (The mothers mentioned: "to get attention; test the mother; imitating another child; taking something out on the parents; seeing if he can get the rule changed; frustrated moods; mother's bad mood; tired; spoiled; showing off; wants to be independent; he's involved with something else and doesn't want to be disturbed; doesn't know right from wrong; he's angry; he's trying to make a joke out of everything; parents are too bossy; he has too much freedom."

   This comprehensive list details mothers' experiences and contains reams of ideas for discussion. For example, "to get attention" is a reason given so frequently for every kind of misbehavior that it may be a thoughtless response. Because it's often used in an accusatory, blaming sense, it's worth talking about.[1]
5. Some parents discipline too little. What is the effect on the child? (He becomes anxious: he doesn't know what he should or should not do; he develops no self-control; he is unpopular with others.)

6. What is the effect on the parents? (They feel badgered and help-less; they dislike the child because they must cater to him and he is unpleasant to live with; they dislike themselves because they fail to control the child.)

7. Some parents discipline too often or punish too severely. What is the effect on the child? (He behaves worse; he constantly fears punishment so he loses all self-control; he is sure he is bad and that his parents despise him.)

8. What is the effect on the parents? (They punish automatically and believe the youngster is much worse behaved than others his age; they're angry constantly; their dissatisfaction with the child and with parenthood carries over into other areas of their lives.)

9. What are some good methods of teaching obedience? (One group mentioned being consistent and sticking by what you say, principles they know but often ignore. Other methods are: mild reward and punishment, isolation, and retribution.)

10. What are rewards and punishments you can use with a pre-school child? (The mothers listed these rewards: special treats, reading to the child, a star chart, a new toy, praise. They named only two punishments: removing something the child values — a toy or privilege; spending a short period of time in his room. They said nothing about spanking, although they all certainly spanked. How, when and why spanking, other punishments, and rewards are used should be reviewed.)

Closing

Summarize the discussion. Suggest that each mother keep a tally count of the number of times daily she corrects, criticizes, or directs her child.

2. Eating, Sleeping, and Trainig

Introduction

Failures of parent and child in these three areas create daily con-flicts and enduring bad feeling. The parent is frustrated, angry, dis-appointed, and defeated. The child is exhausted, infantile, and dissatisfied with himself.

But if eating, sleeping, and training are well-managed, they become a base for good health and self-discipline. When daily life is relaxed and orderly, the child is free to learn and grow.

Discussion Questions

Eating

1. Why do preschoolers refuse to eat? (Their appetite decreases after the first year; they're tired or excited; they practice independence by playing with or turning down food; they dislike new tastes; they want what adults have; they're fed too often and aren't hungry; they are easily distracted; eating has become boring routine and they dislike the confinement of high chair or table; if they're punished for not eating or are forced to eat, the sight of food ties knots in their stomachs; if their parents get excited, coax, and beg, the children enjoy dominating them; the parents substitute food the child demands for food he refuses; the parents feed the child who can feed himself, so eating becomes their responsibility, not his.)

2. What can be done about this? (Put his meal in front of him and leave him to feed himself. When he plays with or throws food, send him away from the table. Give nothing to eat until the next scheduled time. Have him eat alone, not with the family. Give him small quantities of food so he'll ask for more. Provide only nourishing foods; ban filling and frequent snacks. Give favored foods first and graudally add less popular ones.)

3. Should children snack between meals? (A snack half-way between regular meals keeps children alert and cheerful. They should not snack when they choose nor stuff themselves with chips, cokes, ice cream, and cake.)

4. What should they be given? (Fruit juice or Kool-Aid; a cooky or graham cracker; or raisins, carrot sticks, apple and orange slices.)

5. What happens if parents force a child to eat? (He becomes so tense he can't eat anything at mealtime. If this happens, snacks are essential.)

6. What happens if parents feed the child when he can do this himself? (Eating becomes something adults want, not something he

wants. He resists to show his independence. He also turns lazy, waits for service, and loses initiative in other areas of his life.)

Sleeping

1. Why does a child resist going to bed and going to sleep? (Mothers in a sub-group wrote these answers: if the TV is still on, or parents have company, or if one or both parents are still up, they're curious and won't go to sleep; the child could have fears and insecurities.)

2. Why does he call out, asking for drinks and complaining? (The mothers: calling out and asking for drinks are excuses to have more of the mother's attention.)

3. What can be done about this? (Put him to bed early, the same time every night. Spend an hour winding down: he can pick up clothes and toys, take a bath, listen to a story. Then close his door and answer no calls for service.)

4. A common problem is that the child leaves his bed and joins his parents in theirs. What should be done about this? (Take him him back to his own bed at once.)

5. What should parents do when the child cries or is afraid during the night? (A parent can sit with him till he falls asleep. Also, the youngster can have a night light and take a favorite toy to bed with him.)

6. How must rest in bed (night sleep, plus naps) does a child need when he is nine months old? (Sixteen hours.) Thirteen months old? (Fifteen hours.) Two-and-one-half years? (Fourteen hours. This stays the same until he is six, when the nap is dropped. A one- to two-hour rest on his bed replaces the nap when the child is three and older.)

Training

1. Before a child is completely toilet trained he must be able to do three things. What are they? (He must recognize the sensation of a full bladder; he must hold urine till he reaches the toilet; he must release it when he is on the toilet.)

2. Sometimes a trained child begins to soil himself. Why? (He gets busy playing with friends, doesn't want to leave, and thinks he can hold the movement. He can't.)

3. What can be done about this? (Have him try regularly, twice daily, to move his bowels; reward him for success; have him

clean up the mess when he fails.)

4. Why does a child over the age of four wet the bed? (His bladder may be unusually small; he drinks Cokes and tea during the day; he drinks quantities of fluid at night; he fails to use the toilet before going to bed; his parents get him up at night to urinate; his parents are upset when he wets, call him names, shame, or punish him; he is convinced that he cannot stay dry at night.)

5. What can be done about it? (Eliminate stimulant drinks; keep fluid quantities small after supper; have him use the toilet before sleeping; do not get him up; post a star chart for a dry bed with a special reward — a toy, treat, a trip to the zoo — for five successes.)

6. Why does a child you're trying to train let you know after, not before, he wets? (He knows you're interested in wetting, but hasn't caught on to exactly what it is you want him to do.)

7. Why does he wet all over the floor right after you've taken him off the toilet where he wouldn't go? (He was tense with excitement, hoping to urinate, when seated; once off, the drama ended, his muscles relaxed.)

8. What makes a child afraid of the bathroom? (Long sessions on the toilet; the noise and disappearance of water during flushing; an angry, pleading parent; being spanked for failure.)

Closing

Summarize what's been learned. Suggest that each mother choose an eating, sleeping, or training problem and try some of the ideas proposed.

3. Emotion: Crying, Fear, and Anger

Introduction

A preschooler's frequent and noisy emotional displays frighten his parent. He feels guilty when the child cries, worries when the child is afraid, and gets angry when the child is angry.

A mother tends to sympathize with her upset child; a father thinks emotion is infantile. When the youngster screams in public, both parents are embarrassed.

Some parents are sure that their preschooler will never change: instant rage, distress, or fear will mark him forever. This is not so. Age brings better control. But handling the child's emotion well speeds up the timetable.

Discussion Questions

1. Why does a preschool child cry more often than an older child? (He doesn't talk well about problems; he's relatively helpless to improve a disturbing situation; he's too young to inhibit emotion well.)

2. What does your child cry about? (Mothers listed: can't have something in the grocery store; can't have his brother's toy; can't have his father's beer; must go to bed; can't go with sister; when he's afraid; when he's tired; when he's over-ruled.)

3. What do you do? (Mothers mentioned soothing; ordering him to stop; telling him not to be a baby; giving in to what he wants.)

4. What helps him most (Don't mention crying — act as though you neither see nor hear it; distract the child by handing him a toy, pointing to something outside, singing, dancing, or heading for the kitchen and inviting him to come. If the child is crying over a refusal, give the reason for your decision — only once — then distract him.)

5. What frightens your preschooler? (Mothers reported: loud noises, like sirens; strangers who talk to him or pick him up; bugs; shadows: dogs; large road or building machines.)

6. Why does a five-year-old have more fears than a two-year-old? (He's more aware of everything and can anticipate possible harm. A two-year-old notices less and has had little experience with being hurt.)

7. How can you help your preschooler overcome his fears? (Accustom him gradually to what he fears; explain how things work or what is gong to happen; avoid forcing him to do what he fears; stay calm; don't ridicule him; ban TV — violence, including that in cartoons, keeps him afraid.)

8. What makes your child angry? (Mothers listed: can't have his own way; can't reach something, open a door, work buttons;

forced to come indoors; told to go to bed; brother pesters him; sister hits him; playmate grabs his toy.)

9. How does he show temper? (Mothers reported: cries, screams, calls names, kicks, hits, throws things.)
10. How many times each day is he angry? (A few times is normal; a dozen is too many.)
11. How long does it take him to get over it? (He should get over a tantrum in five minutes or less.)
12. What do you do when he's angry? (Mothers said: spank him; put him in his room; let him do what he wants; punish the child who's made him mad.)
13. What are some good ways to help a child get over anger? (Don't let anger change a decision you've made; isolate him until he's calm; have him repair any damage he does when he's furious; find out if events in his life cause tantrums: too little sleep or food, too many bosses, unfair punishment or restrictions.)

Closing

Summarize the discussion. Suggest to the mothers that they try a new way of managing crying, fear, or anger.

4. Independence

Introduction

If a preschooler strives to be independent, he'll learn, compete, gain self-respect, and tolerate hardship. If he succeeds, caring for him is easier and his mother and father have much to be proud of. They also know that when he's eighteen he'll be able to leave home and look after himself.

Too often, however, a child's moves toward independence are labelled bad behavior. He is considered disobedient, stubborn, selfish, or even stupid (when he tries what is difficult.)

Thwarting adult help and dominance, he threatens parent control, disturbs adult patience, initially causes extra work (cleaning up the mess he makes when he tries to feed himself), and wastes time (the mother watches while the child struggles to dress himself.)

If parents get angry, frustrated, or discouraged because of their preschooler's experiments, they may punish him. When his bids for independence always are stifled, soon the child quits trying and relapses into helplessness.

Discussion Questions

1. How does the dependent, babyish child act when he is with his parents? (He lets them feed, dress, and amuse him.)
2. With his brothers and sisters? (He cries when he can't have his own way; he seeks help from parents; he's demanding and selfish.)
3. With other boys and girls? (He resents their competence; he remains an outsider.)
4. With other adults? (He's hesitant and withdrawn; he's uninterested in them and what they do.)
5. How does the dependent, babyish child act when he's told, "No"? (He cries.)
6. When he is asked to help? (He refuses; he runs off.)
7. When he is expected to obey? (He won't; he thinks nothing should be required of him.)
8. What will the dependent, babyish child think about school when he starts? (He'll dislike the rules, the restriction of playtime, the competition of classmates.)
9. About his teacher and what she expects of him (He'll want his teacher to look after him, help him with his boots and coat, and protect him from classmates. He won't try to do assignments because he believes he shouldn't be asked to do hard work.)
10. How does helping a child too much keep him babyish? (He does nothing for himself; he loses confidence; he learns no skills.)
11. Give some examples. (Feeding him beyond the age of fifteen months; dressing him beyond the age of three years — other than shoe-tying, which he learns when he's five; picking up his toys; brushing his teeth; wiping him after a bowel movement.)
12. How does protecting a child too much keep him babyish? (He learns he's entitled to comfort and that he can do no wrong.)
13. Give some examples of overprotection. (Always settling brother-sister fights in his favor; chasing away aggressive playmates; taking his part with an irate neighbor whose flowerbed

he's trampled; not letting him play outdoors when it's cold or hot; driving him when he could walk.)

14. How does telling a child what to do keep him babyish? (He relies on his parents to direct his life; he takes no initiative and assumes no responsibility for what he does.)

15. Give examples of over-direction. (Parents give hundreds of orders daily, telling the child what to wear, with whom he may play, and what to play. They schedule lessons, practices, and parties so that he has no free time to do what he likes.

16. How do daily chores help a child grow up? (He learns how to do many tasks; he's useful; his confidence grows.)

17. What are some chores a three- or four-year-old child can do? (Pick up toys; dust; run errands; clean the yard; sweep; cook — make gelatin, pudding, salads; set and clear the table; wash and dry dishes.)

18. How does taking care of his own needs help the child grow up? (He can get along without waiting for adult service; he's proud of his skills.)

19. What can a three- or four-year-old child do for himself? (Feed and dress himself; brush his teeth; bathe; put clothes and toys away; manage toileting; get snacks and drinks for himself; make his bed.)

20. How much freedom should a three- or four-year-old child have in trying out his ideas, going where he wants to go, and doing what he wants do to? (He can be allowed to do whatever is not dangerous.)

21. Think of some things he should be allowed to do and some things he should not be allowed to do. (Let him walk to friends' homes in his own block — have him phone when he gets there and before he leaves to come home; play in mud puddles; try cooking; use scissors, hammers, and hand saws. He should not climb on roofs, play in the street, use power tools, or go to a shopping center alone.)

22. In trying to be independent, the young child often annoys his parents. What are common irritating experiments between the ages of birth and one year? (He resists dressing and diapering; grabs his spoon and cup from his mother; drops food on the floor.)

23. Between one and two years? (Takes off his clothes; dumps wastebaskets; empties drawers and closets; refuses food.)
24. Between two and three years? (Constantly says, "No"; insists on doing everything himself; wants to "help" parents.)
25. Between three and four years? (Seeks attention with endless talking; refuses to obey and means it; wants to make choices himself.)
26. Between four and five years? (Sasses parents; swears; urinates outdoors; explores playmates' bodies.)
27. What can you do if your preschooler wants to help you bake cookies and you don't want him to? (Let him have his own bowl and dough to mix.)
28. What can you do to encourage independence in your child? (Let him settle his own disputes with siblings and friends; practice eating and dressing; try to do what you think he can't; do chores.)

Closing

Summarize. Suggest that each mother give up doing for her child one task which he can do for himself.

5. Learning and Learning To Get Along

Introduction

Learning facts and learning to get along with people both prepare a child for the world outside his home.

Most parents worry from the day a child is born whether he is bright; they want him to do well in school.

He will if he does things himself, rather than merely watch others, and if his mother and father read to him, play games with him, and work at chores with him. His store of knowledge grows when he hikes in the country, visits a zoo and a farm, goes for a bus ride, and watches planes take off at the airport. When adults talk to him, listen to him, and answer his questions, he stays eager to learn. But if most of the time he stays indoors watching TV and his parents never speak to him except to give orders, he will fail in school.

He learns to get along with people by practice. Playing with other boys and girls, he discovers what they are like and how to lead or adapt. The characteristics of the friends he has affect the way he thinks of himself, how he behaves toward others, and what skills he develops.

Discussion Questions on Learning

1. What did you do yesterday with your child which taught him something he didn't know before?
2. List everything you can do to add to your child's knowledge. (Read to him; take trips and walks; answer his questions; explain how things work; point out what you see outdoors; teach chores; play games.)
3. Sometimes parents spend time every day quizzing their preschooler on the alphabet and having him practice writing his name, counting, and coloring. Does this help or hurt him? (Constant drill burns out a young child. He loses interest in academic tasks and won't work at school when he gets there. Instead, follow his lead: when he asks about a letter or word on the oatmeal box, tell him what it is. When he wants to write his name, print a sample. When he gets out a coloring book and his crayons, let him work away for as short a time and in as scruffy a fashion as he chooses. He'll be taught reading, writing, and arithmetic at school. There are dozens of other things you can teach him.)

Discussion Questions on Learning To Get Along

1. What happens to the preschooler who watches television an hour or more a day? (He's overstimulated; he gets headaches and stomach pains from tension and lack of exercise; he fails to use his imagination and intelligence; he imitates what he sees, both emotionally and aggressively.)
2. What do you dislike about your child's playmates? (Mothers said: they quarrel and fight; run off and leave him; wreck toys; make a mess; hang around too long; talk to me instead of playing with him; complain about him; I have to settle their arguments, tie their shoes, get them something to eat.)

3. Why are playmates good for the child? (He can join his own generation; he tests himself; he deals with rejection and competition; he learns that others differ from himself; he acquires companions and confidantes.)

4. What are some rules which help preschoolers get along better? (No toy-grabbing; everyone helps pick up toys; if they're arguing and not playing, they separate for fifteen minutes; they play alternately at each other's homes.)

5. What are the benefits of outdoor play? (Exercise; fresh air; the chance to run, climb, and use large equipment; a change from being indoors; improved appetite and sleep.)

6. How much time daily does your child play outdoors?

7. What can you do to encourage outdoor play? (Get a swing, sandbox, wheeled toys, warm clothes; make outdoor play a part of daily routine.)

8. How long at a time should preschoolers play together? (Sixty to ninety minutes.)

9. How often should they play together during the week? (Try for a minimum of three times, a maximum of six.)

10. What happens if a child always plays with older boys and girls? (He's bossed or coddled; the play is unsuited to his age.)

11. With younger children? (He bosses them or gives in to them; play is unsuited to his age.)

12. With children of the opposite sex? (He doesn't learn to play as youngsters his own sex do and is ill-at-ease around them.)

13. What kinds of toys do preschoolers like? (Anything they can manipulate, climb on or into: boxes, ladders, buggies, wagons, trikes, swings and slides, sandboxes, imitative toys — shovels, lawnmowers, cooking utensils — dolls, trucks, balls, balloons, crayons, clay, paints, board games, books, scissors, tools. Many toys can be made from throwaway household articles. Books, obtainable at the library, describe games, activities, and toys.[1]

Closing

Summarize. Suggest that parents turn off the TV this week and watch how the child spends his time. Also, ask them to plan to do something with him each day which adds to his knowledge.

MANAGEMENT OF PROBLEMS

Some problems with preventive classes can't be fully solved. But if you expect them, you won't feel so glum when your helping project seems to founder.

Attendance

Attendance will be spotty. Sometimes there'll be a crowd; sometimes you'll all fit easily around one small table. Different mothers will come each week.

Unless a woman brings her neighbor, friend, or sister, there is no close tie between participants and a mother thinks she won't be missed if she skips a session. In order to come, she must shuffle her schedule, get herself and her child ready, and arrange transportation. Going to class wrecks a morning and may not seem worth the effort.

Encourage your mothers to come back each week by thanking them for their good ideas and selling the next program with a few sentences of tempting description.

Effectiveness

It's satisfying to your ego if you're sure that your classes are effective in helping mothers do a better job. In remedial classes, you can compare a child's behavior at the beginning and end of the course. With preventive classes, no such measurement is possible.

You can ask parents to fill out an evaluation sheet at the final meeting. Find out what each mother learned, liked best, wants added, and would like changed. But expect nearly everyone to write only: "Very good! There should be more classes like this!"

Non-Participation

Expect many mothers to say little during their hours with you, especially if the group is large. Knowing they get less from the session if they contribute little to it, you'll regret their silence.

The best you can do is to split the class into small groups each time. Then most mothers will talk and think about the subject, not merely be exposed to it.

Distance Between Leaders and Participants

If you, a psychologist, team up with a teacher or nurse to conduct classes, you add up to a formidable duo. The mothers are awed by your degrees, authority, and knowledge.

Because they don't know you well, their concept of psychologists is shadowy, probably negative. You can boost the profession's image and mellow the mothers if you stay informal, recognize their frustration and guilt, and put humor into descriptions of preschooler's comments and actions. If you take neither yourself nor their mistakes too seriously, they'll feel more relaxed with you.

Limited Time

There's so much to talk about that your classes could go on for months. Because that's not possible, you must choose some topics and forget others. Packing into each short meeting everything you can, you'll skim subjects and this can make you think you're doing a slipshod job.

But remember that each mother latches on to the idea, technique, or attitude which fits her need. That stays with her and directs her toward change.

Also, by coming to your class, she gets acquainted with you and other professionals. Later, if serious problems develop with her child, she may contact you because she knows you and likes the way you think. Had she not come to your preventive classes, she might never have sought help.

Preschoolers and their parents set the foundation for their own and society's future well-being. You can make a difference in how they do it.

REFERENCES

1. Auerbach, A. B.: *Parents Learn Through Discussion: Principles and Practices of Parent Group Education.* New York, Wiley, 1968.
2. Burrows, A. K., and Kronberg, C. L.: Recommendations for the successful development of school and community programs for young children. In Judy, G. L., ed.: *Successful Innovations in Child Guidance.* Springfield, Thomas, 1982.
3. Dinkmeyer, D. C., and Muro, J. J.: *Group Counseling.* Itasca, Peacock Pubs, 1971.
4. Harway, V. T., Magnussen, M. G., and Rager, S.: Following up families who participated in an infancy counseling program and those who did not: Two to four years later. In Judy, G. L., ed.: *Successful Innovations in Child Guidance.* Springfield, Thomas, 1982.
5. Johnson, D., and Breckenridge, J. N.: The Houston Parent-Child Development Center and the primary prevention of behavior problems in young children. *American Journal of Community Psychology, 10*: 305, 1982.
6. Rothenberg, B. A.: *Parentmaking: A Practical Handbook for Teaching Parent Classes about Babies and Toddlers.* Menlo Park, Banster Pr, 1982.
7. Webster-Stratton, C.: Teaching mothers through videotape modeling to change their children's behavior. *Journal of Pediatric Psychology, 7*: 279, 1982.
8. Webster-Stratton, C.: The long-term effects of a videotape modeling parent-training program: Comparison of immediate and 1-year follow-up results. *Behavior Therapy, 13*: 702, 1982.

AUTHOR INDEX

A

Abe, K., 111, 112
Abraham, A., 215, 221
Abraham, W., 162
Abramovitch, R., 104
Adams, G., 283
Adams, R. E., 208, 221
Adams-Tucker, C., 275, 281
Adelson, R., 120, 125
Adler, S., 32
Allen, E. E., 334
Ames, L. B., 67, 70, 76, 85, 95, 113
Ammons, C. H., 138
Ammons, R. B., 138
Anders, T. F., 76
Anderson, B., 165
Anderson, C. C., 138, 281
Anderson, G. L., 281
Anderson, H. H., 281
Anderson, J. E., 76, 85
Andrews, R. J., 162
Andrews, T. F., 85
Anthony, E. J., 85
Apelt, W. C., 162
Araki, F., 95 ·
Arbitman, D. C., 167
Arieti, S., 164
Asher, S. R., 98, 103
Atwater, A. E., 18
Aubry, J., 281
Auerbach, A. B., 334, 355
Austin, G., 26, 32, 39, 51, 58
Ausubel, D. P., 281
Axelrad, S., 297
Ayer, M. E., 281

Azrin, N. H., 107, 112

B

Baehner, R. L., 70
Baer, D. N., 112
Baird, M., 85
Baker, H. J., 162
Baker, J. G., 162
Baker, S. M., 70, 76, 85, 95, 113
Bakwin, H., 58, 70, 76, 85, 104, 109, 112, 125, 143, 162, 222, 281
Bakwin, R. M., 58, 70, 76, 85, 104, 109, 112, 125, 143, 162, 222, 281
Baldwin, A. L., 281
Ball, R. S., 105, 285
Balthazar, E. E., 281
Bandura, A., 138, 250, 281
Bankart, C. P., 138, 281
Barber, E., 162
Barsch, R. H., 162
Beardslee, C., 26, 32
Becker, J. V., 162
Becker, W. C., 281
Beckey, R. E., 95
Bee, H. L., 282
Bell, R. Q., 199, 250
Bender, L., 121, 125, 139, 162, 274, 282
Bennett, H. L., 284
Benton, A. L., 95
Benton, P. C., 162, 163
Bereiter, C., 45
Berg, I., 80, 85, 281
Bernal, M. E., 64, 70
Bernhardt, K. S., 282
Bernreuter, R. G., 281

SUBJECT INDEX